A COMPLETE AND BALANCED
SERVICE SCORECARD

A COMPLETE AND BALANCED
SERVICE SCORECARD

Creating Value Through Sustained Performance Improvement

RAJESH K. TYAGI
PRAVEEN GUPTA

Vice President, Publisher: Tim Moore
Associate Publisher and Director of Marketing: Amy Neidlinger
Executive Editor: Jim Boyd
Operations Manager: Gina Kanouse
Digital Marketing Manager: Julie Phifer
Publicity Manager: Laua Czaja
Assistant Marketing Manager: Megan Colvin
Marketing Assistant: Brandon Smith
Cover Designer: Chuti Prasertsith
Managing Editor: Kristy Hart
Senior Project Editor: Lori Lyons
Copy Editor: Cheri Clark
Proofreader: San Dee Phillips
Indexer: Lisa Stumpf
Senior Compositor: Jake McFarland
Manufacturing Buyer: Dan Uhrig

FT Press offers excellent discounts on this book when ordered in quantity for bulk purchases or special sales. For more information, please contact U.S. Corporate and Government Sales, 1-800-382-3419, corpsales@pearsontechgroup.com. For sales outside the U.S., please contact International Sales at international@pearson.com.

Company and product names mentioned herein are the trademarks or registered trademarks of their respective owners.

Printed in the United States of America

First Printing June 2008

ISBN-10:   0-13-198600-7

ISBN-13:   978-0-13-198600-8

Pearson Education LTD.

Pearson Education Australia PTY, Limited.

Pearson Education Singapore, Pte. Ltd.

Pearson Education North Asia, Ltd.

Pearson Education Canada, Ltd.

Pearson Educatión de Mexico, S.A. de C.V.

Pearson Education—Japan

Pearson Education Malaysia, Pte. Ltd.

Library of Congress Cataloging-in-Publication Data
Tyagi, Rajesh K.
 A complete and balanced service scorecard : creating value through sustained performance improvement / Rajesh K. Tyagi,
Praveen Gupta.
    p. cm.
 ISBN 0-13-198600-7 (hbk. : alk. paper) 1. Service industries—Management. 2. Performance—Measurement. 3. Customer services. 4. Total quality management. I. Gupta, Praveen, 1957- II. Title.
 HD9980.5.T93 2008
 658.3'125—dc22

                                2008005436

This book is dedicated to Robert Kaplan and Ken Norton for developing the concept of Balanced Scorecard

Contents

Acknowledgments

I am grateful to my colleagues at DePaul University, Department of Management, especially Professors Scott Young, James Belohlav, and Ray Coye, for providing me encouragement and invaluable suggestions. My special thank you goes to Dean Dipak Jain, Dean, Kellogg School of Management, Northwestern University, for planting the seed and providing invaluable suggestions to focus on Service performance issues. Comments and facilitation of cases by Professor Dean Schroeder of Valparaiso University and Pavlo Schremeta, Dean of Kiev Mohyla Business School, Ukraine, are highly appreciated. Comments from Professors Robert Rubin, Erich Dierdorff, and Scott Sampson are also acknowledged. I would also like to acknowledge students Umesh Shahi, Arthur Mrzinski, and Pei-Ning Chang for helping me with the topical research.

I also would like to thank Infosys leadership for sharing information about performance measurements.

And I am grateful to my wife, Anjali, and daughter, Keya, for their love and support in this endeavor.

—Rajesh Tyagi, Assistant Professor, Logistics and
    Operations Management HEC, Montréal

I would like to thank my coauthor, Rajesh Tyagi, for his teamwork and making the writing a collaborative experience. Special thanks to my colleague Arvin Sri for his valuable support in research and review throughout the project.

My thanks to my family and friends for their continual support in writing this book. Special thanks to Dean Spitzer and Jahn Ballard for their active support in discussing service performance measures. I am grateful to Jim Spohrer for promoting Service Science.

—Praveen Gupta, President, Accelper Consulting,
    ASQ Fellow, Six Sigma Master Black Belt

Finally, the authors greatly appreciate Shellie Tate for excellent editorial support; and Executive Editor Jim Boyd and his staff for making this book a reality.

About the Authors

Dr. Rajesh Kumar Tyagi joined HEC Montreal as an Assistant Professor of Logistics and Operations Management in June 2008. Previously, Dr. Tyagi was a faculty member at the Department of Management, College of Commerce, DePaul University. Professor Tyagi teaches Service Operations, Operations Management, and Quality Management. Dr. Tyagi has also taught service operations and operations management at Kellogg School of Management, at Northwestern University, and in East Europe and Southeast Asia. His current research and consulting interests are in areas of service delivery chain design, service performance management, measurement of service quality, Six Sigma applications in the services sector, and design of a reverse supply chain. He has more than 12 publications in scientific and technology journals and has presented at various national and international conferences. He is the co-author of *Six Sigma for Transactions and Service*.

Professor Tyagi also co-founded a biomedical device manufacturing company in Singapore. Professor Tyagi is a consultant to an early-stage venture fund and also consults on operations and technology management issues for early-stage companies and established corporations. He obtained his Ph.D. in Engineering at the University of Ottawa, Canada, and his MBA from the Kellogg School of Management, Northwestern University.

Praveen Gupta, president of Accelper Consulting (www.accelper.com), developed the Six Sigma Business Scorecard that has been recognized worldwide for its innovative approach to corporate performance, ease of implementation, and importance to sustained profitable growth. Praveen has also developed a Business Innovation framework and pioneered the Six Sigma methodology at Motorola, and the 4P Model for process management. Integration and adaptation of these methods to service operations have been addressed in continuing work for sustaining profitable growth and creating success opportunities for leadership and employees.

Praveen's experience at working with dozens of companies in the manufacturing, service, and software industries has given him a uniquely holistic perspective on business performance. Praveen teaches his methods and tools at Illinois Institute of Technology and at DePaul University to graduate students in the IT and Management departments.

Praveen has led several organizations in improving their operations and financial performance using the Business Scorecard, Six Sigma, Business Innovation, and 4P model. He frequently speaks in conferences and seminars around the world.

Praveen holds B.S. and M.S. degrees from Indian Institute of Technology, Roorkee, and Illinois Institute of Technology, respectively. Prior to founding his consulting company, Praveen worked at Motorola and AT&T Bell Laboratories.

Besides his books on scorecards, Praveen has authored *Business Innovation in the 21st Century, Stat Free Six Sigma, Improving Healthcare Quality and Cost with Six Sigma*, and *The Six Sigma Performance Handbook*. Praveen regularly writes for various publications and is the Editor of the *International Journal of Innovation Science*, being launched in 2009.

Foreword

by Paul Harmon

Business Process is a hot topic at the moment. Depending on who you talk with, Business Process can include business performance management, business intelligence and executive dashboards, the creation of a business process architecture, process redesign and improvement, six sigma and lean, as well as a host of business process management software systems.

Surveys typically find that senior executives are not very happy with the way their organizations implement their corporate strategies. If you ask, senior managers will consistently say that one of the things they hope to get from BPM is an improved way of measuring corporate performance. If you look at most BPM methodologies, however, you will find them long on redesign and improvement techniques and on business process architecture concepts but surprisingly short on performance measurement.

Most business process redesign or improvement programs talk about the importance of measurements. Some projects, especially those led by Six Sigma practitioners, gather lots of data on process performance. Unfortunately, most of these measurement efforts are project focused. They start with the process and measure improvements in the process. They sometimes relate metrics to measures of customer satisfaction, but they very rarely show how the process measures are actually aligned with the organization's goals and strategies. In other words, most organizations do not have a systematic way of tying specific measures derived from a particular process to the overall goals or strategies of the company. Nor is there a systematic effort to gather measures on all processes in the organization that could enable comparisons between changes in one process and changes in related processes.

This situation is about to reach crisis proportions within the BPM community as companies increasingly adopt BPM software products that are capable of automatically gathering process measures and transmitting them to executive dashboards. During the past year, many of the leading BPM software companies have announced acquisitions of Business Intelligence firms. Those acquisitions are predicated on the assumption that companies will use these capabilities to report metrics to executives, and then provide those executives with advice about trends that can guide executive decisions. It will be ironic if the BPM vendors acquire a lot of fancy technology and then can't offer their clients a systematic approach to determining what process measures their fancy tools should actually monitor and report.

The approach to corporate performance measurement that has been most widely adopted over the past decade derives from Robert Kaplan and David Norton's work on Balanced Scorecards, which they initially defined in the *Harvard Business Review* in the early 1990s. In their original articles and subsequent books, Kaplan and Norton focused on helping organization's broaden the number of things they measured. The "Balanced Scorecard," as conceived by Kaplan and Norton, was a grid that considered Financial, Customer, Operational, and Learning and Growth measures. As they developed their ideas over the course of the past decade, Kaplan and Norton have increasingly sought to tie their Balanced Scorecard measures to an organization's strategic goals. Kaplan and Norton now speak of Strategy Maps and seek to derive measures from a hierarchy of business activities.

Many organizations have explored the Balanced Scorecard approach; some with notable success. Unfortunately, most organizations have used the Balanced Scorecard to reinforce their existing organizational structures. Thus, organizations begin by creating a corporate scorecard. The goals and measures defined on the corporate scorecard are then delegated to divisional or departmental scorecards, and then, in top-down fashion, to subdivisions or functional units within departments. In too many organizations, scorecards have served to reinforce the departmental silos and management practices that are so detrimental to effective organizational performance.

Thus, in 2004, I was happy to discover Praveen Gupta's book, *Six Sigma Business Scorecard*. This book presented scorecards from a process perspective, explicitly typing scorecards to business processes. It also extended the four measurement categories, as many other scorecard users have done, to a more extensive set of measures, including Leadership and Profitability, Management and Improvement, Employees and Innovation, Purchasing and Supplier Management, Operational Execution, Sales and Distribution, and Service and Growth. *Six Sigma Business Scorecard* initiated a very fruitful dialog within the business process community and has led a number of business process gurus to see how a scorecard approach can provide business process developers with a more systematic way of generating and maintaining an enterprise-wide process/performance measurement system.

While business process people have become more excited about the potential of scorecard systems, Praveen Gupta has continued to think about the challenges of aligning process measures with strategies and with corporate performance systems. In *Service Scorecard* Gupta has joined with Rajesh Tyagi to move from a Six Sigma focused view of scorecards to a broader view of processes. At the same time, reflecting a growing recognition among process practitioners that service processes are different from manufacturing processes, Gupta and Tyagi have written a new book that extends the scorecard concept, while simultaneously focusing it on the concerns of service business organizations.

As a generalization, manufacturing businesses generate products, which are then packaged and delivered to customers. Service businesses don't so much create products as they create customer experiences. The actual "product" they deliver is modified as it is delivered, consisting, as it does, of interactions between the customer and the company employees engaged in providing the service. Obviously this isn't a sharp distinction, but it is an important one and it results in particular challenges for business executives who seek to measure the success of service-oriented business efforts. Many books have been written on the problems of measuring manufacturing processes. It's refreshing to find a book that focuses on the problems of monitoring and measuring the activities of organizations that focus on providing services.

Service Scorecard starts with the sevenfold scorecard that Gupta developed in *Six Sigma Business Scorecard* and refines it to support an organization that is trying to measure and organize its service processes. This new book clearly reflects Gupta and Tyagi's experience over the past few years and provides lots of very practical advice on how to organize corporate scorecard development efforts. At the same time, they devote specific attention to how one can organize measures to predict business trends.

This is an important book that appears at a critical time in the development of corporate business process management efforts. It suggests a practical way to meld process management and performance measures into a well-aligned system. It provides BPM practitioners with a way to conceptualize how their efforts can support business strategies. This book shows you how Business Process Management will evolve into the next phase by merging business processes, performance measures, and management evaluations into a seamless whole. Thus, this is a book that everyone involved in process work or performance measurement should read.

—Paul Harmon
Executive Editor, Business Process Trends

Foreword

by Dean Spitzer, Ph.D.

The book that you are about to read, *Service Scorecard: Creating Value Through Sustained Performance Improvement*, represents an important contribution to the literature on performance measurement of services organization. As you know, service has become, by far, the dominant sector in the world economy. But, as you also know, services organizations are often very frustrating to deal with, both to work for and to do business with. We all have our favorite stories of services snafus. On the high end, there are some very effective organizations, but in general the quality of services is remarkable for its deficiencies and inconsistencies. The services exemplars invariably have better measurement systems.

In my recent book, *Transforming Performance Measurement*, I explain that no organization can be any better than its measurement system because management is based on measurement. That is why I am so enthusiastic about this book. If your organization uses even a few of the principles, methods, and tools contained in this valuable book, it will become more effective. The framework proposed in this book is both comprehensive and practical and reflects the state-of-the-art thinking on good performance measurement.

But innovative thinking about performance measurement in services is rare. It was the dearth of good thinking about performance of measurement in services that led me to found the Research Round-table on Services Performance Measurement, with members invited from leading companies, non-profits, government, and academic institutions. Because of their thought leadership, the authors of this book, Praveen Gupta and Rajesh Tyagi, were selected as members.

Praveen is a prolific author, an excellent communicator, an innovative thinker, and a valued colleague. I have read many of Praveen's previous books and have benefited greatly from his wisdom and his counsel. I have frequently cited the *Six Sigma Business Scorecard* in my own writing. This book applies and extends that thinking specifically to services.

By reading this book, you are taking an important step toward the "sustained performance improvement" of your services organization.

—Dean Spitzer, Ph.D.
Author of *Transforming Performance Measurement*
Founder of the Research Roundtable on Services
Performance Measurement

Introduction

As economic focus shifts to service businesses, performance management of service organizations becomes of interest. Most management work has been geared toward businesses comprised of manufacturing supported by associated service operations. Our experience teaches us that as the role of manufacturing in developed or developing economies shifts toward service businesses, performance of services suffer due to ineffective and inefficient management of service resources. For example, customers are more dissatisfied with services in the service economy than with services in the manufacturing economy. There is a consistent and steady decline in the perception of service quality. Customers today get less, and poorer, services in many business sectors—be it telecommunication, fast food, airline, or personal computers—and they feel helpless (Service quality ACSI index of 80.3 in year 1994 compared to an index of 78.3 in year 2004).

Business management for product-driven companies—such as Proctor & Gamble, Motorola, Rubbermaid, Exxon Mobil, Apple, Boeing, or Toyota—is not suitable for companies like Goldman Sachs, Bank of America, American Express, Disney, Starbucks, Southwest, or McKinsey. In other words, service organizations do have their uniqueness that must be managed to achieve sustainable, profitable growth. The main differences between services and manufacturing operations include service focus, interaction with customers and customer participation, job skills, intellectual component, compensation, process and experience management, perception of research and development in services, and performance measurements. Components of the cost of goods sold vary from that of the cost of services due to the lack of physical inventory involved. On the other hand, payroll dollars may be higher for services businesses than the manufacturing business due to the qualification level of service professionals. Even though service functions at the surface level sound and appear to be similar to their manufacturing counterparts, adaptation to service intent becomes an implementation issue that creates a need for the Service Scorecard.

The authors have experience with a variety of scorecards, including the Balanced Scorecard and Six Sigma Business Scorecard, in a variety of industries. Channeling their personal academic and business experience has led them to develop the Service Scorecard. The Service Scorecard builds on the framework used in Six Sigma Business Scorecard, which is a hybrid of Six Sigma and Balanced Scorecard for ensuring completeness and ease of implementation. The authors have written the Service Scorecard book to enable service performance professionals to view their service operations in the business context and manage it for best in class performance. This book benefits from the historical performance management principles and presents the complete model that drives best in class performance, service innovation, and employee engagement. Eventually, service organizations need Service Scorecard to ensure sustained profitable growth for for-profit organizations, or sustained value for not-for-profit organizations. The sustained profitable growth implies that service businesses can grow and make money at the same time, rather than either grow or earn profit year after year through excellence in execution and innovation. Similarly sustained value implies that a not-for-profit must define its value proposition and continue to grow the value creation yearly.

The Service Scorecard book has been organized in three parts.

Part I, "Understanding Service Performance," builds the background in performance management and presents its challenges. Part I also includes a chapter on Six Sigma for services, which introduces the concepts as the Six Sigma intent as incorporated in the Service Scorecard. The intent of Six Sigma is to accelerate improvement in order to achieve superior and best in class performance. At the end of Part I, you learn about the challenges of service performance management, various performance management models, gaps in performance management for service, and the need for the Service Scorecard.

Part II, "Learning Service Scorecard," is written to introduce Service Scorecard. You will learn about Service Scorecard concepts and Glacier elements. Glacier is an easy way to remember all seven elements: Growth, Leadership, Acceleration, Collaboration, Innovation, Execution, and Retention. In service operations, collaboration and retention are two distinct aspects that differ significantly from manufacturing operations. You learn about the Service Performance Index (SPIN), which is based on the overall performance of the service organization and developed specifically for leadership of the organization for identifying opportunities for performance improvement. By the end of Part II, you will understand the framework of the Service Scorecard, its elements, associated measurements, and their applications for driving organization-wide performance improvement.

Part III, "Practicing Service Scorecard," focuses on implementation aspects. It covers the step-by-step approach to implementation, integration with various existing improvement initiatives, and best practices for various elements of the Scorecard. Also, validation of the Service Scorecard demonstrates the importance and relevance of each element, and the causal relationship between each element and SPIN, which is a predictor of the service corporation in achieving sustained profitable growth. In identifying best practices, the authors have identified several successful service corporations that use various elements of the Service Scorecard. Practicing all elements in an organization is bound to make the service organization perform at a much higher level, thus making it a profitable and growing organization. Wall Street rewards profitable firms—however, employees love a profitably growing organization as it facilitates their growth and brings out their best. Finally, profitable growing organizations are fun to work for!

Part I

Understanding Service Performance

1

Performance Management and Scorecards

The service component of the U.S. economy has been growing continually for the past several decades. National economic development moves through stages of growth in agriculture, manufacturing, and service. The dominance of service is influenced by the role of support functions, value-sourcing, and evolving servicing enterprises. These support functions may include sales, purchasing, design, and human resources; value-sourcing really implies sourcing for value irrespective of national boundaries; and servicing enterprises include the service sector, such as finance, insurance, and real estate. More than two-thirds of the U.S. gross domestic product (GDP) has service components. Major corporations, like GM and GE, are shifting manufacturing and focusing more on the service side of the business, to the point where most of their profits are realized through service elements.

The transformation of the U.S. economy from an agricultural-based to manufacturing-based leading to a service-based economy has a profound impact on the way corporate performance should be measured. The agricultural process is inherently nature-dependent and supplemented by machines and people. The process of agriculture was originally learned through apprenticeship. In manufacturing, on the other hand, the definition, measurements, and improvement became more exact and, thus, a science. As a result, the manufacturing processes became learnable, repeatable, and measurable. Thus, the performance of the manufacturing processes improved over time to virtual perfection (i.e., Six Sigma level).

Service Industry Components

The service processes consist of interaction and transaction elements. The transaction-heavy service processes are similar to the manufacturing processes; however, the interaction-heavy service processes have their intricacies. Even the transaction-heavy service processes contain elements of interaction that make their definition and measurement somewhat difficult. The transaction processes are typically high-volume, process-dependent, formatted customer input; thus, they are more efficient and have a low value per transaction. On the other hand, the interaction processes contain low-volume, extensive-people-dependent, flexible customer input; thus, they are more responsive and have a high value per service. Interaction-based services could be classified as traditional services, such as a retail setting or financial services, or as experiences such as theme parks. The length and extent of interaction with the customer separates these types of interaction services.

Based on these types of services, we could describe services as a transaction or as an experience. Considering services as a transaction, the inputs to a service process include customer information, systems, methodologies, interpersonal skills, work environment, and response time. The output of a service process may be a transaction record document or personal service to a customer. The performance of the transaction record can be measured in terms of its accuracy, but the performance of a personal service can be somewhat difficult to measure because of human emotions and perceptions. Considering services as an experience, the firms usually "stage" the experience with customer involvement, and customers leave with a "memorable perception."

A business is a collection of business processes. Each business contains common processes as well as unique processes. The common processes include management, sales, purchasing, human resources, quality, and customer support. The unique processes represent the focus of the business. In financial services, for example, these unique processes could relate to stock buying or selling transactions, loan applications review, dividends distribution, banking services, and many more. Both transaction- and interaction-heavy businesses will contain common as well as unique service processes. The process errors observed in the transaction- and interaction-heavy businesses include information accuracy and integrity errors, product performance errors, delinquencies, errors in the misapplication of a tool, customer service errors, and other human errors.

Business Performance Measurement Challenges in the Service Industry

The leadership of a service organization faces the challenge of measuring business performance. In a manufacturing business, the leadership tracks the number of turns, customer satisfaction, inventory levels, and/or asset utilization. Service businesses, however, do not have inventory levels, the number of turns, or significant assets to measure utilization. The most critical asset—human resources—is difficult to measure. Some companies attempt to remedy this challenge by measuring productivity in terms of revenue per employee, but doing so can have its drawbacks.

As an example, the leadership in one company hired a productivity consultant, and one of us was hired as a quality or performance consultant. During a casual discussion, we were told that whenever the productivity consultant met with employees or analyzed employee productivity, employees slowed down. Measuring human productivity has a negative connotation associated with it and is sometimes perceived to be detrimental to employee dignity. In addition, human productivity is difficult to measure for further improvement. If one measures revenue per employee as a measure of productivity, the only way to improve the productivity without any process improvement is to reduce head count or improve sales. Such action implies that scorecards must identify process-based measurements rather than events or outcome-based measurements.

The Balanced Scorecard

Beginning with the simple measurements of profit, growth, or customer satisfaction, to a series of financial measurements, there has been a perceived continual need for more nonfinancial measurements. The need for measurements is growing due to the increased expectation of more process knowledge coupled with the lack of information about the process. Both for-profit and not-for-profit organizations use a variety of scorecards. Whenever an activity is performed, interest in measurement begins with a need to know the "goodness" of the activity's outcome. Measurements are taken related to the activity's consistency and the "goodness" of inputs to the activity. A challenge with the outcome-related measurements, however, is the lack of information due to the nature of the measurements and their application.

Financial measurements are easier to assess than the output measurements because of commonality across processes and industries. The Balanced Scorecard was introduced by Robert Kaplan and Ken Norton in the early 1990s as a framework for diversifying measurements beyond financial measurements. Since its inception, many companies have implemented or attempted to implement the Balanced Scorecard; however, its impact is not known yet. The Balanced Scorecard consists of four perspectives: Customers, Financial Operations, Internal Operations, and Learning and Growth. After reviewing its performance in the field, the following observations are apparent:

- The Balanced Scorecard was designed as a Strategic Management System and thus geared toward the organization's executives instead of toward operations. As a strategic management system, it does incorporate various aspects of the organization; however, it is not useful at the operations level.
- Employees at the operations level cannot relate to the Balanced Scorecard, thus causing a gap in communication between executives and employees.
- The Balanced Scorecard does not relate to the organization's structures; thus, it appears to be an imposed set of measurements. No actual business is organized as four perspectives with clear responsibility for each perspective. Therefore, successful

implementation of the Balanced Scorecard appears to be questionable in the absence of clearly identified responsibilities.

- The Balanced Scorecard does not provide guidance for implementation at the process level. Although it can identify measures at the process *output* level, it does not clearly help in identifying relevant measurements at the process level, where all the opportunities in performance improvement reside.

- The Balanced Scorecard does not address the intangibles of an organization and thus remains incomplete. It does not address the issues of leadership, employee innovation, and improvement.

In several conferences we have asked the audience to raise their hands about using the Balanced Scorecard. Invariably, everyone raised their hand to demonstrate their use of the Balanced Scorecard. When we asked them how good they felt about the Balanced Scorecard's impact on their company's bottom line, no hand went up. In other instances when one of us asked about implementation of the Balanced Scorecard, we rarely saw any hand go up. Instead we got responses like, "It has been implemented in our Finance department," or "It is for our management." Such responses simply show that people are calling their measurements "the Balanced Scorecard" without using it as intended, implying that the Balanced Scorecard has been unable to address real business needs.

During the past 10 to 15 years, the business model has significantly changed. Factors such as globalization, increased competition, arrival of the Internet, outsourcing, and strength of Asian economies have all disrupted the current business model. In addition, the Balanced Scorecard has not changed its methodology since its inception. Although continual change is now fundamental to a business, the Balanced Scorecard has maintained its status quo. The measures of business performance within the Balanced Scorecard must change to represent the present reality.

Because the Balanced Scorecard, consisting of the four perspectives of Customers, Internal Operations, Financial Operations, and Learning and Growth, is the known measurement system to date, its variations have been implemented in several industries, such as human resources, healthcare, municipalities, and information technology. The conceptual breakthrough highlighted in the Balanced

Scorecard led to diverse measurements. For example, when implemented at Halifax Regional Municipality in 2004, the Balanced Scorecard was diversified based on the priorities of the municipality's business strategies. Challenges faced in diversifying the scorecard included too many priorities, conflicting demands, and operational versus strategic emphases.

Business Performance Evolution

According to Dean Spitzer, the author of *Transforming Performance Measurements*, performance measurement has evolved into a purely technical area using methodologies (i.e., the dashboard). Measurement specialists lead the measurement initiative, and everyone else in the organization just becomes an observer of performance measurement. The complete cycle of performance measurement must instead be implemented effectively to realize its dual purpose of organizational learning and business transformation.

According to documents at the Performance Measurement Resources Center at The Enterprise Solutions Competency Center, which provides support for the Department of Defense Executive Branch, the current business environment is very different from what it was ten years ago. Performance measures drive accountability, visibility, and transparency; inspire and motivate all employees; provide direction for the organization; and encourage alignment from top to bottom. Strategy sets the direction for execution, and performance measurement allows for improvement. In a nutshell, performance measurement is the process of developing indicators using metrics for driving progress toward business goals.

Fundamentally, enterprises realize that their primary challenge is the disconnect that exists between strategy and execution. Strategy, initiatives, resources, and risk are addressed at the senior executive level of an organization, but they are not directly tied to the day-to-day activities. As a result, organizations can measure performance, but they are unable to manage it.

One of the reasons an organization has a performance measurement system without a significant impact on the bottom line is a lack of understanding of the role of measurements. Table 1.1 shows how the measurements have historically been utilized. These measurements were reviewed for various aspects such as basic purpose, driver, methodology, type, example, outcome, challenge, and beneficiaries. The need for a different set of measurements is apparent when you study the trend from the industrial age to the knowledge age. Interestingly, even the purpose of establishing measurements subtly changed from productivity, quality, and profit to profitable growth.

TABLE 1.1 Evolution of Performance Measurements

Aspects	Industrial Age	Quality Age	Information Age	Knowledge Age
Objective/Scope	Increase productivity	Improve quality	Improve bottom line	Sustained profitable growth
Driver	Basic needs	Expectation	Shareholders driven	Customer value driven
Methodology	Metrics	KPIs	Balanced Scorecard	Business Scorecard
Type	Output	In-process	Organization wide	Supply Chain
Purpose of Establishing Measurements	Quantity— Units (Cost per unit)	Yield % Good (Defects per unit)	% Profit (Profit per unit)	% Profitable Growth (Value per unit)
Outcome	Fulfill customer needs	Get customer business through quality	Increase market value through profit	Achieve business growth through innovation
Challenge	Orders shipped	Quality received	Financials achieved	Performance achieved
Beneficiaries	Producer	Consumer	Shareholder	Stakeholders

Productivity increase was required to keep up with the customer demand, which led to sacrifices in quality and resulted in focusing on quality improvement. The quality improvement was related to the cost of poor quality deducted directly from the profit, thus leading to a focus on profit. Excessive focus on profit led to adverse actions, such as layoffs, outsourcing, supplier squeeze, price wars, and the eventual demise of the business.

While the business progresses through its life cycle, experience and information are gained, technology is developed, and responsiveness becomes critical. Now customer delight—not just customer satisfaction—is expected. The explosion of knowledge has led to informed customers, intense competition, and more demand for better, faster, and more (not cheaper) value. This shift requires operation optimization, continual innovation, and mass customization. As a result, the leadership must become adept at multitasking, comprehending business complexity, and responding optimally.

All of this evolution in business development highlights the need for profitable growth, which requires measurements that represent all segments of the business—objective and subjective, machines and people, and strategy and execution. Kaplan and Norton's Balanced Scorecard was designed to improve the bottom-line performance of companies by focusing on nonfinancial measures of the vision, strategy, objectives, targets, and actions. Experience shows that most Balanced Scorecard measurements follow the "SMART" (specific, measurable, action, realistic, and target) principle. However, the real business also consists of difficult-to-measure, difficult-to-quantify, knowledge-driven, and subjective measurements. Service industries and operations are bound to have more subjective performance measurements.

The *Six Sigma Business Scorecard* book (Gupta, 2006) presented a holistic business scorecard framework consisting of seven categories and ten measurements. The seven categories and measurements are shown in Table 1.2.

As with any scorecard, the Six Sigma Business Scorecard needs to be adapted to various industries. The seven categories are applicable to most businesses; however, measurements need to be customized to represent needs of various industries. For example, in banking industries or similar service industries, physical inventory may not exist; thus, the purchasing performance could be measured differently.

TABLE 1.2   The Six Sigma Business Scorecard

Category	Measurements	Significance (%)	Comments
Leadership and Profitability	Profit CEO Recognition	15% 15%	12% profit implies 100% score. CEO recognition is accorded for significant value creation.
Management and Improvement	Rate of Improvement	20%	Each department must set an aggressive goal for improvement.
Employees and Innovation	Number of ideas per employee	10%	Idea generation implies employee engagement; thus, it is critical that employees continually input their ideas for improvement.
Purchasing and Supplier Management	Quality (Sigma) Cost of Purchase	5% 5%	The aim is to have suppliers achieve higher quality. Cost of Purchase is measured as % of sales.
Operational Execution	Quality (Sigma) Cycle time variance	5% 5%	Internal operations must aim toward established performance targets. Cycle time variance requires setting delivery or activity completion targets.
Sales and Distribution	% new sales	10%	Emphasis on new sales for revenue growth.
Service and Growth	Customer Satisfaction	10%	This could be a measure of multiple internal measures leading to customer satisfaction and loyalty.

Evolving business conditions continually highlight the outsourcing processes, growing collaboration or partnerships trends, and intellectual engagement of employees. In addition, service processes do have different dimensions and attributes of their own, especially in terms of the roles of people and machines. Unlike in manufacturing, which is equipment- or machines-heavy, service processes are more people-driven. Table 1.3 demonstrates the differences between service and nonservice businesses.

TABLE 1.3 Service and Nonservice Business Differences

Business Attributes	Nonservice Businesses	Service Businesses
Customers	Customer requires tangible outputs, measurable performance, and ability to easily get it corrected; customer is less engaged from operations.	Customer requires intangible outputs; it is difficult to measure performance and easier to redeliver rather than repair; customer is likely to be involved in the delivery operations.
Outputs	Products, parts, or systems create experience.	Experience creates the output.
Processes	Series of operations involving machines, material, method, and people.	Series of activities involving people, material, tools, and methods.
Inputs	Tangible raw material.	Intangible information.
Suppliers	Many suppliers depend upon the complexity of the solution.	Fewer suppliers with stronger relationships.

Recent emphasis on business governance, such as the Sarbanes Oxley (SOX) Act, has imposed compliance requirements regarding the business performance. Accordingly, public companies are required to evaluate and disclose the effectiveness of their internal controls and be audited by a third party to disclose their performance specifically relating to financial reporting. Privately held firms, on the other hand, have not been affected by the SOX Act. Industry perceptions of the SOX Act indicate it has an associated cost that has adversely affected business performance. However, the general perception is that SOX has improved awareness of the dependability of the reported business performance. Thus, having effective performance measures will help any type of governance regulations.

The post-information age trend is to *use* information or extract business intelligence. This initial emphasis on using the information led to the concept of dashboards. While dashboards remain, the necessary business intelligence is lacking without a comprehensive business scorecard model. Most of the dashboards are creative in displaying and reporting the information; however, they are difficult to utilize on the operations side due to an inability to extract business intelligence from them.

Thus, there is a growing need for intelligent scorecards that can predict information. According to Jeff Hawkins in his *On Intelligence* book, intelligence implies the ability to predict. Therefore, holistic and comprehensive business scorecards that include leading indicators (rather than lagging indicators) provide the intelligence to optimally manage business performance.

The Six Sigma Business Scorecard, as shown in Figure 1.1, offers a predictive indicator of business performance, called BPIn (Business Performance Index), that is determined based on a set of ten measurements used to identify areas for improvement and to set goals to achieve overall business performance. The BPIn, which is based mainly on the operational measurements, can provide a good indicator of the company's financial performance. An operations-based index can predict the financial performance, so the management team can take preventive actions to achieve the desired financial results.

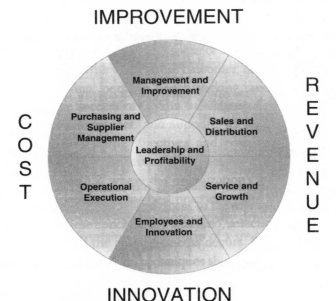

Figure 1.1   Business Scorecard Architecture
(© Accelper Consulting 2005)

The BPIn can also be used to determine the corporate sigma levels, which are essential to sustain Six Sigma initiatives at a corporation. In the absence of the business-level performance measures, any corporate strategic initiatives become difficult to track, thus affecting their chances of success. According to Kaplan and Norton, only about 10 percent of strategies are successfully executed.

Service Scorecard

The Service Scorecard should balance cost and revenue, improvement and innovation, management and employees, and execution and growth. This Service Scorecard must also balance the objective and subjective measurements, which are sometimes difficult to measure but that must be measured.

No performance scorecard with only objective measures can present a complete picture of the performance, because all businesses incorporate tangible and intangible assets. Actually, the ratio of intangible to tangible assets increases from manufacturing to service operations. In other words, service operations deal with more intangibles than tangibles, because the service operations are more dependent on people and, thus, are more subjective in nature. In the manufacturing sector, the objective is to reduce the cost of each widget and make it more reproducible. However, in the case of service operations that are more customized, more flexibility and variations to delight customers are required.

With the integration of technology and globalization, certain shifts occur from manufacturing to service operations (i.e., from the Business Scorecard to the Service Scorecard). For example, the manufacturing operations deal with suppliers of parts, material, and services. In the service industries, however, the focus is on intangible relationships involving various stakeholders and even customers. Establishing partnerships and collaborating with customers and suppliers is the goal.

Another shift occurs from manufacturing to service industries in the sense of execution. In manufacturing the focus of execution is excellence first before timeliness to minimize waste. In the service industries, however, the focus is often on responsiveness before perfection. Customers being served like to feel cared for before being served. Thus, the focus of execution in service operations must be on agility, care, and creativity in delivering customers what they love to have, which may be different every time a customer needs service.

The Service Scorecard Architecture presented in this book has seven categories or elements: Growth, Leadership, Acceleration, Collaboration, Innovation, Execution, and Retention (GLACIER). The Service Scorecard was created for achieving the fundamental strategy of any business: sustained profitable growth. Instead of focusing on making money (or profit at any cost), the leadership must focus on realizing profitable growth. This shift requires the utilization of other aspects of the business. A good performance scorecard must trigger critical aspects of the business for achieving its fundamental strategy, which must be constantly articulated for successful internalization by everyone on the executive team.

Growth requires critical thinking at the leadership level for assessing industry position and caring for customer needs. To grow the business, the leadership must clearly understand what its customers would love to have. Only when we care enough to listen to the customer's love-to-have requirements will we establish a successful and profitable relationship with the customer. Knowing the future needs of current customers and the needs of potential customers allows the service provider to develop new solutions to serve its customers.

Leadership is considered great when it can bring out the best in its followers, be it 1, 10, 100, or 1,000s in number. Unless people are mobilized to achieve the fundamental business strategy and objectives, sustaining profitable growth will be a daunting task. One of the best known ways to bring out the best in people is to recognize the best of people. Good breeds more good, and success breeds more success; thus, recognition of success will bring out more success. Besides, the leadership must ensure that the business is profitable while it is growing; otherwise, employees will perceive their work as a waste of their time.

Acceleration is defined as the rate of improvement to achieve ideal or desired business objectives. Accelerating improvement and reduction in waste will continually contribute to the bottom line of the company. Besides, customers ask for better, faster, and more value— not cheaper service. To provide more value faster and better requires each department manager to focus on producing more, better and faster. Ultimately, the best corporate performance will be governed by the worst departmental performance. Basically, the worst of a company is the best it can deliver to its customers. Acceleration in performance improvement continually raises the bar for higher value to the customer.

Collaboration is an imperative when accelerating performance. If a department or process has a goal to improve 5 percent per year, people usually wait for the change to come by itself; they generally do not challenge themselves to achieve improvement. The 5 percent improvement is not aggressive enough to challenge them and cause them to seek help. However, if the goals for improvement are set aggressively, collaboration from other departments, processes, or people will be required to accelerate improvement. Achieving 50 percent or more improvement requires passion to collaborate for achieving desired results.

Innovation is an outcome when people collaborate. When people work together, new ideas abound, creativity is cultivated, and innovative solutions are the outcome. Innovation to achieve growth through R&D (research and development) functions has been inefficient and slow at best. Typically, an R&D department develops a new product or service that is delivered through operations with a ton of challenges. The resulting quality and efficiency degradation leads to unsatisfactory results and delays delivery of products or services. Thus, the involvement of operations throughout the service life cycle accelerates improvement at any level.

Execution represents producing or providing service with optimum resources on time and delighting the customer. In service businesses, the customer experiencing joy matters because people are involved. Customers tend to be sensitive to receiving service without a smiling attitude. Thus, in service execution, people processes must be designed to facilitate agility, care, and creativity, as well as a sense of going the extra mile to please the customer. Basic process management principles still hold true for service processes as well; the people aspects just need extra attention.

Repeat business from customers receiving service, or Retention, is fundamental to survival as well as achieving sustained profitable growth. The cost of new customer acquisition in the service sector is much higher than that of keeping a repeat customer. Thus, effort must be invested in listening to the customer for growing requirements and customer feedback to identify opportunities for improvement. Repeat business pays for the expenses, and the new business pays for the profit. A service business cannot survive without repeat customers. Thus, specific strategies must be developed to bring the customer back continually, irrespective of the nature of the service.

Establishing the Service Scorecard Measurements

Identifying and establishing Service Scorecard measurements requires that we identify the purpose of the Service Scorecard and its expected value proposition. Is the purpose of the scorecard to display some information in the form of some dashboard, or to analyze and use the information to identify and exploit opportunities for improvement? The Service Scorecard can be used for realizing the fundamental business strategy of achieving sustained profitable growth, to monitor profit, or to communicate information with stakeholders. To establish measurements in different areas, answering the following questions can be helpful:

- What does one do?
- Why does one do it?
- Who does one do it for?
- How will one know one has done it?

The measures are identified based on strategic outcomes, client benefits, and the process outputs. Another way of establishing measurements for an element of the scorecard includes answering the following questions:

1. What is the purpose of the Service Scorecard for an organization?

2. What is the purpose of each element of the scorecard?

3. What is the expected deliverable as a result of each element of the scorecard?

4. What is the measure of success for each element of the scorecard?

5. What are the activities to be performed in implementing the required measurement?

6. What are the critical elements of the activities to be performed?

7. What are measures of success for critical elements in question 5?

Opportunities abound for a service operation to be striving for excellence. In the so-called "service economy," our experience shows more customers are dissatisfied with the service due to a variety of reasons. The Service Scorecard can create the "love" for customers, improve business performance, and foster high employee participation and joy.

Take Away

- The service sector is an important sector in world economy.
- Service can be defined as a transaction or as an experience.
- Measuring the performance of services is challenging, and traditional models are inadequate for this purpose.
- The Six Sigma Business Scorecard needs to be adapted to the services context.
- The Service Scorecard Architecture has seven elements: Growth, Leadership, Acceleration, Collaboration, Innovation, Execution, and Retention (GLACIER).

2

Performance Challenges in the Service Sector

The service sector is the dominant component of all major developed economies. In addition, the service sector is also growing in developing economies such as India, Brazil, Russia, and China. These developing economies have also experienced productivity improvement and growth in the double digits. Understanding performance measurement at service firms in these economies is an integral part of managerial decision making leading to corporate value enhancement.

The advantages of implementing a performance measurement system include the presence of a robust decision support system for managers, timeliness of relevant information, improved quality of information for decision making, more effective and clear communication among various stakeholders, and the alignment of goals. Performance measurement challenges in the service sector range from people issues to having a well-defined understanding of service processes and the differences between the service and nonservice sectors. Achieving good measurements of customer satisfaction or service warranties are also difficult but important.

Hence, a robust performance measurement system is a prerequisite for performance improvement and management leading to productivity improvement and business effectiveness. Performance measurement systems are designed and implemented to monitor and maintain influence over companies, which in turn helps firms achieve business goals and objectives. At the basic level, a performance measurement system asks four basic questions: (1) What has happened in terms of corporate performance? Does everybody know what has happened? (2) Why has it happened? Does everybody in the firm have the same understanding of the managerial drivers? (3) Is it going to continue? How long will it continue? (4) What are we going to do about it? What are the organizational barriers?

Even though implementing a Performance Measurement (PM) System is proving to be a difficult task, many service firms are doing so. Problems usually arise either at the design stage or the implementation stage. Design issues lead to poor data quality, as measuring what is easy to measure is pursued instead of measuring what should be measured. Challenges at the implementation stage are much more related to the existing firm culture and the infrastructure of the information system. The implementation stage also needs to consider human issues. Effective implementation in a service sector has to consider these challenges in addition to considering the uniqueness of the service sector.

Examples and Drawbacks of Performance Measurement Systems

Performance Measurement (PM) has grown over the past few years with the creation of frameworks, such as activity-based costing and the Balanced Scorecard. Lately, different forms of performance measurement systems have received their share of criticism. Much of the criticism of traditional performance measurement systems stems from their failure to measure, monitor, and control multiple dimensions of performance, due to an almost exclusive concentration on financial (and lagging) measures of performance. Although PM systems prove to be helpful to firms, they have yet to be a plainly definable and meaningful concept. Some of the specific criticisms include the following:

- Multiple interpretations of PM systems across the organization. The goal and usage of the system are not clearly defined.
- Lack of common understanding among various stakeholders.
- Lack of alignment with business goals and strategy. The PM system is not aligned with corporate strategy and is not updated and changed as strategy changes.

- Lack of understanding of business context. A standard cookie-cutter approach is used but not adapted to a particular business context. The business context will vary based on the service sub-sector, the firm's maturity, the firm's size and geographical diversity, and the firm's variety-of-offerings portfolio.
- Lack of relationship between measures and business performance. A causal relationship is missing between what is measured and what is important for the business performance.

Recent examples of popular measurement systems are the Balanced Scorecard, the Performance Prism, and the Performance Pyramid. The Balanced Scorecard is the most widely used performance measurement system. A recent study showed that 60 percent of companies in America have tried the popular Balanced Scorecard. Due to various shortcomings, the Balanced Scorecard elements need to be adapted in the service context. For example, the Balanced Scorecard lacks employee focus, a partnership mindset, service innovation, and a clear emphasis on leadership quality. The Balanced Scorecard was not designed specifically for service firms and is not predictive in nature.

Unilever added "people development" as a fifth dimension to the Balanced Scorecard. Partners' or service chain partners' contributions and their impact on performance measurement are either missing or not adequately addressed in existing frameworks. Business interdependencies are increasingly becoming more important, and a robust system should include service chain partners (or suppliers) as stakeholders.

Service innovation is poorly defined and often not reflected in popular performance measurement systems such as the Balanced Scorecard and Performance Prism. Employees at the operations level are unable to relate to the Balanced Scorecard, thus causing a gap in communication between executives and employees. A performance measurement system designed specifically for the service-dominant context—one that includes explicit measures to implement the scorecard—is needed.

Performance Measurement for Service

To design a performance measurement system, we need to understand characteristics of services, various business subcontexts in the service domain, and uniqueness presented in this context. The characteristics of services, including the intangibility of services, simultaneous production and consumption, and proximity to the customer, are thoroughly discussed in the literature. Classification schemes may be helpful when identifying the order of priority of service quality dimensions, because they are based on dimension of contact, customization, and labor intensity. For example, the Haywood-Farmer three-dimensional model puts every service into one of eight cubes. Another classification considers dimensions such as nature of the service delivery and availability of service outlets. Based on the nature of services, one could also classify service among three categories: transaction, services, and experience. Table 2.1 presents a comparison among these three categories. The degree of customization and customer participation is the highest for experiences.

TABLE 2.1 Understanding Services

Transaction Services	Services	Experience
High volume, less variety	High value, more variety	Overall experience, high variety
Productivity	Quality and performance	Overall perception
Invisible to customer	Visible to customer	Partnership, co-design
Often in push system	Responsiveness, push-pull boundary in the middle	Customer driven and pull system
Automation, standard processes	Back room has some transactional process	People to people
High "service inventory," less work needed after arrival	Medium "service inventory" Consistency standard leading to better service recovery	Very little "service inventory"

Process View and Experience View of Services

Within the next few decades, the major productivity improvements and growth opportunities are expected to take place in the service sector. Major corporations like General Motors and General Electric are shifting from manufacturing to the service side of the business, because most of their profits are realized through the service component. Adopting a process view of services has implications on the corporate strategy of a service firm.

Process-oriented disciplines, which are common in manufacturing settings, may share certain basic concepts, such as breaking down processes into logical steps and sequences to facilitate their control and analysis. The process view, however, does not include the customer viewpoint and customer preferences. Blueprinting, which is designing a process flow diagram including the customer visibility line, is a method of mapping out a service system. Service blueprinting is much more valuable in the service context, because customers are the integral part of the system.

The service industry has designed jobs in parallel with Taylorism and Fordism manufacturing practices (for example, splitting up the high and low customer contact activities within a job to cut costs). This practice is also known as the "decoupling process," where (a) low customer contact (face-to-face or person-to-person) activities are removed from the customer's line of visibility, and (b) such activities are standardized and often centralized in a remote location (for example, a call center and processing center in the financial industry) to achieve economies of scale. The service blueprint will show above-the-line and below-the-line steps of the process.

Customers do not view high-contact services as a collection of processes. As evident from the preceding discussion, the process view represents the provider's perspective. Customers consider services as experiences. The experience view of service takes the psychology of customer-employee interaction into consideration. Increasingly, service firms are even attempting to convert a transaction into an experience to achieve better customer retention.

Strategic View of Services

As mentioned previously, performance systems often lack an alignment with the business context. Therefore, an understanding of the service strategy and business context is a necessary first step in this direction. Service strategies will depend on the target customer segment. Similar to the view of transaction and high/low contact services, R. Metters and V. Vargas in an article in *Business Horizons* (2000) suggested the following strategic approaches for service firms: cost leadership, cheap convenience, dedicated service, and premium service. The *cost leadership* approach is used when the business strategy on services is to compete on price; therefore, the decoupling process is used to reduce costs. In the service industry, cost leaders generally centralize their services, causing cost to decrease while reducing the work variance. Job duties become highly specialized and do not necessarily promote cross-training. When dealing with standard-type customers, this approach can be highly efficient; when dealing with special requests, however, it can create a sense of chaos. The use of technology in this particular system helps with labor reduction. Even though this strategy is cost efficient, there are negative effects, including a loss in flexibility, response time, and quality.

The *cheap convenience* competitive approach is used when firms aim to enhance customer convenience while remaining cost efficient. The use of back-office work is limited, and the front-end workers are cross-trained to do the back-end work themselves; this process greatly cuts the number of workers. Because the workflow patterns are not predictable, however, this model can potentially hurt customer service, creating a bottleneck in customer queues.

The *dedicated service* competitive approach offers greater variety and flexibility than the two approaches described previously. The decoupling process is used to enhance the front-end office capabilities; the cost consideration is a secondary concern. The firm can place employees in the front- or back-end office depending on their work personalities (people-oriented or task-oriented), as well as centralize back-end tasks by region and designate specific teams to specific organizational front-end areas.

This *dedicated service* model fosters long-term relationships between front- and back-end office colleagues; it reduces the overlap in work and promotes the employee with a more personalized responsibility. Employees will be more willing to go the extra mile for the customer and colleague. The back-office employees are cross-trained in different departments to eliminate bottlenecks; furthermore, management is encouraged to set in place an incentive program that rewards the back-end employee for supporting the front-end employee.

The *premium service* competitive approach provides a superior level of personalized customer service. The goal in this approach is to go beyond the transactional orientation to a relationship orientation, maximizing customization and responsiveness. The use of back-end operations is seen only when there is an overwhelming advantage provided by scale economies. In this model, hiring the proper employee, offering superior training, and ultimately retaining these employees are extremely important objectives. If employees leave the organization, they could potentially take their clientele with them due to the relationship they have formed. Customers form a loyalty relationship with the front-end employee, not necessarily with the organization itself; the use of back-end employees is seamless to the client. A managerial challenge is to ensure that the front-end employee is maintaining conformance with quality standards and brand image.

The ultimate success of each of the respective approaches is dependent on considering the market in which the firm is situated, as well as executing the selected approach that fits the current marketplace and customer base. If the type of company, target customer group, and market segmentation are not considered and studied appropriately, the decoupling decision will fail.

Performance Measurement Challenges in Services

In the early 1980s, the academic and business communities argued that existing measures were not appropriate given the modern manufacturing environment. In the early twenty-first century, the existing frameworks do not adequately address the modern service-dominant economic environment. Service-dominant logic and related concepts are increasingly becoming accepted even in product-centric firms. The majority of performance measurement systems in use today were developed in the manufacturing setting. Attempts have been made to force-fit these frameworks into the service-dominant context.

Our understanding of service performance measurement itself is evolving. For example, service inventory discussed in the previous section has been redefined for the services context. As Andy Neely and Rob Austin assert, "Rather than add yet more confusion and complexity, there is a need to step back from recent developments and reflect upon where the field of performance measurement has been and where it is going." Observation is especially relevant for the field of service performance measurement. A comprehensive performance measurement system specifically for services must be developed. Specific challenges associated with service firms' performance are listed here:

- **Inherent variation among customers, servers, time periods, and service processes**—Customer variability is an added variability that should be incorporated. Various classifications of performance measures are available: objective versus subjective measures, internal versus external measures, and core versus noncore or supporting process-based measures. In this section, the impact of customer variability on core measures is considered. The core process of the service delivery system includes added variability, which is nonexistent in manufacturing-based systems. Manufacturing systems include demand variability. Customers often co-produce services and introduce added variability. Due to customer involvement in the service product process, four types of variability are introduced, as shown in Table 2.2: (1) arrival/request of the customer, (2) capability of customers with respect to their expected involvement, (3) effort employers are willing to exert, and (4) subjective preference of customers for how service should be delivered.

  Active customers introduce all four types of variability, and passive customers introduce type 1, 2, and 4 variability. How is customer-introduced variability relevant to performance measurement? Performance measurement needs to be context-dependent, and the reduce-accommodate strategy creates business contexts.

TABLE 2.2 Customer Variability Management

Arrival/Request	Capability Process	Effort Employer	Subjective Performance
Create complementary demand Move demand to off-peak pricing	Target customers based on internal capability	Target customers based on motivation and preferences	Set consistent expectations
Persuade customers to adjust preferences influence Outsource customer contact	Experienced and skilled employees Employees training	Build service inventory Prepare customers	Communicate expectations
Reservation (by type)	Customer self-service	Experienced employees	
Cross training	Automation	Automation	
Buffer labor	Self-service	Self-service	

(Frei, FX, *Harvard Business Review*, 2006 Nov:93-101)

- **Prominently including the engagement of employees—** Human capital is a critical asset at a service firm. Employee engagement drives the financial performance and innovation potential of a service firm. A recent Watson Wyatt survey report showed the relationship between its Human Capital index and shareholder value. Specifically, five key human capital practices are associated with a 30 percent increase in shareholder value: recruiting excellence, clear rewards and accountability, collegial flexible workplace, communications integrity, and prudent use of resources. The survey represented 60 percent of firms in service settings. Employee engagement/development has been often overlooked in the existing performance measurement framework. Employee engagement is critical in the service-dominant context, and its impact on financial performance should be even greater.

- **Including the service innovation dimension—**Our understanding of innovation and the innovation process in services is derived from the manufacturing setting. However, performance measures like R&D spent per employee or numbers of patents per employee are meaningless in a service-dominant context. The service innovation topic is not yet explicitly integrated into the academic world. Questions about service innovation that demand answers include the following: Do services innovate any differently? How does innovation happen in the service-dominant context? How is progress of service innovation measured? How can innovation performance be improved? In manufacturing settings, innovation can be classified as product-related or process-related. Service firm innovation places emphasis on human skills and collaboration with service chain partners. However, services can innovate along a third dimension, namely organizational change. This dimension of innovation is nonexistent in the manufacturing context. Services also have a tendency to innovate incrementally as opposed to being discrete or step-wise innovation as evident in the manufacturing setting. A performance measurement system needs to capture these inherent differences.

- **Maintaining a partnership focus**—A service offering often includes elements that are offered by partners. The performance of a service firm is directly impacted by the quality of relationships it maintains with its partners. The concept of relationship takes a different meaning in the services context, because these companies are partners and not merely suppliers of a standard component of an offering. A robust performance measurement system should include the element of partnership management.

- **Existing in a solution-dominant world**—Customer solution perspectives need to be included into the performance system. In essence, a *pure* product or *pure* service world does not exist these days. The either/or dichotomy of products and services has been replaced with a solution-dominant context, as shown in Figure 2.1. Managers should identify the needs of the customers and provide appropriate solutions. The solution could include some product and some service component. We define a *solution* as an integrated and customized system of products, services, and knowledge co-produced with customers and partners to achieve better customer outcomes than the sum of the parts. Key points to note are that the innovation process is a collaborative process, and the outcome or customer need is a starting point. We also need to consider the experience aspects of customer-service firm interaction. Typical success indicators used in a product-centric world are product revenue, product profitability, and market share. A solution-centric world will likely include measures such as customer experience, value created, and satisfaction and loyalty. Figure 2.1 shows characteristics of solutions and experiences.

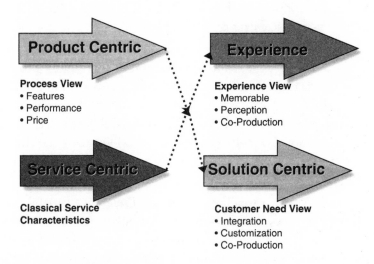

Figure 2.1   Solution-centric view

Major Challenges

The following section provides a discussion on the importance of customer-introduced variability. Customer-introduced variability is unique to service situations due to customer involvement at service production and design stages. The section provides an understanding of different types of variables and strategies to managing these situations.

Customer-Introduced Variability

Frances X. Frei, in a recent *Harvard Business Review* article, suggests how to manage customers' involvement in service operations to deliver consistent quality at sustainable costs. In a product world, a firm faces variability only in the production process. In service settings, customers introduce additional variability, because they are often an integral part of the production process.

All variability can be classified into five categories that create operational issues for a company. The first type is the *Arrival* variability, which involves queuing management such as cashiers at retail stores, call centers, and emergency rooms. The second is *Request* variability, which involves options and substitutions. The option for white or wheat toast at a typical cafe is an example.

The third category is *Capability* variability, which is the difference in customers' knowledge, skill, physical ability, or resources to perform their tasks that affect the quality or cost of service. For example, a patient's ability to describe his symptoms will affect the quality of the healthcare he receives. The fourth is *Effort* variability, which is the difference in additional work that customers are willing to offer. Whether or not a shopper returns her shopping cart to the corrals in the parking lot has an impact on the store's service quality and cost.

The fifth type of variability, *Subjective Preference* variability, involves customers' opinions in terms of what good treatment is (which can differ among customers). Although some people think it is helpful that a salesclerk talks to customers, others think it is soliciting. To reduce the impact of these customer-introduced variabilities and enhance the competitiveness of service, managers must use a systematic process to diagnose problems and fine-tune interventions. Whenever customer-introduced variability creates a challenge for a company, managers often assume that they had to either accommodate customers' various desires and behaviors at high cost or refuse to accommodate them at the risk of customer defection.

Service Inventory and Service Delivery Systems

The customer interface can be made-to-stock (MTS) products or made-to-order (MTO) products. MTS products in the manufacturing world have an inventory to absorb the variability in demand. MTO products typically compete on delivery time and customization; these processes generally have low utilization. These types of products include assemble-to-order, make-to-order, engineer-to-order, configure-to-order, pack-to-order, and print-to-order. Similar principles can be applied to services. Service inventory, recently discussed in the literature, is all about the placement of the push-pull technology and how it defines the amount of work that is completed and stored before a customer requests service. This variable is what seems to make the service inventory much more unique when compared with the product inventory.

Since the dawn of the new push environment that is present today, keeping too much inventory within a company can end up being costly and unnecessary. What the service inventory provides is work readily available to its customers before they even request the service. The reason that this new methodology is becoming increasingly more relevant is that the environment went from a *pull* environment to a *push* environment. In other words, companies no longer build product in response to actual demand; rather, they wait for the consumer to come to them in order to meet their needs. The service industry has technically always been a form of a push environment, because such companies wait for the consumer to come to them with a request for service. The service industry needs to be viewed in the context of how firms compete and create value for their customers by contributing a certain number of attributes.

How well a service delivers these attributes to customers is critical to the company. The four main attributes of a service are quality, speed, customization, and price. Quality is increased as the push-pull boundary is moved toward the market. Shifting this push-pull boundary lets the company account for failures that allow it to respond efficiently.

Combining speed and price together, service inventory allows for greater customization that will quicken the time of receiving the service along with reducing the cost. The reason behind the quicker customization and lower cost is due to how relatively cheap it is to hold and maintain service inventory, thus allowing service providers to have greater pricing flexibility. Whether companies deliver these four attributes properly depends on the process choices that the company decides to make.

During this process design, managerial decisions are based on certain drivers of performance: the placement of the push-pull boundary, the level and the composition of resources, and access policies. The push-pull boundary determines how much work is done and stored in anticipation of demand. Resources are used to perform the actual work of delivering a service. And access policies are used to govern how customers are able to make use of service inventory and resources. Where the push-pull boundary is located is one of the major decisions under consideration within the process design. Table 2.3 provides an overview of the impact of service inventory on service attributes for services and experiences.

TABLE 2.3   Service Inventory

Service Attribute Desired by customers	Impact of Service Inventory on Performance SERVICES	Impact of Service Inventory on Performance EXPERIENCES
Service Inventory	Medium service inventory.	Low service inventory.
Quality	Provides for consistency and conforms to standards.	Conformance to a standard is not important.
	Provides standard and simple response to service failures.	Individualized response is expected.
Speed	Medium level of service inventory reduces amount of work needed after customer arrival (lower capacity requirements).	Speed is slower as more steps have to be completed.
Customization	Customers use preferences for customization. Allows greater customer control.	Customers co-design the experience and provide multiple inputs to customize the experience.
Price	Service Inventory helps in self-service and reduces cost of service provided.	Customers are willing to pay higher prices.

(S. Chopra and M.A. Lariviere, "Managing Service Inventory to improve performance," *MIT Sloan Management Review*, 47: 57-63, 2005)

The service industry allows for a company to take advantage of the economies of scale. The service industry can perform better because those businesses are constantly dealing with customers on a semipersonal basis and knowing what that customer is looking for in terms of customization. With regard to economies of scale, consider the Radian Group of Philadelphia. This insurance group stores the information collected from its customers in its own database, thus making it easier to exploit economies of scale much more cheaply and quickly for its customers. One way in which Radian's service inventory relates to product inventory is by limiting what the company can deliver to its customers quickly, which is true of all service inventories when compared to product inventories.

Supply chain management must focus on *how much* inventory should be held for the company in regard to product inventory in manufacturing. For service inventory, on the other hand, the decisions really rely on *what kind* of work to store. In other words, a service provider must decide what types of offerings are needed to build inventory and at what stage the service should be completed.

Two instances in which a service provider should consider service inventory for its company are (1) when it can find a positive in enhancing its competitive position over other service providers, and (2) when it sets a standard set of access policies for the company ensuring that it can maximize its success. Knowing where to push the push-pull boundary for a service provider is important, because where that boundary is set determines the success of the company. Service providers should set this boundary where they find their service inventory providing structure and support to their service. The service provider should find the greatest results at this level. In this case, a service provider's inventory will be maximized, thus helping out its economies of scale.

Managing service inventory is a great way to enhance a company's economies of scale. When related to managerial decisions, service inventory is important, because it can end up being costly or detrimental to customer satisfaction for a company if too much inventory is held or not enough is present. The service inventory decision is part of the service *delivery design* decisions and is discussed while presenting Six Sigma applications in services.

Service Guarantee and Service Recovery Challenge

If properly designed, a service guarantee enables a service organization to gain control over all aspects of service delivery and related processes. A service guarantee (with clear goals/objectives and an information feedback network) assists the organization by identifying items that need performance improvement. Committing to error-free service can force a company to provide error-free service. Why do most existing service guarantees fail? In the customer's eyes, a service guarantee loses its power in direct proportion to the number of conditions and exceptions it possesses. Ideally, the service guarantee should have the following traits:

- **Be unconditional**—The service guarantee should promise the customer unconditional satisfaction without exceptions. If the company cannot guarantee all the elements of its service unconditionally, the company should unconditionally guarantee the elements of its service that it can control.
- **Be easy to communicate and understand**—The guarantee should be written in simple and concise language that specifically identifies the pledge. This assists both the customer and employees in understanding expectations.
- **Be meaningful**—The service guarantee should ensure the aspects of the service that are important to the customer and offer a financial payout if promises are not kept.
- **Be easy (and painless) to invoke**—Customers should not have to expend additional effort to invoke the guarantee, nor should the customer be made to feel guilty about invoking the guarantee.
- **Be easy and quick to collect**—The customer should not work hard to collect on the guarantee. The process should be quick and easy.

The following reasons outline why a service guarantee works:

- The guarantee pushes the entire company to focus on the customer's definition and perception of good service.
- The guarantee sets clear performance goals and standards that boost employee performance and morale.

- The guarantee generates reliable data (through guarantee payouts) noting poor performance, thus improving the reliability of the system.

- The guarantee forces the organization to examine its entire service delivery system and related processes for potential breakdown. It helps identify causal relationships and makes the system foolproof.

- The guarantee builds customer loyalty, sales, and market share.

We should note both the real and the perceived power of an unconditional service guarantee, because it forces a company to focus on its customers, set clear standards, and generate feedback (to use in continuous improvement and to help understand why certain items failed).

Case Studies of Performance Measurement in the Service Sector

The explicit example of the trade-off is Southwest Airlines. While traditional airline companies are making expensive investments to accommodate the customer-introduced variability by providing international flights, offering multiple-cabin classes, instituting several levels of refunds for tickets, providing reserved seats, providing full meals with multiple kinds of beverages (including alcoholic beverages), transferring passengers' luggage, flying into larger airports in major cities with a "Hub and Spoke" flight routing system, and networking with travel agents, Southwest is saving money by focusing on domestic flights, with one class, no refund tickets, no assigned seats, simple snacks and beverages, no luggage transfer, use of secondary airports with a "Point to Point" flight system, and use of a direct booking system though the Internet and phones. Although its operation certainly reduces the range of service and additional benefits for some, the quality of the main service (in this case, a safe and comfortable flight with smooth booking, checking, and boarding procedures) has been maintained, thus explaining why Southwest continues to be profitable even after the 9/11 attacks.

The same concept of limiting service options is applied to the cruise ship industry. EasyCruise seeks to attract young, budget-conscious travelers in Europe who are less interested in flashy entertainment and spacious cabins than in getting off the ship and enjoying destinations they might not have been able to afford to visit otherwise. Because EasyCruise does not offer lavish meals and expensive shows, it is able to charge lower prices. Hence, these low-cost players alter customers' behavior permanently and get people to accept fewer benefits at a lower price.

Another great example that altered customers' behavior drastically in the transportation industry is Zipcar, which completely changed the car-rental system. Instead of applying a rental concept, it created a sharing concept. Members of Zipcar can pick up a car in their neighborhood and use it for a couple of hours without the cost and hassles of owning a car. Users just need to apply online to be a member. They can check vehicle availability and reserve a car via the Internet or telephone. After the reservation they receive an access card, which they can use to unlock the doors by just holding it to the windshield. Each vehicle records hours of usage and mileage, which is uploaded to a central computer via a wireless data link. The rental fee is as low as $8 an hour including driver's insurance. (There is an annual membership fee according to each plan.) Also, members get reimbursed for typical car maintenance items, such as car washes and window wiper fluid refills.

Zipcar can provide such a flexible service with low cost simply because the company does not have to maintain offices and large parking garages. However, an even more significant shift is occurring in the customer's behavior. In fact, Zipcar is a perfect example of managing customer-introduced variability with low cost, yet in an uncompromised manner. What if users do not return the car on time? What if users cause damage to the cars? Such provisions of renting a car take up a big portion of the cost for the traditional rental-car companies.

On the contrary, Zipcar's business model became feasible based on the users' mutual trust. This "sharing" concept functions simply by spontaneous cooperation of users for their mutual benefits. Users manage their arrival variability by reserving a car online. They manage their request variability by choosing a pickup location and a type of car from the existing list. They manage their capability of applying for a membership, making a reservation, finding a car, unlocking doors, and paying fees. They manage their effort to keep the cars clean for other users and return them to the pickup spot. They manage their subjective preference from a value-for-money standpoint.

Although Zipcar's business model has not yet been accepted by mass society, after early adapters start telling of their experience, the power of word-of-mouth will rapidly enhance the possibility of business penetrations. Because the business was designed to set a mutually beneficial operating role for customers, they find an explicit value in the service.

Another tactic for trade-off that manages customer-introduced variability is the self-service system. Until a couple of years ago, no self-service gas stations existed in Japan. Because of law regulations, customers could not pump gas into their cars and had to sit and wait while a staff person filled up gas in the car, cleaned car windows, and picked up garbage for them. Consequently, customers paid extra service fees to the gas stations.

However, deregulation made an epoch turn in the gas station industry in Japan. As of December 2005, there are now 4,900 self-service stations and 43,000 traditional full-service stations in Japan. Full-service stations are decreasing every year, with a 20 percent decrease from 53,000 stations in the year 2000 alone. On the contrary, self-service stations are increasing, with 12 times more now compared to 400 stations in the year 2000.

As with Zipcar, the business model altered customers' behavior in Japan. Customers appreciate their cost benefit rather than becoming critical about service quality. A partial reason for this phenomenon is that companies handed over the control of service quality to the customers. Customers now do not have to pay for an unnecessary service, because these additional benefits are optional. They pay for the fundamental quality of products or services and take responsibility for fulfilling the quality of supplemental services themselves.

Challenges in performance measurement systems within the service sector will vary based on the subsector. For example, the health-care sector has its own additional challenges related to regulations and privacy issues. Professional service firms need to focus much more on human capital and knowledge management issues.

The size of the firm will also play a role during the design and implementation stages. A small firm in the early stages of development will have its own set of unique challenges as opposed to a mature multinational firm with global presence. Some of the challenges are becoming more apparent now due to the changing nature of business. The extent of outsourcing leading to a fluid definition of service firm boundaries is creating additional challenges in terms of ownership and accountability. As discussed previously, the importance of partner selection and the quality of the partnership relationship is becoming increasingly important.

Take Away

- Existing performance measurement systems often have been criticized for providing a standard cookie-cutter approach.
- Understanding of both process and experience views is necessary to design a performance measurement system for services.
- Challenges to designing performance measurement systems for services are the following: added variability due to customer involvement, importance of employee engagement, and service innovation and inclusion of partnership focus.
- A fresh understanding of "service inventory" and "service delivery system" is necessary to implement a performance measurement system.
- Understanding the importance of a service guarantee is also important to implement a performance measurement system. The service guarantee is one way to build customer loyalty, collect information, and improve the system.

3

Six Sigma for Services

As discussed in the previous chapters, significant differences exist between an offering provided by a manufacturing firm and that provided by a service firm. Salient characteristics of service operations systems are customer participation in the service process, the interdependent and dynamic nature of the service system's steps, the intangibility of the offering, and the perishable nature of the offering. The previous chapters also mentioned a few types of performance management systems. One of these methodologies, Six Sigma, has been applied extensively in the manufacturing context. The application of the Six Sigma methodology within the service context, however, becomes a challenging task due to the differences presented previously.

Imagine working in a manufacturing company where mistakes are constantly made and daily shutdowns occur because of poor operation problems. The product manufacturing takes place far from where customers buy their products. Now, imagine a service firm (such as a bank, an airline, or a retail store) and how mistakes in this environment will affect the normal operation of the firm. For example, an airline experience includes finding a parking space, queuing in for check-in, the process of checking in, going through the security check, boarding the plane, having the in-flight experience, deplaning, waiting and getting the luggage from the belt, and taking a cab. The relative importance of many of these steps will matter.

Many customers will make a decision about the level of quality service they receive within minutes of being encountered, and their level of dissatisfaction/satisfaction will carry over to the next steps. The term "zones of tolerance," which describes an acceptable level of service at each stage, complicates a multistep system. These zones of tolerance are also dynamic. For example, a customer arriving at a hotel to find that his or her reservation has been lost, and that the frontline staff person is rude and unhelpful, experiences multiple steps of service. For this customer, the zones of tolerance for those stages will be narrower as compared to the zones of tolerance if those missteps did not happen. Similarly for a very good start of a service, zones of tolerance may be wider at the later stages.

Most large, worldwide service firms initiate and adopt some form of service quality initiative. These initiatives are metrics-driven and provide information to the performance management system in place. These initiatives include ISO standard certification and the Baldrige Award application. Broadly speaking, a firm can choose from the following methodologies:

- **Total Quality Management (TQM)**—A total quality management system includes basic quality tools and associated methodologies.
- **ISO 9000**—Process-oriented international certification. The certification brings standardization and process-oriented thinking into the picture and is usually audited by a third party.
- **Capability Maturity Model**—The maturity model, consisting of five levels, is adopted by information technology (software) firms. Few firms around the world have achieved Level V certification. The certification shows the maturation of project management and quality management processes at these firms.
- **The Malcolm-Baldrige Award Model**—This model is used to improve the overall competitive business performance of a firm and is popular in the U.S.
- **Six Sigma Method**—This methodology, introduced by Motorola and made popular by General Electric, improves business performance.

Six Sigma and Service

Six Sigma could strangle the culture of innovation at firms such as 3M. Six Sigma is a structured methodology and brings standards, methods, and templates into play that could directly work against the culture of innovation at a particular firm. Such a firm should consider the importance of service innovation and firm culture while adopting and implementing such an initiative. No matter which combination of methodologies a firm chooses to adopt, an alignment with the operations (and corporate) strategy is a necessary and required condition for the initiative to succeed.

Additionally, a service firm's operations strategy should also be in alignment with its corporate strategy. The operations strategy of a particular firm will depend on its business context, the life cycle of the offering, and other contextual variables. The operations strategy of a service firm is based on what the firm decides to offer its customers in terms of price, quality, response time, and level of customization.

Any Six Sigma initiative needs to take a firm's operations strategy into consideration. For example, a firm following a cost-based operations strategy, such as Wal-Mart, will have much more emphasis on processes and methods as opposed to a firm following a differentiation strategy, such as Disney World. Disney World provides empowerment to employees, and thus the structure is much more flexible. Although a firm's management could determine the business objective without the help of the Six Sigma methodology, the analysis and discipline provided by a measurement system help achieve the objective and measure the progress toward this objective.

Six Sigma Methodology Overview

DMAIC (Define, Measure, Analyze, Improve, Control) is an established methodology in a manufacturing context. Considering the importance of innovation and challenges to implementation, a newly proposed Six Sigma methodology called DMAIE (Define, Measure, Analyze, Innovate, Embed) is presented here. The established Six Sigma methodology DMAIC is compared with DMAIE. The DMAIE methodology can be applied to both transaction-based and experience-based services. Table 3.1 offers a side-by-side comparison of the DMAIC and DMAIE methodologies. A description of each step in DMAIE follows.

Table 3.1 Comparison Between DMAIC (Traditional) and DMAIE (New) Methodologies

DMAIC Methodology Phase	Comments	DMAIE Methodology Phase	Typical Tools Used
Define: Need identification, project selection, stakeholders analysis	Identify relationship with corporate performance	**Define**	Identify customer viewpoints and degree of participation. Define what exactly will be measured.
Measure: Measure, and collect information	Identify "right" measures	**Measure**	Turn qualitative indicators into measurable. Define vice recovery effectiveness. Use perceptions and zones of tolerances.
Analyze: Develop hypothesis, identify root causes, and validate hypothesis	Identify key "causal" relationships	**Analyze**	Benchmark internally and externally.
Improve: Develop ideas to improve, test ideas and make solutions standard, and measure the outcome	Brainstorm and identify solutions	**Innovate**	Apply service innovation techniques such as TRIZ, brainstorming, mind mapping, and Brinnovation™.
Control: Establish control measures and control charts	Use control charts	**Embed**	Institutionalize and consider human aspects of implementation.

Define and Develop

The first step in the Define and Develop phase is to revisit the strategic alignment of a service firm. Often the first step steers the whole Six Sigma initiative in a certain direction. As described in Table 3.1, the first step involves tools like project selection, a service operations audit, process flowcharting, and service blueprinting. The framework to understand and improve a given service delivery system becomes important in this phase.

The Define phase also includes defining the service delivery system and service operations aspects in detail. The service delivery chain must be designed to support the strategy of the firm, as well as fill its customer needs to be successful. The strategic position of the firm in relation to the customers' needs may be defined in terms of speed of response, variety/customization, level of interaction, willingness to pay, and quality.

Like the product supply chain, the service delivery chain is designed to respond to the degree of service demand and variability in function of the service characteristics, customer needs, and service capabilities. The service chain capability should provide the appropriate level of performance in the dimensions of responsiveness to customer needs and change demand, as well as the cost incurred to provide a service. The service chain capability consists of four key drivers:

1. **Service capacity network,** which represents the level, location (degree of centralization), flexibility, and ownership of the service capacity.

2. **Service inventory,** which takes into account the steps of service to be completed before and after the customer arrives (degree of completion and distance from the customer).

3. **Service delivery channel,** which accounts for how the service will be delivered: direct or remote; person-to-person, person-to-machine, and machine-to-machine channels; and possible combinations of the different channels.

4. **Information,** which represents how information will be used to support the offered service, in terms of lower cost, flexibility, responsiveness, and appropriate allocation of the information gathered.

Measure

A way to measure services is through the collection of data. Two types of measurements can be taken: hard measurements and soft measurements. In hard measurements, information is quantitative. For example, an airline can measure the number of late flights, and a package carrier can measure the number of missed/lost packages. This quantifiable amount is used to measure performance in the service industry both now and in the future. Soft data, on the other hand, are not so easy to measure. Examples of soft data include measuring friendliness, professionalism, courtesy, and helpfulness. Companies attempt to monitor their soft data by making a minimum number of eye contacts and smiles between the employee and the customer. Along with tracking hard and soft data, rewarding the employees is also a part of the empowerment approach.

The Measure step includes deciding the measurement strategy, measuring the appropriate indicators, and setting the baseline and goals based on these measurements. The measurement system needs to be aligned with the service delivery system. The measurement system should not be too rigid and needs continual updating. Managers need to include appropriate internal and external measures, and appropriate qualitative and quantifiable measures. Often the challenge lies in finding the relationship between outcome measures and causal factors. This step also requires us to define a baseline or a benchmark for adopted measurements. The measures developed in this step will directly contribute to metrics for a typical performance management system.

Analyze and Innovate

The Analyze step includes analyzing available information for further action, identifying failure modes, and identifying root causes and opportunities leading to the best course of further actions. The step utilizes multiple tools and techniques. The Innovate phase, a new step in the methodology, provides a process to make breakthrough or incremental improvements. Because the Innovate step is new, few tools are available for it.

Embed

The Embed step includes providing employee training, managing projects, creating templates, and disseminating best practices. This step helps institutionalize the project learning at the firm. Six Sigma projects should be managed just like any other projects.

Design for Six Sigma for Services (DFSS)

Design for Six Sigma for Services methodology is a five-step process: Define, Measure, Analyze, Design, and Optimize, or DMADO. Following is a description of each step of the methodology.

Define and Measure

This first phase establishes the goal and sets the direction for all future activities. At the very beginning of the project, the project team needs to answer a few basic questions: Why do we want to design this new service? What is our vision? Who is the customer? How does this service differ from existing alternatives in the market? From where will the resources originate? When will the service start and be launched (start and finish dates)? An understanding of the time-to-market period and expected payoff from the project will help provide answers to some of the questions posed.

The objective of the measurement phase is to collect information regarding customer preferences, delivery system process elements, and service delivery details. The measurement phase initial activities are geared toward gathering additional data and information on customer preferences. Following are some of the tasks of the measurement phase: capture the voice of the customer, develop a value-based measurement system, perform benchmarking, and plan and collect the data.

Analyze

In the Analyze phase, the alternative concepts for the service process and delivery that will perform to these requirements are determined. After these concepts are analyzed, selection of the best ones for the next stage of the design process occurs. For concept generation and evaluation, creativity techniques should be used. Examples of creativity techniques are brainstorming, Pugh's Concept Selection Matrix, TRIZ, and mind mapping. For developing process flow and logical relationships, techniques such as SIPOC, workflow model, and flowcharting should be used.

Design and Optimize

The next step in the process is to develop enough details that the design can be evaluated for performance and feasibility. Associated risks with the design are also better understood in this step. The challenge for the team is to make the choices that simultaneously balance the benefit as well as cost and risk elements; such choices also must be compatible with previous, high-level decisions. The Design phase is supported with tools such as Systems Engineering Design Reviews and FMEA (Failure Mode and Effect Analysis).

The Optimize step often has a heavy engineering connotation. However, the Optimize step should be seen as a communication, implementation, validation, and continuous improvement phase. In general, optimization requires identifying the objective, setting decision parameters, and providing constraints.

After this brief background on the DFSS, a description of the axiom-based service design model follows.

Axiom-Based Service Design Model

The axiomatic approach to service design is based on the assumption that a fundamental set of principles determining good practices exists. The axiom-based service model provides a framework for our DFSS approach, as well as the criteria for evaluation. Axioms state self-evident truths, which cannot be proven but have no counter examples. Axioms are abstraction of existing knowledge imbedded in many things that managers can use or observe routinely.

Nam Pyo Suh (2001) in a book titled *Axiomatic Design: Advances and Applications* identified design axioms that govern all types of designs. To comprehend Suh's independence axiom, understanding the concepts of functional requirements (FR) and design parameters (DP), as well as their hierarchy, must be mastered. Both functional requirements and design parameters exist at several levels. Generally, lower-level requirements (i.e., FR) are more detailed in nature. Functional requirements are met when those customer requirements that design must satisfy are captured without redundancy or overlap.

They describe the objective of the design for a specific need in the simplest possible form. Design parameters are those variables that define a solution for meeting the functional requirements.

Axioms of service design are based on maximizing customer value and meeting business objectives. Following is an axiom-based service design model consisting of *two* axioms.

1. **Service interactions should be designed to generate or exchange quality information.** The ultimate objective of service interaction is to ensure customer satisfaction, leading to customer loyalty and achievement of the business objectives. The nature of customer interactions with a provider depends on the type of service channel utilized by the provider (face-to-face, human-to-machine, or machine-to-machine) and the type of tools and information provided to the customer.

   Interactions usually take place at all stages of services; at every stage both customers and providers may have different reasons for interacting. At the initial stage, the provider is trying to understand the customer expectations, and the customer is trying to assess the capability of the provider to make a buying decision. During the service recovery step, a customer wants to "get it right," and the provider is not only "making it right" but also getting information to minimize future failures. A successful interaction will meet the objective of both of the parties. The first axiom states that we need to design service interaction such that quality information gets generated and communicated to both the parties at all stages.

   For further understanding of interactions, defining what the attributes are that define quality of communication for services is important. The following attributes, which are well described in the service quality literature, define the quality of interaction from the customer's perspective: Responsiveness, Empathy/Understanding, and Assurance. The importance of an attribute is related to the method of customer contact (i.e., channel) used and the customer segment targeted. From a provider's perspective, the following attributes will define the quality: Speed, Usability, and Comprehensiveness.

For example, if a customer goes to a garage to get his car repaired, the clerk at the desk will collect information from him about the symptoms of the problem, which will help in diagnosing the cause and providing an estimate of repair charges. The clerk will also collect other information that will be required for billing and for the provider's internal processes. During this interaction, the customer will be satisfied with the interaction if he feels the clerk was very responsive, was willing to listen to his problem, seemed to understand its severity or urgency (empathy), and was able to provide him satisfactory answers. Finally, the customer must feel assured about the capability of this garage being able to repair his car based on this interaction.

From the garage owner's point of view, he would like to minimize the clerk's time spent in collecting and recording the information correctly (efficiency), collect only that information which will be useful for repairing this car or for his business in some other way (usability), and make sure that all the required information is collected the first time (comprehensiveness). The garage might also want to provide a comprehensive diagnosis free or at a lower cost with the expectation that the customer will return to the same garage for future repairs. Future revenue likely depends on the diagnosis provided at this time.

2. **Customer interactions should be secure and efficient.** The customer should also be able to trust the system. This second axiom assumes that the first axiom is valid, and that the interaction has resulted in generating quality information. Efficiency in an interaction has the following three attributes: Accuracy, Resources Spent, and Relevancy. Accuracy is regarding the facts contained in the information, and it can be measured based on errors in interpreting the data generated from customer interaction. The resources a provider spends on processing information are important, as they define the cost and time it takes to process information. Security and trust in the provider are becoming increasing issues in an era of information overload. The provider needs to assure its customers that the information collected is required for the transaction or service and will not be misused, will be handled in a secure manner at

all time, and will be discarded when the information is no longer necessary.

This second axiom implies that we remove all non-value-added steps. Process flow concepts that are applicable to manufacturing are readily applicable to services. A service blueprint is a modification of a process flowchart and involves drawing a customer visibility line in the middle. Separating what the customer sees or experiences at the front stage is the distinguishing feature of a service blueprint.

While thinking about efficiency improvement using a process flowchart or service blueprints, managers have the following three measures in mind: average flow rate or throughput, average flow time for a flow unit, and average inventory. The preceding parameters interact through a relationship called Little's Law, as follows:

Inventory = Flow rate/Flow time

In general, managers want to increase throughput, decrease process cost, and reduce inventory of the system. For example, a hotel like the Ritz-Carlton, catering to the high-end customer, collects information about customer preferences during the first visit. The information is used in the future to improve the quality of service and to customize the service to suit the customer's needs. The information collected during the interaction should be used efficiently and kept secure. During the second visit, the provider removes the non-value-added steps of collecting the same information.

Using Axioms for Designing Services

The objective of Design for Six Sigma is to design service processes and communication methods that minimize the likelihood of defects per million opportunities (DPMO). Defining "defect" may be the first challenge for managers in a service organization. Certain defects will be customer segment specific and will often represent a gap between customer perception of the service and customer expectations before entering into the system.

Every element of the service process needs to be designed such that it adds perceived value by the target group of customers. A mechanism to track the corporate progress in terms of value captured and expenses incurred should also be instituted. The following frameworks have been discussed by different authors: the ISO 9000 framework, the Six Sigma Business Scorecard to estimate the corporate performance, and 7-S to analyze corporate returns on investment. To define service value, first we need to understand the value of an attribute as explained by the Kano model, a model often used in the field of total quality management:

- **Must Be**—The customer expects these attributes in the service as a minimum. If they are not fulfilled, the customer will perceive a limited (or even zero) value. Even if they were completely fulfilled, the customer would not perceive a very high value.

- **Satisfiers**—These attributes have a linear effect on value. The more these attributes are met, the higher the customer perceives the value.

- **Delighters**—These attributes do not cause dissatisfaction when not present but increase the value when present.

All the preceding three types of attributes can again be divided in two categories from a measurement point of view:

1. Higher the Better (HTB)
2. Lower the Better (LTB)

Occasionally we may find a Nominal the Better (NTB) type attribute for service; however, a NTB measurement can also be considered as LTB by taking its deviation from the target as measurable quantity.

To calculate Service Value, the following steps must be performed:

1. Identify all the Must Be attributes.
2. Divide them into HTBs and LTBs and establish lower and upper limits respectively. Ensure that the service has all Must Be attributes above the lower limit or below the upper limit.

3. Identify Satisfiers and Delighters.

4. Develop a common measurement scale for all the attributes.

5. Divide all Satisfiers and Delighters into two groups: HTB and LTB.

6. Calculate the ratio of HTB to LTB.

To increase the value of service, we need to increase the ratio of HTBs to LTBs while ensuring that all the Must Be attributes are present at least at their minimum level. Any organization that strives to stay ahead of the competition must grow the numerator, where the numerator measures the level of fulfillment of the attributes that customers demand more and more. Examples of these attributes are accuracy and response time. The denominator measures resources. This ratio could be used as an indicator of the value of the service system at an organization. Managers need to be responsive to customer needs and changing demand.

Consider an airline with a delayed flight. Several passengers on this flight are likely to miss connections. Considering the preferences of its customers during service recovery, an airline should try to provide the following capabilities:

1. Additional and flexible capacity should be offered in the form of an agent at the gate and more aggregated service capacity in the form of agents at a service desk. The step adds resources in the denominator.

2. Information on other connections that may be suitable for each passenger must be readily available. The information database consisting of customer travel preferences could be used for this purpose. Therefore, integration between the service recovery system and the service delivery system is necessary to provide the best possible service at the lowest possible cost. Passengers may automatically be booked on these flights to save time if they agree to the new connection. Other services could be provided in the form of hotel bookings and calls to people the passenger wants to inform. This step increases the numerator and reduces the denominator.

3. Initial service recovery is preferably delivered through the person-to-person direct channel, even though it increases cost because service recovery requests are likely to be different for each customer. A high level of interaction can improve the customer's perception of service recovery. This step increases both numerator and denominator.

4. Information systems must be structured to support each of the other choices. For example, information could be used to identify passengers who will miss their connections and arrange for alternative flights.

The objective of all these steps is to maximize the value provided to customers at the lowest possible cost.

Implementing Six Sigma in Service Organizations

The Design for Six Sigma for Services—Define, Measure, Analyze, Design, and Optimize (DMADO)—highlights the conflicting corporate needs and has long-term strategic implications. Decisions are made on a portfolio basis. As a next implementation step, you should look at a Six Sigma implementation road map. The focus of the map is to implement Six Sigma from the top down. The road map identifies the potential opportunities for corporate improvement and defines appropriate projects to make the improvement happen. Opportunities depend on the likely payoff of the project. However, the length of time-to-market has direct implications on the expected payoffs that a service firm can expect.

A company is composed of people who work together to achieve a particular goal or goals. Whether it is to accumulate higher profits, to achieve awareness, or to be the best in the industry, achieving a goal still takes a team that works together to achieve that goal. For the approach of Six Sigma to work, all key executives must commit to its foundation. The Six Sigma method involves much improvement, lots of innovation and creativity, and a measurable change in current practices. If key executives do not agree with the drastic changes that will take place, the Six Sigma method will not be able to reach its full potential. A plan, or a road map, must be put in place for the company to improve.

To start the process of Six Sigma, the executives must be trained. Figure 3.1 shows an example of a road map for Six Sigma implementation. Executives must decide what needs to be improved and associate projects that will reflect in such changes and increase profits. These changes must be clearly illustrated in measurable and quantifiable terms.

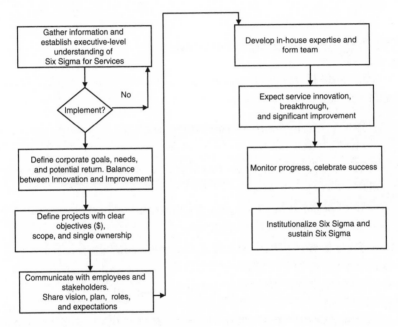

Figure 3.1   Implementation road map

After company leaders understand that Six Sigma works from the top down and that the company members will apply the Six Sigma methods, the leaders must clearly define a performance baseline. This baseline can be accomplished by conducting interviews of management, owners, and a number of employees. If data cannot be collected, a company must find a way to establish an estimated or relative baseline. Certain tools can aid in establishing these baselines. For example, ISO 9000 is a framework that processes and gathers data.

The Six Sigma Business Scorecard estimates corporate performance. The 7-S methodology uses seven attributes of an organization to understand its framework. Lastly, a company can use its financials to study the company's returns on investments.

The Six Sigma Business Scorecard and ISO 9000 are well known throughout corporations. On the other hand, the 7-S framework uses seven attributes for understanding an organization and does not enjoy such notoriety. All the aforementioned methods, however, are excellent ways to set a performance baseline for a company.

Six Sigma Enhancements

The DMAIE methodology overcomes the deficiency of the traditional Six Sigma methodology and has the following advantages:

- It is a system approach, and the corporate alignment is considered while executing the methodology.
- The methodology considers the design of an effective service delivery system.
- The service innovation process is an integral part of the methodology.
- The method is data driven and objective in nature.
- The method considers the interpersonal and project management aspects of the implementation system.

The axiom-driven Design for Six Sigma (DFSS) approach is a combination of axioms, methodology, and tools. This combination produces a service design capable of the six-sigma performance level. The DFSS approach for service design described in this article has the following key differences compared to the traditional approaches: (a) Managers follow a well-documented methodology and do not jump into designing the system right away; (b) Managers begin with a top-down integrated design approach by first learning about segment-specific customer preferences, organization-related constraints, and expected payoff from the project; and (c) Whenever in doubt or in need of verification, managers go back to the basic axioms.

Take Away

- Six Sigma methodology has been successfully applied to services.
- New Six Sigma methodology uses DMAIE steps: Define, Measure, Analyze, Innovate, and Embed.
- One of the challenges in applying Six Sigma methodology is the balance between improvement and innovation.
- A new Six Sigma methodology incorporates "innovation" as a distinct step.
- Design of Six Sigma approach is a combination of axioms for service design, tools, and methodology.

4

Performance Management for Services

In the next few decades, the major productivity improvement and growth opportunities are expected to take place in the service sector. Major corporations like General Motors and General Electric are shifting their focus from the manufacturing side to the service side of the business—to the point where most of their profits are realized through service elements of the business. In manufacturing, the definition, measurements, and improvement became more exact—in other words, a science. As a result, the manufacturing processes became learnable, repeatable, and measurable. Service businesses do not have exact inventory levels, number of turns, or significant assets to measure utilization. Service firms also face the dichotomy of understanding both the customers' perspective and the providers' perspective. Usually, the customer-oriented view is experience-based, whereas the provider-oriented view is process-based. Customers do not care about the process as such but instead view it as an experience.

The field of performance management evolved in the twentieth century with financial indicators like the DuPont ratio and Economic Value Added (EVA). *Financial* indicators such as profit, return on capital employed, or EVA are often used as indictors of the financial health of a firm. Financial indicators are lagging indicators of firm performance and represent only the historical performance of a firm. The General Electric Company in the 1950s incorporated *nonfinancial* measures, such as product leadership, personnel development, employee attitudes, public responsibility, and balance between short-range objectives and long-range goals.

Performance Management Challenges in Services

Understanding the characteristics of services, the various business subcontexts in the service domain, and the uniqueness presented in the service context is imperative. Characteristics of services, such as the intangibility of services, simultaneous production and consumption, and proximity to the customer, have been discussed by various authors.

Services should also include the transaction and experiences perspective. Requirements are very different for these two types of systems. We described specific challenges at length in the preceding chapter.

In this chapter, utilizing elements of existing models and reflecting on the field of performance management in a service-dominant context are the goals. This chapter addresses three questions:

1. What are existing performance management frameworks that are relevant for the service-dominant context?

2. Can a performance management framework that is relevant for the service-dominant context be developed?

3. What will this framework look like and how will it be implemented?

Comparative Analysis of Performance Measurement Systems

Many performance measurement/monitoring and control frameworks exist for the manufacturing context. Examples of popular measurement systems are the Balanced Scorecard, Performance Prism, Six Sigma Business Scorecard, and Performance Pyramid. A few popular auditing frameworks are the Deming framework (www.deming.org), Baldrige Award (www.quality.nist.gov), European Quality Model (www.efqm.org), and maturity models for software firms. Specific to service firms, a lack of comprehensive study in this area is present. Only two comprehensive studies that were designed specifically for the services context have been identified. For example, the Service Profit Chain model is a strategic tool and includes a service profit chain management audit. However, no measures are provided in this model. Table 4.1 shows an evolution and timeline of various performance models.

TABLE 4.1 Online Resources and Evolution of Models

Year	Model	Web Site URL
1946	Quality Association	www.asq.org
1986	ServQual Model	—
1987	Malcolm Baldrige Award	www.nist.gov/quality
1987	ISO 9000 standard	www.iso.org
1988	SEI-CMM Capability Maturity Model	www.sei.cmu.edu/cmm/cmm.html
1990	Balanced Scorecard	www.balancedscorecard.org
1992	EFQM Excellence Model	www.efqm.org/
1994	Service Profit Chain Model	www.serviceprofitchain.com/index.htm
2000	Performance Prism Model	http://www.valuebasedmanagement.net/methods_performance_prism.html
2000	Performance Measurement Association	www.performanceportal.org
2003	Six Sigma Business Scorecard	www.accelper.com

Balanced Scorecard

In Paul Niven's book, *Balanced Scorecard Step-By-Step*, he educates his readers about the Balanced Scorecard. The Balanced Scorecard essentially attempts to handle two main issues: the problem of effective organizational performance measurement and successful strategy implementation. Often when a company is dealing with loss, whether it is financial, commercial, or customer-related, one can look to management for both a problem and a solution. Many organizations put too much emphasis on financial measurements as an indication of performance. Financial measurements do not relate to all areas of an organization. To say that financial measurements are directly correlated with performance is a flawed concept; however, financial measurements do play a large part in determining performance.

The Balanced Scorecard recognizes the importance of financial measurement but also understands its limitations. Financial measures provide a great review of past performance. Predicting the future based on financial measures alone is erroneous because many conditions fluctuate; therefore, it is vital that environmental situations and other circumstances be taken into account. Often the data provided by these financial departments are actually just some numbers on a spreadsheet by the time they reach other departments. Unless the data are interpreted, many departments find it difficult to relate the information to their departmental decisions and strategies.

The scorecard has four areas of defining perspectives. Vision and strategy are at center stage, and the customer perspectives, the internal process perspective, the learning and growth perspective, and the financial measures surround vision and strategy.

Incorporating all four perspectives into one's strategy is not necessary; rather, selecting which perspectives relate to the story of one's strategy and working from there are best. For example, the four perspectives might very well capture all aspects of the strategy that an organization deems are necessary. If the organization has competitive advantage in a specific area, however, it may be best to consider adding a different perspective.

In developing key perspectives, having a grasp of the company's background and its mission is important. Digging into annual reports and reviews may also be beneficial. The Balanced Scorecard is balanced throughout all facets from design to implementation. Therefore, balancing all research by having both reports and reviews, as well as conducting interviews to gather valuable input from senior-level executives, is important.

In the measurement of the success of one's perspectives, specific questions should be stated to represent the scope of the objective. The results from measurement of these perspectives should be the capturing of cause-and-effect relationships and the identification of lagging and leading measures. In order for a Balanced Scorecard to be successful, it should contain a mix of both of these results. Lag indicators represent the consequences of actions already taken. On the contrary, lead indicators are measures that drive the results achieved in lagging indicators. For example, sales of a product may be a lagging indicator, while what drives sales (whether they are poor or prosperous) are leading indicators. Leading indicators predict the performance of the lagging measure.

In addition to these performance measures, financial measures are an important component of the Balanced Scorecard. These measures may not have perfect positive correlation to growth and profitability, therefore indicating whether strategy implementation is, in fact, leading to bottom-line results. The Balanced Scorecard is a system that creates value though one's organization strategy. A company's chosen financial perspectives link together to form a chain that encompasses value across all facets of an organization.

After the process is designed and launched for implementation, proper scorecard reporting techniques must be understood. As society becomes more technology-dependent, reporting techniques and data warehousing are best left to current advanced technologies. When the Balanced Scorecard was first introduced, very few software industries provided any management tools for the scorecard's strategic system. As the Balanced Scorecard gained in popularity, software companies recognized its growth potential and took hold of the opportunity to cater to the market of those in need of Balanced Scorecard software solutions. In defining data and automating the Balanced Scorecard, the organization can use such software to draw detailed conclusions and create relationships among its performance measures.

The Performance Prism

The Performance Prism considers five perspectives on performance management: Stakeholder Satisfaction, Strategies, Processes, Capabilities, and Stakeholder Contribution. In this model, the following questions must be answered:

- What drives stakeholder satisfaction?
- What is the relevant optimal strategy?
- What are the critical processes?
- What are the core capabilities of the firm?
- What drives stakeholder contribution?

The 1990s showed a dramatic surge in mergers and acquisitions, with results varying from augmentation in the profits to a diminution of the company. On the positive side of mergers and acquisitions, increased profits and corporate expansions occur that benefit shareholders, officers, and the company overall. On the flip side, the negative impact of mergers and acquisitions is that the outcome is unpredictable and the future outlook of the company is not stable. Conflicts of interest within the company are often the result, and such instability can lead to a long-term decline of the company. Companies such as Disney, BMW, and AT&T exemplify how mergers and acquisitions are not always a successful proposition. In fact, several authoritative studies have found that a merger has no better than a 50-50 chance of creating value for the acquirer—some suggest less. If true, then from 1999, when the worldwide value of M&A deals was a staggering $2.3 trillion, there will be at least $1.15 trillion of value eventually destroyed.

Adopting effective post-merger integration (PMI) tracking and measurement systems on a wide scale would greatly improve the economic value that is derived from mergers and acquisitions. In essence, the five main points of the PMI are these: Stakeholder Satisfaction, Strategies, Processes, Capabilities, and Stakeholder Contribution. Each of these facets shares the commonality of communication with the shareholders. Shareholders are the key to the success of any company; when they are satisfied, the success and expansion of any company can be fulfilled. The PMI is able to identify stakeholders and cater toward them. Maneuvering in such a way ensures stability within the company, because the interests of those who are directly involved are addressed, and such involvement paves the path for cohesiveness and prosperity.

Six Sigma Business Scorecard

The Six Sigma Business Scorecard, presented by Praveen Gupta, was developed to monitor growth and profitability through a set of measurements beneficial in today's business environment. To develop a Six Sigma Business Scorecard, the executive team must outline the business process flow, identifying key processes and establishing measures of their effectiveness. Then measurement components are selected for critical inputs, in-process tasks, and outputs of the process. Following are a few of the basic guidelines to the help in the development of the Six Sigma Business Scorecard:

1. Understand the intent of the Six Sigma Business Scorecard.
2. Commit to using the Six Sigma Business Scorecard by integrating Six Sigma in a revised vision of the company.
3. Create a Business Performance Index (BPIn).
4. Establish short-term and long-term improvement goals for a profit center or the company.
5. Establish measurements for each category of the Six Sigma Business Scorecard for each profit center.
6. Establish the relationship between profitability and Six Sigma Business Scorecard measurements.

Competitive pressures, customer expectations, and the role of well-informed management require that businesses establish practical measurements that add value to the business. The Six Sigma Business Scorecard provides a framework and a set of initial measurements, which are essential for any organization needing guidelines for developing a growing business. This scorecard can be used by businesses for performance improvement and as a leading BPIn. This index is based on the business's real performance rather than the market's idea of that performance. The BPIn should provide greater assurance in corporate performance, because it is based on more complete information instead of just financial information.

The major differences between the Six Sigma Business Scorecard and other performance measurements are that it requires a lot of involvement and accountability from leadership, it emphasizes the management's responsibility for achieving a major rate of improvement, and it encourages employee involvement for innovation. Overall, the Six Sigma Business Scorecard is balanced for cost and revenue, growth and profitability, internal and external research and development, objective and subjective measurements, human and material resources, production and nonproduction processes, and management and employees. The measurements are designed to observe the corporate performance effectively and can benefit any organization that uses them correctly.

Scorecards Versus Quality Programs

The quality programs provide a methodical discipline for improving critical business processes that augment customer value propositions and amplify productivity. Two quality approaches used most in society today are the European Foundation Quality Management Excellence Model (EFQM) and the Baldrige National Quality Program. Both of these approaches were created to assist organizations in bettering themselves. Organizations determine their strengths, weaknesses, and other key factors in various categories in comparison to a benchmark on what is adequate for a "good practice."

The Baldrige categories include leadership, human resource focus, strategic planning, process management, customer and market focus, information and analysis, and business results. Both models have categories that have more external performance indicators, and the results relating to business are given more weight. The Baldrige Program and EFQM look at internal process performance and focus on continuous improvement.

EFQM Model

The criteria for the EFQM and Baldrige Program include many different factors, all of which have different percentages on how much of the total should be focused on the individual factors. The EFQM criteria include leadership, people, policy and strategy, partnerships and resources, processes, people results, customer results, society results, and key performance results. EFQM is Europe's most prestigious award for organizational excellence. The Award is the highest form of recognition an organization can receive because it comes from its own peers. Top executives from leading businesses and public service organizations visit the candidate firms and after a thorough examination select the few outstanding achievers.

Malcolm Baldrige Award

The Baldrige Award (the Malcolm Baldrige National Quality Award) is an award presented to various businesses by the United States National Institute of Standards and Technology. The award recognizes organizations that demonstrate exceptional total quality management throughout the company. Various companies have successfully used the Baldrige Award framework to conduct an assessment of their organizations and use that information to improve their businesses and increase efficiency. The assessment process is extremely critical to a successful organizational change. An organization can use a Baldrige-style assessment to its fullest potential in many ways.

Conducting the assessment process is what essentially evaluates the quality level of a given organization. The organization may design the assessment in many ways. To create the right assessment for a given organization, the company must choose the correct options to arrive at a process that is right for the organization. A good assessment takes three things into consideration: the criteria, the people who perform the work, and the process they use. Selecting suitable criteria is one of the easier parts of the assessment process because it is quite straightforward.

If an organization's leaders want to use the Baldrige Award as a framework for an internal assessment, they must choose which aspects of the Baldrige assessment they want to use and alter many things.

They should consider modifying the language in which the award assessment is written to ensure that the criteria will not seem alien to their employees. The criteria of the assessment should be familiar to employees and should not use a large amount of business-oriented language if employees are not accustomed to it. Also, the organization must decide whether to choose simple or complex criteria. Other factors to consider when selecting criteria for an internal assessment are widespread acceptance (which makes it easier to share information if many others are using the same criteria), availability of support materials, availability of expertise, and award eligibility. If organizational leaders use some of the Baldrige Award criteria for their own assessment, they must consider these factors to ensure the presence of people knowledgeable about the criteria. They must also make certain that outside material is available to help the organization better understand the criteria.

After the criteria for the assessment are chosen, the organization must select the best assessment process. The main consideration in this decision is how thorough the organization needs the assessment to be. This depends on how long the organization has been working toward improving quality. If the organization is at an early stage of quality improvement, a basic assessment is sufficient, because a full-scale assessment is not yet needed. On the other hand, an organization that has continuously worked on quality improvement for years requires a more in-depth assessment to produce specific opportunities for further improvement.

The next step is to choose one of the four types of assessments that range from simple assessments to more advanced assessments. One type of assessment is a Mini-Assessment. It is delivered in a workshop format, in which employees of the organization are guided through an evaluation of the company using the information they have in their heads. The criteria are simple in this type of assessment, and there is minimal data gathering because no formal report is generated.

The second type of assessment is a Facilitated Assessment. This assessment is carried out by an internal team that is trained, guided, and supported by an external facilitator. The trained team then conducts interviews with employees and reviews key documents. These data are then used to create a report summarizing findings that is later presented to executives. After the data are presented, a planning workshop is held to develop a plan to improve quality management using the key findings. The third type of assessment is known as a Joint Assessment and is essentially the same as the Facilitated Assessment. The only difference is that the external facilitators are a part of the entire process and work with the internal team as full members.

The last type of assessment is an External Assessment. This is the most thorough type and is an internal assessment conducted by external experts. The internal team creates an application report that is used by the external experts to understand what the organization is attempting to accomplish. The external team then completes its own assessment of the organization and presents its findings to executives. Each of these types of assessments has various pros and cons; the organization that is conducting the internal assessment must decide which type best suits its needs.

As with the criteria used from the Baldrige Award framework, the assessment type can also be altered to better fit the organization's needs. The organization can choose to compress the time frame of the assessment, use a questionnaire survey, simplify the documentation required, and tailor the education and training of the assessment team. After an assessment type is chosen and altered to the needs of the organization, and the assessment team is trained, the data-gathering stage begins.

Data gathering is a vital step in developing an understanding of what is going on within the organization. The employee interviews are where the data gathering is conducted, and performing well-conducted interviews that will reinforce the credibility of the assessment is important. Data gathering is also the most expensive part of the assessment because of the time and effort required for the interviews. To make the overall assessment as successful as possible, the organization must make sure that its data-gathering strategy is on point. An open atmosphere must exist so that the employees feel comfortable sharing information. The interviews must be focused on the areas in which the assessment team needs information, and the team should use both group interviews and single interviews to ensure adequate representation of the various levels of employees. After the assessment team understands these requirements, they can begin conducting the interviews.

The team will begin by conducting interviews with employees at various levels and gathering key documents to complement the information obtained from the interviews. For these interviews to be conducted in the most effective and efficient way, the interviews should be scheduled in advance, the interviewer should be prepared beforehand, and the interviewer should conduct a valuable interview. After an interview is done, the data-gathering stage is almost complete. The last step is debriefing.

Debriefing should be done after every interview as well as with the entire assessment team during the data-gathering process. Debriefing helps answer any of the team's questions, better focuses the team's interviews due to feedback, and creates a summary for all team members so that they know the progress of the assessment. After the data-gathering stage is complete, the implementation of the assessment results takes place. To see the improvement plans through to completion, the organization must have a system to support implementation. The first two steps are to (1) create the system to support the implementation of the assessment results, and (2) develop an improvement team.

The improvement team is the key to a successful implementation. Developing a successful improvement team involves five steps: formation, preparation, execution, completion, and holding the gains. The formation of the team should include clear objectives that reflect the organization's goals, the assignment of a senior executive as the sponsor, selection of a suitable team leader and team members, allocation of sufficient time and resources, and a progress monitoring system.

After the team is formed, the preparation stage begins. The team is trained and develops a plan of action for its proposed improvements. When a plan is in place, the team must begin the execution step. Execution involves putting the proposed plan of action into place, and it can take weeks, months, or longer. When the team members feel as though they have accomplished their goal, the implementation process is complete. The improvement team should present its progress, findings, and any other relevant information to senior executives. Although the team's task is essentially complete, the team must make sure that the solutions put into place are not lost over time. The most effective way to do so is to ensure proper integration of the improvements into the existing system of process management.

The Baldrige Award promotes quality awareness and successful quality strategies. Using an award such as the Baldrige Award as a means of improving quality and bottom-line results in a given organization can prove to be extremely beneficial. It can help improve organizational performance practices and will ultimately serve as a tool for understanding and managing performance. An organization can take the Baldrige assessment process, tailor it to the specific organization, and execute a successful assessment of the organization's practices and quality management. The results of such an assessment can be used to form strategies of improvement and can be implemented into the current organizational system. The ultimate results can be vast and can include the following: improving value to customers, market success, improvement in overall organizational effectiveness and capabilities, and organizational and personal learning.

Capability Maturity Models

The Software Engineering Institute (SEI), developed an initial version of a maturity model and questionnaire at the request of the government. The model consists of five maturity levels. Organizations and business units go through an audit to achieve a certain level. Level I is the lowest level, and Level V is the highest possible level of achievement. Only a select few have achieved Level V certification. Levels evolve into a disciplined process (Level I), leading to a standard consisting of the process (Levels II and III), followed by a predictable (Level IV), and continuously improving process (Level V). Software firms received prestigious achievement of Levels IV and V by following through years of a disciplined approach. However, achieving Level IV or V does not guarantee the quality of the offering in the customer's view. Figure 4.1 presents all these levels.

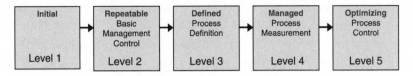

Figure 4.1 Levels of Capability Maturity Model

Other Models

General Electric's growth model should also be mentioned in this section. Innovation and leadership are integral components of GE's model. However, the partnership element is still missing from the conceptual model. The process explains how specific initiatives fit into a larger organic growth process. The elements of the growth model are these:

- **Great Technology**—The firm should have the best products, content, and services (New Product Introduction Ecomagination).

- **Commercial Excellence**—The firm develops world-class sales and marketing talent, and demonstrates the value of "one GE brand."

- **Globalization**—The firm creates opportunities everywhere, and expands in developing global markets (Emerging Markets).

- **Growth Leaders**—The firm inspires and develops people who know how to help customers and GE grow (Growth Traits).

- **Innovation**—The firm generates new ideas, and develops capabilities to make them a reality (Lean Six-Sigma Net Promoter Score).

The Deming quality prize in Japan is based on individual firms' circumstances. There is no clear framework used to judge the winner for the Deming Prize. Another scorecard, Future Scorecard, incorporates a futuristic open perspective and the need for aligning the scorecard with the strategic planning process. Both internal and external perspectives are incorporated.

A comparison of three frameworks is presented in summary form in Table 4.2. Only EFQM, the Baldrige criteria, and the Service Scorecard are included, because these frameworks are very similar. The Service Scorecard, presented in this book, goes beyond the audit function, however.

TABLE 4.2   Criteria of Two Leading Quality Models Compared with Service Scorecard

EFQM Criteria	Baldrige Categories	Six Sigma Business Scorecard
Leadership (10%)	Leadership (12%)	Leadership and Profitability (30%)
People (9%)	Human Resource Focus (8.5%)	Employees and Innovation (10%)
Policy and Strategy (8%)	Strategic Planning (8.5%)	Management and Improvement (20%)
Partnerships and Resources (9%)	Process Management (8.5%)	Purchasing and Supplier Management (10%)
Processes (14%)	Customer and Market Focus (9%)	Operational Execution (10%)
People Results (9%)	Information and Analysis (8.5%)	Service and Growth (10%)
Customer Results (20%)	Business Results (45%)	Sales and Distribution (10%)
Society Results (6%)		
Key Performance Results (15%)		

Performance Management Development

A generic process of developing a performance management system could be described in the following five steps:

1. **Define the objectives of the system.** Describe the need for and utility of a measurement system, the type of system desired, the definition of core offerings, how the system will evolve over time, and how the system will interact with the existing system and infrastructure in place.

2. Identify core requirements of the system and relate them to the core business process service and/or core competencies and/or key success factors. This step forces one to think about causality and the impact of any changes.

3. Develop the Service Scorecard. This step will define what will be measured and how it will be measured. A few simple rules while selecting metrics include the following: (a) Fewer metrics are better, (b) Metrics should be linked to the business drivers, (c) Metrics should present past, present, and future (leading) indicators, (d) Metrics will be adjusted and changed as strategy evolves, and (e) Each metric should have a target goal and/or a desired range.

4. Establish baseline, threshold, and success factors. This step should clearly define the upper/lower bound of each measure.

5. Focus on implementation. No cookie-cutter approach should be used, and top management support is crucial for a successful implementation. The implementation challenges are similar to any other management change project. The implementation stage goes through a starting stage, a development stage, and a usage stage. The development stage brings customization of key performance indicators and success factors.

Take Away

- Hardly any existing performance measurement system was intentionally designed for services.

- Examples of existing measurement systems are the Balanced Scorecard, Performance Prism, and Six Sigma Business Scorecard.

- Some quality programs, such as the Malcolm Baldrige National Quality Award and European Quality Award, have become de facto auditing tools for performance measurement.

Part II

Learning Service Scorecard

5

Understanding the Service Scorecard

Businesses utilize measurements for monitoring performance. Financial measures conventionally are the most frequently used business performance measures by executives. Financial measures depend on the state of the industry, strategy, operations management, leadership, macroeconomic conditions, corporate culture, and many other factors. Managers use dozens of financial measures. Some financial measures are industry-specific, whereas others depend on the financial structure of the business. Some financial measures are governed by the regulatory requirements, and still others are contingent on the leadership preferences. Eventually, financial performance depends on what actually happens in or to the business.

For years many businesses were using the widely known Balanced Scorecard, which was first used in the late 1980s. Corporations use the Balanced Scorecard in its various forms and adaptations, but they still preserve its four perspectives, which are Customer, Internal Operations, Financial Operations, and Learning and Growth. Of course, like any tool, the Balanced Scorecard has been used ineffectively or partially, when a business has used only one or two of its perspectives rather than using it as intended. Many success stories, as well as many unsuccessful implementations, abound about using the Balanced Scorecard.

Infosys Technologies provides business services to clients globally by leveraging its technology. Infosys's approach focuses on new ways of combining IT innovation and adoption while also leveraging an organization's current IT assets. Infosys works with global corporations to build new products or services and to implement prudent business and technology strategies in today's dynamic digital environment. Behind its success, Infosys has deployed a very comprehensive corporate performance measurement using the enhanced Balanced Scorecard concepts.

The Infosys measurement system is summarized in Table 5.1. The figure consists of three columns listing Infosys's framework elements, business objectives, and corresponding performance measures. Some of the measurements represent a good cross section of the business, including resources, capital, ethics, improvement, rework, collaboration, diversity, revenue, cost, margin, and client. Overall, the Infosys framework includes six elements, 32 objectives, and 39 measures. Infosys's five-year CAGR averages about 40 percent for revenue and profit.

TABLE 5.1   Infosys Measurement System

Framework	Sample Objectives	Performance Measures
Values and Ethics	Be a responsible corporate citizen	Contribution to Infosys Foundation
Financial Performance	Improve profits	% improvement margin
	Achieve revenue growth	Revenue
	Reduce operations cost	Accounts receivable
	Improve return on capital	Return on capital employed
Client/Market Focus	Grow large accounts	% revenue increase from large accounts
	Enhance client satisfaction	Annual client satisfaction index
		# of significant client references
	Strengthen brand position	% of revenue from services introduced in last two years
	Broaden business footprint	
Operational Excellence	Improve quality and productivity	Rework cost as % of total effort
		% utilization
	Optimize resource utilization	
	Strengthen internal collaboration	
	Leverage intellectual property	

TABLE 5.1 Infosys Measurement System

Framework	Sample Objectives	Performance Measures
Talent Management	Recruit quality talent	% of recruits receiving top grade in a comprehensive test
	Develop and retain competencies	% of annualized attrition
	Strengthen perform-ance ethics	Variable payout as a % of budgeted payout
	Develop workforce diversity	
Scale Infrastructure	Scale infrastructure	% of schedule slippage of critical projects

Printed with permission from Infosys

In 1981, 14 churches in the greater Seymour area joined forces to meet an urgent need for elder care. The community came together to build a home for the elderly so that the elderly could remain where many of them had spent most of their lives. The 14 collaborating churches share the basic values of care and respect for others and support for the community. To implement these values within the long-term-care field, the organization also had to become a high performer. To this end, Good Shepherd Services (GSS) incorporates business best practices using the Malcolm Baldrige National Quality Award framework, which has a significant emphasis on process management and measurements.

To sustain the success of GSS in fulfilling its fundamental objectives of care, share, respect, and support, its leadership developed short-term and long-term objectives and corresponding measures without using a predefined scorecard framework. GSS measurements are shown in Table 5.2, where the organization's focus appears to be to improve performance using best practices, raise funds, and control expenses. Data used at GSS are more activity driven and financial in nature rather than contained in the form of a scorecard.

TABLE 5.2 GSS Measurement System

Action Plan	Performance Measures
Long Term	
Improve quality of life through best practices	Benchmark using national indicators, reports, and surveys
Reduce dependence on government funding	Percent of income from nongovernment resources
	Amount of gifts and pledges received
Fundraising and revenue generation	Number of presentations, tours, and consulting activities
Dissemination of best practices	
Short Term	
Provide wellness programs for staff	Maintain low insurance premiums
	Deploy wireless network
Use technology for productivity	Issue new bond with lower interest rates
	Improve financial picture
Lower interest payment	Fund site visit by MBNQA examiners
Control expenses	Increase endowment fund
Fund for improvement	Secure additional consulting agency staff
Build endowment	Revenue from consulting
Improve management capabilities	Secure formal relationships with other organizations
Secure resources for contingency	Increase media coverage of the corporation
	Culture/Climate assessment
Practice corporate mission and philosophy	
Showcase GSS	
Pursue best practices	

Elements of Service-Based Businesses

Recognizing the uniqueness of service operations, Parasuraman, Zeithaml, and Berry identified ten dimensions of service quality as elements of the framework called ServQual. The ten dimensions are tangibles, reliability, responsiveness, competency, courtesy, communication, credibility, security, access, and understanding. These dimensions have gained a significant traction in evaluating various services, including the healthcare, banking, and education sectors. Further analysis of the consumer responses led to five key dimensions of service quality, which are reliability, responsiveness, empathy, assurance, and tangibles. These dimensions are more applicable when evaluating a service, not necessarily the service business.

Service operations and businesses are different from manufacturing or product-based businesses. Even some services businesses are product-based services. Services can be of a transaction or interaction type. Thus, service could be tangible as well as intangible, influencing the customer experience and time of the experience.

Intangible services tend to be delivered in real time. The typical service value chain may include demand forecast, supply management, delivery, and service after delivery. Many of the functions of service organizations are similar to those of nonservice organizations, such as leadership, management, processes, sales, marketing, finance and accounting, and quality. Some of the unique aspects of service are in design, supply, operations, and delivery.

If a business can be structured in three major components, as shown in Figure 5.1, management and support functions are similar between service and nonservice businesses; however, the operations tend to be significantly different. The management processes include the management system, performance measures and accountability, reviews, and audits. The support processes may include training, quality, purchasing, sales, marketing, and accounting. The operational processes include design, production, acquisition or delivery, field performance, customer service, and quality control.

Operationally, services have transaction and interaction components. Interaction is required to gather customer information or request for service, to deliver service, and to service after delivery. The transaction aspect of the service has more to do with the production of service, such as in finance or the food industry. Both the transaction and the interaction aspects are necessary to deliver a service. Typical service operations involve more interaction and less transaction. The transaction aspect is becoming more technology-dependent, and interaction is always more people-dependent. Sometimes, however, there is a mutually overlapping zone where transaction is more in person, and interaction is more technology-dependent.

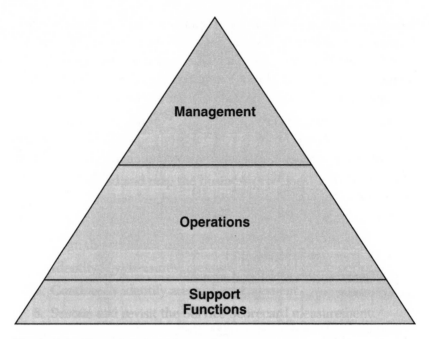

Figure 5.1   Hierarchy of service performance

Typically transaction-based services tend to be high volume and low value, whereas the interaction services tend to be low volume and high value. Interaction- and experience-based services are people-based and are visible to customers. Customers are often involved in coproduction of services. Interpersonal skills of employees are crucial.

The commonly known service sectors include finance, insurance, banking, distribution, telecommunication, food, construction, airlines, education, and healthcare. Even the nonservice sectors have a significant service component. Today, almost every business has a "service" aspect. In the so-called service economy of today, however, the quality of service appears to be diminishing. The customer perception of service is not certainly favorable. Of course, exceptional service is present, too, such as at the Ritz-Carlton hotel or Lexus auto dealerships. One of the challenges in improving the perceived value of a service is in managing business effectively and making necessary resources available.

Rationale for Service Scorecard

The Balanced Scorecard, first used in the 1980s, was developed before the advent of the Internet. In the past 20 years, a lot has changed in the business world, such as outsourcing, the sheer rate of change, technology deployment, communication, operational organization, financial structures, and global competition. Organizational expectations have also changed, due to the increasing role of globalization and information technology. The purpose of the Service Scorecard is to ensure that business performance can be audited and used for diagnosing corporate health, identifying gaps, and establishing higher targets, to strive for excellence and sustained success for both profit and not-for-profit organizations.

When an organization implements a Service Scorecard, its impact must be clearly understood in terms of return on investment. In other words, the Service Scorecard must become a leading indicator of the corporate success. The scorecard must be adaptable for service organizations based on their business model.

For example, there are cost-driven companies that focus on selling at the lower price, such as Wal-Mart, IKEA, Southwest, Motel 8, and Shouldice Hospital. Some organizations thrive on differentiating themselves from their customers, such as Disney, Hard Rock Cafe, Dell, Ritz Carlton, and Macy's. At these companies innovation is a critical aspect of managing business. Finally, there are organizations that must be responsive to customer needs where faster is preferred over better or cheaper. Companies like FedEx, UPS, fast-food restaurants, hospitals, and mortgage providers depend on their speed of service along with the quality and cost.

Benefits and Challenges of the Service Scorecard

The applicability of the Service Scorecard is an important consideration in realizing its benefits. For start-up to small businesses, a complete scorecard may not make sense; thus, they can utilize only the applicable aspects of the Service Scorecard. Mid- to large-sized corporations, or a profit and loss (PNL) center of around 300 people or more, can benefit using the Service Scorecard. However, the large or multidivision corporation can benefit tremendously using a holistic and predictive Service Scorecard. Use of the Service Scorecard can lead to the following benefits:

- Provides clear performance targets at the function and business level
- Benchmarks performance against best practices
- Identifies opportunities for improvement
- Uses Predictive Service Performance Index (SPIn) as a leading indicator of financials

Along with its benefits, the Service Scorecard can face its challenges, such as a culture of ad hoc performance; resistance to change; maintenance and communication of business performance; decision making using the scorecard; and data integrity. Another challenge of implementing the Service Scorecard is its use of subjective measures. Especially in the service business (compared with the manufacturing industry), people play a bigger role than do machines, so the measurements related to humans become more important. Of course, institutionalizing the Service Scorecard requires a strategic commitment to measure, monitor, and adjust the business performance.

Many organizations already have too much data that rarely get analyzed effectively. Typically measures get implemented and dropped after some time due to the difficulty in obtaining good data. Wrong data, too much data, limited analysis and feedback to users, outdated data, and data-entry errors are some of the reasons that performance measures are debatable. Another factor that must be addressed in establishing the Service Scorecard is the variability in the method of collecting data (which can be adversely affected by person-to-person variation) or data gathering error. In service operations, the person-to-person variation is normally fixed by establishing documented procedures for various activities, their verification, and data collection.

Many organizations launch their scorecard or performance measurement initiative, but the information is not disseminated to employees. Executives feel that performance measures connect them to the operations, but employees at various operations think they are disconnected from the measurements, because they are not involved in the planning and use of the data. Employees are asked to collect data that does not benefit them. Thus, reporting and communicating the Service Scorecard and its performance measures is critical to make the scorecard a valuable tool. Business Intelligence (BI) has become a competitive advantage through a timely and effective decision-making capability. Well-reported data can lead to identification of opportunities, a sense of accountability, the desire to earn recognition, and healthy in-house competition.

Results of Using the Service Scorecard

With the previous understanding of the Service Scorecard, a commonly asked question is "How many resources are required to implement a Service Scorecard?" Resources include directors, C-level executives, middle managers, and employees besides the required IT resources. If an organization already is benefiting from an existing set of measurements, implementation of the Service Scorecard must be viewed as an effort to add missing elements to get a compete picture of the business. If a business has no corporate performance measures, the Service Scorecard provides an initial framework to launch a strategic improvement initiative. If an organization already has perfected the performance measurement system, the Service Scorecard may be used to identify any gaps (just in case a measurement or two could be more helpful).

Implementing the Service Scorecard does not guarantee performance improvement. Instead, managing business performance using the Service Scorecard through specific action brings improvement. It involves regularly reviewing the performance with management, employees, and stakeholders to set the expectation of improvement, identify actions to change processes with opportunities, and monitor the improvement for ensuring success. In many organizations, the leadership is unwilling to either justify reviewing the performance using the scorecard or take an interest in improvement. Reviewing performance using the scorecard seems too tactical or detailed compared to performing the standard strategic review. However, to manage thin margins or maximize opportunities to sustain profitable growth, the leadership must look into details. The CEO will look at the performance, identify areas performing below expectation, and commit high-profile resources to get problems fixed immediately.

The Service Scorecard was designed for executives to lead improvement in service organizations to sustain profitable growth. The Service Scorecard was designed to identify a set of measurements that are critical to the performance and when aggregated provide an overall indicator, called the Service Performance Index (SPIn). The SPIn can be a good indicator of the expected business performance, because it incorporates all aspects of business and provides a holistic view of the performance.

Trending the SPIn using the regression analysis could be a good predictor of the financials, because operations drive the financials. Normally with the current measurement system, the financials drive the operations (that is, it's a number-driven management approach). When operations drive the business, an action-driven management process is occurring. Eventually, numbers do not make business; instead business makes the numbers. Actions produce financials.

Design of the Service Scorecard

The seven elements of the Service Scorecard are shown in Figure 5.2: Service Scorecard Architecture (Gupta, 2003). The seven elements are Growth, Leadership, Acceleration, Collaboration, Innovation, Execution, and Retention. The seven elements were put together in a model (GLACIER) that represents certain intangible attributes of a service business. Similar to a glacier, the service business is continually changing according to the customer-defined boundaries, adapting to the specifics or kinks of customers, recognizing being part of a larger ecosystem (thus maintaining holistic perspective), maintaining transparency through clarity to details at the bottom, and renewing with seasonal variations.

IMPROVEMENT

INNOVATION

Figure 5.2   Service Scorecard architecture

Each element of the Service Scorecard represents a significant aspect of business and has interdependency with the other elements. Thus, when a business is implementing a Service Scorecard, removing an element can create challenges. A business is not made of strategy, though it is important in setting direction. Instead, a business is composed of processes such as sales, delivery, service, quality, management, accounting, and finance. Therefore, the Service Scorecard elements represent key business processes and aspects. A good scorecard must address the following ten attributes:

1. Strategic support
2. Business relevance
3. Simple flow-down
4. Clarity
5. Executable
6. Opportunistic

7. Predictive

8. Dynamic

9. Benchmark

10. Balanced

A scorecard must be developed as a tool for executives to operationalize the fundamental strategy and adapt to the business needs. The Service Scorecard has been optimized to the fundamental strategy of an organization (that is, sustained success) as defined by the intent of the business. For profit organizations, the fundamental strategy becomes *sustained profitable growth*, and for not-for-profit organizations, the fundamental strategy becomes *sustained value growth*.

The business relevance of the scorecard makes it familiar to employees and improves its acceptability and visibility in the organization. Simple flow-down prevents development of complicated strategy maps and deploys process management. The process mindset is critical to produce desired results with a certain level of confidence. Otherwise, execution of strategy remains successful around 10 percent of the time. Without transforming business objectives into process objectives, strategic results cannot be realized.

The Service Scorecard has been designed with a holistic approach and is simple to comprehend, because it is aligned with various roles (that is, leadership, management, and employees). If the scorecard is not designed this way, it remains in the boardroom or executive offices and never gets power of execution. Having defined roles of inspiration by the leadership, improvement by the management, and innovation by the employees, the Service Scorecard promotes empowering interaction and effective execution of the fundamental strategy throughout the organization.

The power of a scorecard lies in identifying opportunities to increase value realization and predicting the expected performance in the future with some confidence. The Service Scorecard design allows managers to monitor process performance in terms of accuracy, reliability, errors, and quality; responsiveness in terms of delivery time, capability, fulfillment of customer needs, and customer service; and cost in terms of value to the customer for the price paid for the service. Each process, depending on its nature and objectives, will have its unique focus and appropriate measurements to ensure desired success and customer excitement for the service.

Changing customer requirements leads to changing business processes and thus changing scorecard measurements. The seven elements, or the architecture, of the scorecard can be applied across boundaries; however, specific process-level measurements must be suitable to the nature of the business process. Thus, we must continually evaluate scorecard measurements for their suitability to the business objectives and usability in identifying opportunities for realizing more value. A dynamic service scorecard can be continually used over years without losing the benchmarking capability, which is critical to know for achieving the leadership position in the industry. Best-in-class companies review their position in the industry, determine the gap from the leading companies, and identify internal opportunities for improvement to set goals for accelerating improvement.

Finally, the scorecard must be diverse enough to represent various components of the business. In bygone days, businesses used to measure only the financial performance. Balancing financial and nonfinancial measures was a breakthrough in the 1980s; today, however, such a balance may not be enough. The Service Scorecard is balanced for financial and nonfinancial analysis, cost and revenue, profit and growth, employees and management, improvement and innovation, subjective and objective aspects, tangibles and intangibles, and retention and new business. To manage a business effectively, an organization must focus on the relevance and adequacy of the scorecard rather than a simple balance of financial and nonfinancial measurements.

The GLACIER

The seven elements of the Service Scorecard represent a cross section of a service business in the technology-driven global environment. These seven elements grouped together establish the SPIn. Each element and corresponding measurement has a specific intent that must be understood while these elements are being established. Measurements mentioned in this book are baseline measures and should be customized for the specific services context. These measures are in no way prescriptive measures. The basic architecture of the

Service Scorecard remains the same, though. Many more measurements could be added to these measures; however, the practicing organization must be responsible for establishing *necessary* measurements to determine the SPIn and identify opportunities for improvement and the realization of sustained success. When the Service Scorecard is implemented, some of the measurements will be applicable under the current business environment, while new measurements will need to be created to achieve the fundamental strategy in the knowledge age fueled by the Internet. Immediate rejection of new elements or measurements will perpetuate the past, hinder progress in the coming years, and jeopardize corporate survival.

Growth

Growth and profit are considered contradictory propositions in many businesses. Actually, they are two sides of the same coin. While strategizing for corporate success, the leadership must focus on profitable growth—not just the profit. Most organizations are so heavily focused on profit that they do not have dedicated resources to growing revenue. Interestingly, revenue growth requires exploiting new opportunities through new customers and new services. Thus, innovative thinking must prevail to realize sustained revenue growth.

As organizations strive to improve efficiency, reduce waste, and realize excellence, the newly available unused capacity must be utilized to capitalize on the benefits of the improvement effort. The improvement effort in a profit-centric or short-term-oriented organization leads to right sizing, thus hindering future growth.

Growth can be measured in many ways, such as revenue growth through mergers and acquisitions, or through additional business from existing customers. The additional business received from existing customers offers lower profit margins. Such a situation also increases dependency on existing customers, making it a risky growth to sustain. The growth through mergers and acquisitions, though common, has also not been an effective strategy in achieving the intended objectives. The profitable growth through new services provides better margins and creates a process for sustaining the growth.

Several organizations now have allocated an executive to lead the business growth. Some corporations have specific measures for revenue growth from new services. Still, however, the challenge remains as to how to innovate new services, thus requiring institutionalization of innovation throughout the organization.

Leadership

Leadership plays a crucial role in creating the organization's vision, developing strategy, executing the tactical plan, and ensuring success. However, in most organizations the leadership is measured through overall financial performance driven by the shared value and market trends. Such a perspective results in an inconsistent direction conflicting with the corporate vision and values, fluctuating outcomes, and cycles of performance instead of sustained success.

Currently practiced measurements do not highlight the role of the executive leadership, which plays such a critical role. Therefore, leadership has been incorporated into the Service Scorecard to ensure the effectiveness of this vital role. An organization can incorporate many leadership measurements based on its expectations. Establishing measurements for a corporate CEO is difficult, given the multitude of responsibilities both inside and outside the corporation.

After sifting through various tasks and their priority, however, we concluded that leadership success depends on executives' ability to bring out the best from employees at all levels. This challenge involves charisma and soft skills to motivate people. Considering the various activities that executives perform to inspire their employees, a common and simple act of inspiration is recognizing significant employee accomplishments toward the fundamental strategy.

Many organizations do recognize employees for their significant contribution; however, the act has not been institutionalized to drive significant accomplishments from more employees. Thus, a measurement of employee recognition is established in the Service Scorecard to inspire *significant contributions* from individuals or teams. Here the intent is not to give away awards to employees, but rather to create an environment where more employees elevate their performance to the higher level.

Of course, another measure for leadership is to ensure Return on Equity (ROE). No corporation can survive sustained unprofitable growth. If the leadership plans to ensure profitable growth, then actions that ensure margins through customer qualification, operational excellence, innovation, and employee participation are performed. This growth requires physical and human assets. In some service businesses, the human assets are more significant than the fixed assets. However, current accounting practices do not sufficiently account for these intangible assets. Therefore, measures such as Return on Assets (ROA) may not reflect the true nature of the corporate performance of a service firm. To ensure ROE in service businesses, the leadership must integrate all assets deployed to achieve sustained success and thus preserve and reward shareholders to achieve superior return on equity. The two measures for leadership are Employee Recognition for significant added value and ROE.

Acceleration

Every business starts small with an innovative idea. As the business grows, it diversifies, the service mix changes, the customer list grows, operations expand, management styles strangle, and corporate culture dilutes. During all this growth and turmoil, inefficiencies creep into the execution of the fundamental strategy of sustained success or profitable growth. Resource waste is an opportunity to improve profitability, streamline processes, and aggressively pursue reduction of waste of any kind. Most organizations improve continually but not fast enough.

The purpose of creating the acceleration element is to pursue elimination of waste to bring business performance toward virtual perfection. Customers always expect more for less and faster, which strains the effort to realize sustained profitable growth. To keep up with the customer demand, the business strategy must be to provide more value through the service for a price rather than reducing the service and its cost for a lower price. Waste is like money lying around; why not grab it in the business if it truly belongs to the business? Thus, reduction in waste and improvement in performance must be accelerated to keep up with the growing customer demand for more.

Rate of improvement is a measure of acceleration. Each department must establish a goal to achieve higher performance delivered faster and more cost-effectively. The challenge of establishing an aggressive goal depends on the industry position, internal opportunities, and available resources. However, the goal for improvement must be aggressive enough such that it forces employees to think beyond their comfort zone and do something differently. The objective is to have each department manager establish aggressive goals for improvement to engage employees intellectually and produce higher value for customers.

Collaboration

Growth and acceleration demand that teams are deployed to achieve sustained success. An organization's success depends on the performance of its suppliers, service providers, or channel partners. Collaboration is an act to make partnerships value-added. Companies have extended customer relationship management (CRM) and supplier relationship management (SRM) into partnership relationship management (PRM). In a globally distributed organization, collaboration adds a critical dimension to a business's sustained success.

Collaboration can be with suppliers, customers, consumers, employees, or anyone who can contribute to a solution for providing services to customers. For service businesses, collaboration's success depends on the reliability of collaborating partners, mutual trust, and partner satisfaction. If a service business is positioned to deliver unique service experience to its customers through differentiation, the collaboration's success depends on the volume of the service and its reliability. Thus, the total cost of services becomes an important consideration in providing unique services.

When the business is required to service its customers fast, the success of collaboration with its service partners depends on synchronization of processes and resources to ensure cost-effective delivery and accuracy of the service. Accuracy or reliability of service, mutual trust, and partner satisfaction are important measures of collaboration with service partners.

If collaboration is to add value toward sustained success, then clear expectations, communication channels, process designs, and performance measures must be such that the cost of service and its accurate delivery are available to the customer. IT consulting service providers, for example, collaborate with their partners for specific application, technology, or industry expertise.

Innovation

Innovation is a critical aspect to maintain leadership in service. Service innovation is not about producing an innovative design or product; instead it has to do more with thinking innovatively at the activity level and at the same time providing the desired experience to customers. Employees must be trained to respond to the customer's unique need to innovatively ensure a pleasant experience. Four types of innovation based on the scope of activities and depth of discovery have been identified by Gupta recently. The four types of innovation are fundamental, platform, derivative, and variation. These types of innovations are adapted to the service context. Types of service innovations include business model, market, operations, process, experience, and on-demand innovation.

Service innovation can vary from platform to variation depending on the stage of service. At the business level, more fundamental or platform-type innovations are required; at the business-to-business level of service, more derivative innovations may be needed; and at the customer experience level, variation-type innovation can be helpful. Such a breakdown of innovation can help in allocating resources to the innovation strategy to achieve business objectives.

For longer-term growth, resources must be allocated to develop new service platforms, while employees must be trained in innovative thinking for developing unique custom solutions. Such unique solutions must be delivered on demand in real time to earn customer loyalty and repeat business. Platform and derivative types of innovations can contribute to the strategic long-term growth, while the variation-type innovation can affect the cash flow.

To promote continual service innovation, employees must be engaged intellectually; that requires continual learning through culture, support, and incentives. An expectation of employee ideas for improving processes must be present, and approaching service delivery in innovative ways must happen. Besides revenue growth and CEO recognition, the number of employee ideas generated and implemented is a good measure of innovation in an organization. Conventional problems with idea management or suggestion programs must be overcome through establishing a process for managing employee ideas and achieving excellence in idea management.

Execution

Execution simply means excellence in service delivery. Excellence can be defined as achieving service targets. Thus, for key service processes, establishing performance targets must be a first step toward flawless execution. After the target is defined, the process to deliver the service must be established using the 4P model as described previously. The process must expand on its preparation aspect for achieving desired error-free results. Good preparation will facilitate excellence in service delivery.

Process activities must be organized and sequenced such that they do not accelerate errors and reduce the service delivery time. When contracted, customers want service that fulfills their needs when they want it. Accordingly, the service accuracy (or error rate) and cycle time (or speed of service) will be effective measures to ensure superior execution.

Retention

Customer retention is easier than customer acquisition. In service businesses especially, if customers' experiences are pleasant, they will come again for service; however, if the customers' experiences are normal or dissatisfactory, they are prone to defection. Customer retention actually begins by listening to customers before delivering their service. The feeling of care matters to customers. Listening is important to learn what customers' true needs are, and dialoging is critical in developing an innovative solution on demand. Many times customers are part of the service operation; thus, engaging them to create a pleasant experience is a good practice.

The challenges with listening to customers are that they say so many things, express too many expectations, demand unrealistic service, or assume a lot. Professor Kano has established three categories of customer requirements. The three categories of customer requirements are Assumed, Market Driven, and Love to Have. The assumed requirements are unspoken and tend to act as dissatisfiers. If a customer receives an assumed minimal service, he ignores it. If the assumed service is not delivered, however, the customer is agitated and ready to defect.

For example, receiving water in a restaurant could be considered an assumed requirement when customers are eating out. The market-driven requirements imply listening to those requirements carefully, jotting them down if there are too many, and ensuring that they are fulfilled through superior service. The more these spoken requirements are fulfilled, the more the customer is satisfied. The love-to-have requirements imply caring for the customer's total experience, thus generating excitement through dialogue and innovating a unique persona experience that brings the customer back and inspires him to share the experience with others.

Experience has shown that customers will return when they (a) have no choice, (b) have alternatives to receive the level of service, or (c) simply love to come because they enjoy the experience. Customer retention requires that customers enjoy the service experience, which implies caring to learn about their experiential needs such as emotions, value, responsiveness, or uniqueness. Earning and measuring customer loyalty is a good measure of customer retention. The customer loyalty can be determined by the customer-specific revenue, customer referrals, or a measure of customers' experience. Customer defection and complaints can be considered errors in the process of customer retention.

Service Performance Index, SPIn

Implementing elements of the Service Scorecard and corresponding measurements can help aspects of the organization improve and innovate to achieve sustained success. However, these elements are interdependent and affect each other. Thus, integrating these measurements brings various functions together, harmonizes their priorities, and builds teamwork. The Service Performance Index is an aggregate performance measurement that can be correlated to the financial outcomes or the business objectives.

Although every function is important, the significance of every function is not equal. Thus, significance level has been established to ensure responsibility and accountability commensurate with the impact. Table 5.3 shows the significance of each element and corresponding measurement of the Service Scorecard, as well as the element's contribution to the SPIn. The significance has been established such that a balance is maintained among various factors. For example, leadership is assigned a significance level of 30 percent, and managers are at 20 percent. Together they account for 50 percent of the performance of an organization.

TABLE 5.3   Service Scorecard Measurements Example

Element	Measurements	Base Significance	% Score	SPIn Points
Growth	Revenue growth from new services	10	70	7
Leadership	Employee recognition	15	40	6
	Return on Equity	15	70	10.5
Acceleration	Rate of improvement	20	50	10
Collaboration	Reliability of partners	5	80	4
	Trust	5	60	3
Innovation	Ideas	10	60	6
	Satisfaction			
	Involvement			
Execution	Accuracy	5	85	4.25
	Responsiveness	5	90	4.5
Retention	Customer Loyalty/ retention	10	60	6
	SPIn			**61.25**

*Gupta, Six Sigma Business Scorecard, 2007

This significance of management and executives demonstrates that expectations exist at all levels of the leadership. If the leaders' performance is not up to par, businesses do suffer. For execution and innovation, employees are responsible, but for driving improvement and achieving business objectives, the leadership team is responsible. The SPIn value signifies overall performance of the business and available opportunities for improvement initiatives, such as Six Sigma and Reengineering. Finally, the SPIn can also be used to benchmark various divisions or businesses to achieve excellence and maintain leadership position in the marketplace.

Take Away

- The Service Scorecard is a predictive framework that is specifically designed for services context.

- The Service Scorecard provides a view of the health of the corporation and provides an indication about the future performance.

- The basic architecture of the Service Scorecard consists of seven elements.

- The Service Performance Index (SPIn) provides an aggregate indication of the performance.

6

Designing a Service Scorecard

This chapter describes the requirements of a performance measurement system (PMS), the measurement alignment process, existing PMSs for services, and elements of the Service Scorecard. A PMS is used to provide a company with useful information to help manage and control the corporate performance of the company. The information provided by the system is used to enhance the shareholders' value. The information provided by the system must be correct, presented in a timely manner, easily understood by all stakeholders, representing a common language, and accessible to the associate who will benefit from the information. In the long run, a company will have a specialized knowledge management system supporting its PMS.

Continuous evaluation of the system requires aligning the PMS with corporate strategic planning. By combing the system with strategic planning, businesses can "rethink" their business processes to succeed and compete with today's competitive environment. Changes can be introduced and fine-tuned. A failure to align with the corporate planning leaves the company having many conflicting initiatives, objectives, strategies, and action plans. Traditional literature on the strategic planning process describes this process as consisting of four main components for it to be most effective. These are the four components:

1. Employees creatively rethinking the business and organization as to how it can improve. Employees consider the business landscape, new developments, competitive environment, and macroeconomic environment, and brainstorm various possibilities about the future.

2. Creating a shared understanding of the "critical few" strategic issues to properly run the business. To arrive at the shared understanding, employees create a few plausible scenarios. Each scenario will require a different response from managers and a different type of fine-tuning to the system. The initial part of the exercise is also called "scenario planning." One can consider various external (or macro) factors and internal (business context and customer-related) factors during this step.

3. Defining a set of associated objectives, strategies, and measurements for the company. Prepare a plan to achieve the objective using the most plausible scenario.

4. Continuously readjusting these components in case the scenario and the environment have changed.

An effective PMS considers this type of planning process. By focusing on these components, the firm's employees and all stakeholders will have a clear understanding of the organization's vision and will be able to understand what the key objectives are to achieve this vision of success. By clearly communicating to employees and other stakeholders, the plan sets the expectations and milestones.

An Empirical Investigation of the Measurements Alignment Process

PMSs rely on the selection of the right measurements, data collection, information management, and the knowledge management system in place. Selecting the right measurements is a first step in this direction. Measurements can be (a) related to a strategic decision, (b) partial or aggregate, or (c) in units of money or other units. A performance measure can be defined as a verifiable measure that consists of an actual measure—the numerical value that identifies the minimum threshold of performance and the context within which the measurement operates.

Measurements and measurement systems do not operate in a vacuum without a business objective. A good measurement system maintains alignment and coordination with other functional units of the organization. This alignment deals with consistency of strategic goals during the planning process. Coordination deals with the consistency of measurements in various areas, including within the strategic business context. A measurement system will adapt to a particular strategic business context. This strategic business context is shaped by the corporate strategy, its customer, and its competition. For example, a mature firm in a stable market will face different issues as compared to a growth firm in a growing market or a not-for-profit firm or a firm with high contact with its customers.

Measurements should have the same meaning and connotation across the organization. In general, there is a need for common language and terminology that is easily understandable by all stakeholders for various managerial decision-making systems. Few issues should be noted with the common measurement systems. Often, measurements lack strategic focus and intangible components and solely focus on financial outcome and quantitative outcome.

The thinking of including nonfinancial measures is now well established. Nonfinancial measures, however, should be aligned with the strategy of the firm. Similarly, qualitative components, which are relevant in the service context, should be incorporated into the measurement system. Another common issue with measurements is their response to a particular observation. Generally, a particular measurement is flowing down as a proxy for a particular strategic intent. Often the cause-effect relationship is not that straightforward and has not been established.

Seven deadly sins of performance measurement are described by Michael Hammer in a recent article. A few sins of performance measurement are described in this section. The first sin, *vanity*, is related to measuring what one makes look good. Measuring what is necessary to measure is needed as opposed to measuring what could look like a really good number. The second sin, *provincialism*, involves suboptimization at the business unit or functional level. Measurements need to optimize overall corporate performance. *Pettiness*, another sin, relates to measuring some small component of what really matters in the big picture. The deadliest sin, *frivolity*, relates to a lack of seriousness about measurement in the first place. In summary, measurements should emphasize the end-to-end business process and focus on the drivers of the enterprise value creation. A cookie-cutter approach to measurements selection is bound for failure.

Balance Between Innovation and Continuous Improvement

As discussed, an understanding of the strategic objective of a firm is critical while designing a PMS. Organizations need to balance current and future needs. The ambidextrous organization principle, presented by Charles A. O'Reilly III and Michael L. Tushman, discusses the importance of an ambidextrous organization in the business world. Ambidextrous organization is good at both creating innovation and sustaining current business opportunities. Many companies are failing at this duality because they are not embracing the new innovations and technology or the organization barriers exist for a successful implementation. According to this article, the only way to succeed in the business world today is by exploiting the *present* and exploring the *future* (that is, an ambidextrous organization). Doing so allows companies to accept new innovations and keep the traditional aspects of their businesses the same.

A recent report in *Business Week* magazine about the impact of Six Sigma implementation on the innovation culture at 3M also makes the same argument. Each organization needs to find the appropriate balance between improvement and innovation and accordingly devise appropriate systems. Understanding the need for an ambidextrous organization is critical when designing and implementing a PMS.

An ambidextrous organization analyzed in the O'Reilly-Tushman article is CIBA Vision, which sells contact lenses and other eye-care products to optometrists and consumers. CIBA Vision was a successful company until Johnson & Johnson came out with the first disposable contact lenses. Disposable contact lenses were a new innovation compared to the traditional contact lenses that CIBA Vision was selling. CIBA Vision needed to adopt the new innovation in contact lenses to remain profitable. The R&D was now focused on finding innovations in contact lenses instead of promoting traditional contact lenses. The firm faced challenges in the area of change management and integration.

Similarly, Microsoft created separate organizations for MSN.com, Gaming and Xbox, and Mobile Windows. Separate organizations exist for Windows and Office products. These examples illustrate the importance of companies willing to integrate traditional business ideas with new innovations to stay successful in the business world today. The employees, and the leaders of the company, should be open to being ambidextrous. Sometimes being ambidextrous means a company must dismiss some of its workers if they are not willing to change with the company. Management should be aggressive and work hard to make the company and its employees ambidextrous and willing to share ideas across departments.

Analyzing the Requirements of Performance Measurement Systems

A successful PMS is a set of performance measures, a decision-making process, and a feedback learning loop that helps to manage, control, plan, and perform the activities undertaken in the company. This information gained from the PMS is turned into accurate and relevant information for decision making and feedback learning. The system is aligned with other systems already in place, such as a corporate planning system, knowledge management system, and human resources system. Three questions vital to a PMS are

1. *What* should be measured?
2. *How* should the measurement be undertaken?
3. *What* response is appropriate?

The *What* question decides what measurements are relevant for the measurement system. Criteria need to be established outlining the balance between financial and nonfinancial measures, leading and lagging measures, and internal and external measures. The answer to the second question of *How* provides (a) a basis to the methodology for measures, and (b) guidance in frequency of measurement and mode of measurement. The answer to the third question of *What* response provides a response to the information collected. The decision response process should be aligned with corporate decision making.

Not all PMSs are created equal. Broadly speaking, three different classes of PMSs exist. The first class of systems emphasizes being fully integrated with existing systems and processes. This class of systems requires a focus on all stakeholders, both internal and external. The second class places the focus on the customer and is constantly striving to improve—not just to monitor. The third class of systems is focused on internal measures only, such as the cash flows and return on investment. Some requirements are fulfilled by all three classes.

Providing accurate information is the most important requirement of a PMS. Other requirements are supporting strategic, tactical, and operational objectives; guarding against suboptimization; and including a limited number of performance measures. Usually, a firm starts with a class-three PMS. As the system matures, it moves on to the class-two PMS and eventually graduates to the class-one system.

The third class is obviously the most basic class of systems. This class is classified as "mostly financial." This class has some basic requirements that should be fulfilled by a good PMS, which is in all the classes. An additional requirement for a third class is using traditional performance criteria that control different costs, return on investments (ROI), and cash flows. These class-three performance management systems are profit-oriented and optimizing against cost efficiency and mainly short-term results. The main focus for this basic class is internal operations, and this class is one-dimensional.

The second class of PMSs is often classified as "balanced." This class is multidimensional, where the focus is internal, and external needs are fulfilled. Financial and nonfinancial criteria are used covering cost, quality, delivery, and flexibility. Short- and long-term horizons are considered as well. The vital information of this class goes to the specific people without any delay. This class supports innovation and is very customer-oriented. The second class aims to improve rather than monitor.

The performance measures within the first class must support improvement and stand up to the highest standards. The needs from all the customers, shareholders, competitors, suppliers, employees, and society are important for this first class. The PMS is updated when needed and directly presented to the people who require it. Performance measurement databases should be fully integrated. This is causal-relationship dimensional, and the focus is for all stakeholders.

A firm should be continuously evaluating the needs and requirements of the system. In case any of the requirements for a PMS is not fulfilled, an evaluation must be done. As a next step, one should determine whether the type of system used is appropriate for the current stage of the firm. Stage here refers to the maturing of the offerings portfolio, the firm, and the firm in relation to the use of a PMS. If a company does not meet the requirements, the focus should be directed to the areas of need. If a company does fulfill all requirements, the possibility of moving up to the next class is taken into consideration.

Typically, a company utilizes scenarios to define its possible alternative approaches to future developments in the external environment, which are then used to form both a current strategy-based assessment and a futuristic strategy-based development. In developing these approaches, the focus has changed from a traditional market-based approach to the resource-based approach. The resource-based approach identifies new concepts of organizational resources, such as intangible assets and an intellectual capital. Scenario management plays a vital role in developing diverse methods of systems thinking, future open thinking, and strategic thinking. The essence of all of these scenarios is not to invent a completely new strategy, but to examine the suitability of the existing strategies with the help of external scenarios.

Performance Measurement Systems for Services

Comprehensive PMSs designed specifically for services are lacking. Only three systems that were designed specifically for the services context can be identified: the ServQual Model, the Service Profit Chain Model, and the Service Model presented by Fitzgerald et al. The Service Quality Model (i.e., ServQual) focuses on the customer satisfaction aspects of service quality and is not a comprehensive performance management model. The Service Profit Chain Model is a strategic tool and includes a service profit chain management audit. The Fitzgerald model is a PMS, but no measures are provided in this model. None of these models is comprehensive.

ServQual Framework

The 1991 version of the Parasuraman et al. ServQual Model is discussed here. These authors have contributed significantly to the service quality literature. The model uses a questionnaire to identify service quality gaps from customers' perspectives. A set of 22 questions representing different service quality dimensions is administered. The questionnaire has two parts. One part asks about the expectation of the service, and a second part receives responses about the perception of an actual service experienced. The final section has questions on the relative importance of quality dimensions. Analysis of the survey provides gaps in a service system according to the model. The current version of the model includes the following five dimensions:

1. **Reliability**—Ability to perform the promised service dependably, accurately, and as promised.
2. **Responsiveness**—Willingness to help customers and provide prompt service.
3. **Assurance**—Knowledge and courtesy of employees and their ability to inspire trust and confidence.
4. **Empathy**—Caring, individualized attention the firm provides its customers. Ability to put oneself in customers' shoes.
5. **Tangibles**—Physical facilities, equipment, *servicescapes*, and appearance of personnel.

Service Chain Framework

Heskett et al. presented a Service Profit Chain Model. This model has three levels. Level one describes the process wherein a company chooses a certain strategic market position, and a service concept is the end result. The service delivery system needs to be aligned with the operations strategy of the firm, which in turn should be aligned with the corporate strategy.

Level two refers to employees and customer satisfaction. Employees play a critical role in the process. Employee satisfaction and loyalty lead to customer loyalty and satisfaction. Level three describes appropriate financial ratios or a profit model. An audit developed according to the Service Profit Chain Model is performed in the following five steps:

1. Identify the organizational unit.
2. Assess the relative importance of dimensions.
3. Assess current practice in the marketplace.
4. Identify and measure the gaps.
5. Establish priorities and take actions.

Service Model

The model presented by Fitzgerald does not have any specific name attached to it. Fitzgerald et al. conducted the most comprehensive study in this service context. The model proposed by them for service firms included measures related to *results* (financial measures and competitiveness) and measures that related to *cause* (quality, resource utilization, and innovation). These six dimensions can be classified into two broad categories: SBU strategy results (financial performance and competitiveness) and determinants of the strategy's success (resource utilization, quality of services, innovation, and flexibility). The concept of causality is included in this model. In addition, the business unit is considered the main unit for performance management in this model. Fitzgerald et al. provided some guidelines for measurement types that could be used in service businesses.

Other Service Models

An example of a scorecard in the service context is provided by Christopher Ryder Jones. The service excellence scorecard was created to help Gulf Bank provide exceptional service to its customers.

Gulf Bank has around 700 employees with 31 branches in Kuwait and is also Kuwait's second-leading and rapidly growing commercial bank. This scorecard communicates drivers of customer satisfaction, delivery channels, performance standards, and measurement and reporting systems, which in turn provide consumer feedback and process measurements. Performance was measured for 16 drivers of customer satisfaction, including branches, ATMs, the telephone, the Internet, consumer loans, and credit card services. Gulf Bank implemented its service excellence program by creating reports and communicating those reports to managers and branch employees. The results were then integrated in business Key Performance Indicators (KPIs) and turned into employee incentive schemes.

Christopher Jones illustrates how the Gulf Bank created the scorecard for service excellence. It was meant to help the growth of potential customers, to retain current customers, and to gain maximum profit from those customers through superior service. In 2003 the service excellence program at Gulf Bank was launched. Key elements of this program are the reports that were to be prepared for the management of service quality performance. The three key requirements for these reports are the following:

1. Provide a focus on the principal drivers of customer satisfaction and retention.
2. Drive action by channel and product managers.
3. Be straightforward in communication and usage.

A survey was carried out from the institute of Banking Studies in Kuwait to determine key drivers of consumer satisfaction. The key drivers were excellent staff, efficient operations, convenience, competitive costs, and excellent image. The excellent staff should work quickly and efficiently. They must also be knowledgeable, polite, and friendly. Efficient operations components included accuracy of transactions and statements and availability of a full range of service. When consumers were looking for convenience, they wanted less waiting time, as well as reliability, comfort, and effective services. Regarding competitive costs, customers wanted lower charges for loans and lower service charges. Excellent image basically demanded an excellent reputation and corporate image.

Many insights were gained from implementing the service excellence scorecard. The first insight was to incorporate service quality management with overall business management. The second insight was the recognition of service attributes, which were imperative to consumers. The last insight was that great paybacks occurred from defining service excellence in numerical terms and implementing competitive benchmarking wherever it was feasible.

Elements of the Service Scorecard

The Six Sigma Business Scorecard, a newly developed business scorecard presented by Gupta, offers a comprehensive performance-measurement methodology to create a predictive performance model. This scorecard fulfills a majority of these requirements. A causal link to corporate outcome still needs to be established, however. The Service Scorecard, presented in this book, is an adaptation of the Six Sigma Business Scorecard but is designed for the service sector. The Service Scorecard is a unique business-performance model to quantify, predict, and manage service-oriented corporate performance. Figure 6.1 presents a hierarchy of the service performance system. At Level I, we have leadership driving sustainable and profitable growth of the firm. The next level represents the value chain of different stakeholders from partners to employees to customers. The final level is the execution and design of the service delivery system. The design of the service delivery system includes managerial decisions such as service capacity, service inventory, and service delivery channels.

The elements of GLACIER (Growth, Leadership, Acceleration, Collaboration, Innovation, Execution, and Retention) provide a systems perspective of the organization. The scorecard includes processes and methods at the operational level (execution), as well as strategic decisions at the corporate level (leadership) and the tactical level (engagement and innovation). The architecture of the scorecard also includes all the stakeholders in the service chain—customers, employees, managers, and service chain partners. This architecture is the foundation of the scorecard. As a next step, one would adapt the Service Scorecard appropriate to the business context. For example, a for-profit firm will have different measures than a not-for-profit firm.

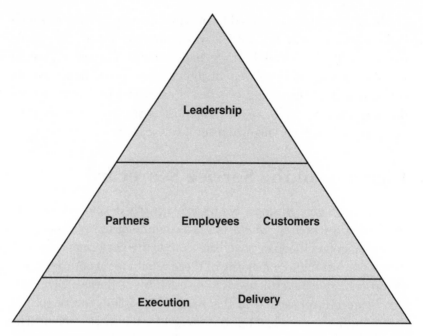

Figure 6.1   Hierarchy of service performance

As the scorecard is adapted to the situation, one should take into consideration all the issues discussed in the previous sections. Some salient features of the scorecard are the following:

- The Service Scorecard architecture is only the starting point. A firm will not take a cookie-cutter approach and will not use the same standard measures as another firm.

- Measures presented in this book are only to showcase the application of the Service Scorecard.

- The Service Scorecard will include 10 to 14 measures at the top level.

- Measures are common across the organization and are clearly understood by all stakeholders.

- The Service Scorecard will benchmark against direct (indirect) competition.

- The Service Scorecard will include internal and external measures.

- The Service Scorecard will include lagging and leading indicators.
- The Service Scorecard measures will be aligned with the strategic intent of the firm.
- The Service Scorecard will be revisited at or during annual strategic planning exercises.
- The Service Scorecard will be aligned with the corporate decision-making process.

Service Scorecard measurements identify operational opportunities for sustaining profitable growth and productivity improvement. Opportunities for profit and productivity improvement are addressed using Six Sigma and Lean principles, and growth is achieved through service innovation. The service innovation begins with employee ideas, and excellence in idea management will ensure continual flow of employee ideas for developing new services.

Table 6.1 shows measures under various categories in the service context. Various categories represent elements of Service Scorecard. In this treatment on the subject, the aim is to utilize elements of existing models and measurement systems and reflect on the field of performance management in the service-dominant context. In other words, three questions are addressed here:

1. What are existing performance management frameworks that are relevant for service-dominant context?
2. Could a framework that is relevant for the service-dominant context be developed?
3. What will this framework look like and how will it be implemented?

TABLE 6.1 Typical Measures by Service Firms

	Measures	Relationship with Corporate Performance
Leadership	Return on net assets	Leadership with performance
	Operating profit, ROI, ROA	
	Revenue per employee	
	Rewards and recognitions	

TABLE 6.1 Typical Measures by Service Firms

	Measures	Relationship with Corporate Performance
Customer Retention	% repeat business	Customer satisfaction with financial performance
	Customer satisfaction	
	% orders lost due to late delivery	Customer satisfaction with customer retention
	Customer satisfaction due to delivery speed	Customer satisfaction with market share
	Gains and losses of customer/accounts	
	Customer retention	
	Customer complaints	
	Customer recovery	
Strategic Planning	Strategic planning	Planning with financial performance
	Relative market share	
Employer Engagement	Staff costs, profit per service	Employee satisfaction with customer satisfaction
	Investment in training, training effectiveness	Employee satisfaction with financial performance
	Overall employee satisfaction	
	Extent of training	Employee satisfaction with productivity
	Absenteeism, turnover	
	Grievances/complaints	
	Work system effectiveness	
	Values added per employee	
Execution	% on-time project delivery	Execution with performance
	Service rework	
	Service errors	
	Cycle time and service response time	
Growth through Innovation	Number of new services	Innovation with growth
	New service introduction lead times	Growth with performance
	% new to existing ratio: existing offerings	

TABLE 6.1 Typical Measures by Service Firms

	Measures	Relationship with Corporate Performance
Partnership	Quality performance	Partnership with performance
	Satisfaction	
	Trust	
	Flexibility	
	Cost savings, price	

The overall objective of an effective performance management system is to control, manage, plan, and perform the business undertaken by the entity. An effective performance measurement system has various requirements:

1. **System:**
   - System requirements provide accurate, timely, relevant information and are easily accessible to those who need the information.
   - The system considers other stakeholders, for example, customers, suppliers, competitors, employees, investors, and society.
   - The system is dynamic in nature. The system should be dynamic in nature to align with the changing strategic direction.

2. **Measures:**
   - Measures are derived from strategic objectives.
   - Both financial and nonfinancial measures are included. Short-term and long-term objectives are included.
   - A limited number of measures are included in the system.
   - For each measure, a clear causal link to corporate outcome should be established.
   - Indicators are easy to measure and comprehend.

3. Decision Making:

- Measures provide guidance for decision making.
- Measures are aligned with the strategic decision-making process.

After the Service Scorecard architecture is ready, implementation of the scorecard is the next step. The implementation process, as shown in Figure 6.2, has the following steps:

1. Understand and map the business processes. The step involves understanding key business processes using existing tools.
2. Match business processes with the scorecard.
3. Align the organization to accomplish the vision/strategy.
4. Identify key measures; measure and monitor the performance
5. Continually identify areas of improvement.
6. Sustain and revisit the Service Scorecard measurement.

Design of Service Scorecard is the focus of this chapter. Implementation steps are discussed further in other chapters.

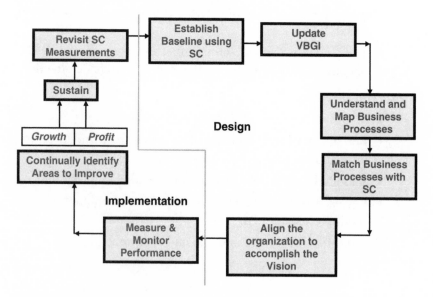

Figure 6.2   Scorecard design roadmap

Take Away

- The measurement system should be aligned with the strategic objective of the service firm.

- Measurements should find the right balance between the need for innovation and continuous improvement, leading and lagging indicators, and subjective and objective measures.

- The purpose and intent of the measurement system needs to be understood upfront clearly.

- Examples of frameworks for services are ServQual, Service Profit Chain, and Service Model.

- Service Scorecard architecture needs to be adapted to the specific context.

7

Leadership and Acceleration

Corporations implement scorecards to monitor and drive performance for sustaining profitable growth. Operations lead to financial outcomes, and stronger financial performance supports operations. Therefore, the success of the Service Scorecard depends on how it is being used by executives for reviewing operational and financial performance. To ensure the active participation of executives and middle management, the Service Scorecard has leadership and acceleration elements.

The leadership element is critical to set the bar, demand performance, and align the organization to achieve business objectives. The Service Scorecard can be implemented successfully by utilizing the following areas:

- Technology for ease of data gathering and reporting
- People for their participation in developing goals and taking actions
- Process level measurements to provide feedback in real time
- Leadership at the process level
- A culture of excellence to strive for the best
- Teamwork to ensure broader implementation and positive interaction

In most organizations, the performance measurement task is assigned to the IT department or the assurance organization to ensure its implementation. Such implementations lack teeth to get anything done except reporting numbers. For example, there was a reporting manager who used to publish monthly performance reports religiously within the first week. At one point the manager took a vacation, left a stack of reports close to the door of his office, and notified all interested parties to pick up their copy. On his return from vacation, he was surprised to find the stack of reports without one copy missing. He then stopped publishing the report, and no one bothered to ask about it. Such an example is not an uncommon attitude about the scorecard.

With the technology available today, scorecards are displayed as dashboards, so people look at the dashboards. They are accustomed to seeing green, yellow, and red zones on dashboards. When it comes to implementation based on the yellow or red zones, excuses such as "it's old data," "the problem no longer exists," or "it's the other departments' fault" are not uncommon. The leadership element is designed to eliminate such excuses, reward superior performance, and establish unquestionable accountability for performance.

Most businesses strive for continual improvement. One of the challenges with continual improvement is that managers are used to setting up realistic and marginal goals for improvement. They spend time reporting the achievement of those goals without being sensitive to the impact of improvement on corporate financials. At many companies, managers report improvement month after month, but employees do not see any improvement. They see reports of improved profit, but they also hear about upcoming layoffs. When such ironic incidents occur, questions inevitably arise. Either the improvement is not enough to overcome the financial challenges, or the growth is not enough to benefit from the improvement effort.

Today every company has some form of improvement initiative, be it lean manufacturing, Six Sigma, TQM, or another similar initiative. When a customer looks to establish a relationship with a supplier, it reviews competing bids for price, the quality management system (QMS), and service. At the time of evaluation, discriminating among potential suppliers is very difficult, because they all have QMS certifications, competitive prices, and customer service departments. All suppliers are incrementally improving in a roughly equal manner; thus, it becomes difficult to discern a good supplier from a bad supplier. The rate of improvement in a supplier's performance, as measured by the Service Scorecard, can provide great insights about its internal operations, culture, leadership, and likelihood of being a dependable supplier.

Acceleration is required to achieve excellence, synergize departments, and demand passionate leadership commitment to achieve business objectives. Typical continual incremental improvement initiatives lead to employee boredom, management apathy, and leadership ignorance. Such incremental improvement initiatives become a champion's job, and the champions look for justification for one's existence through myriad improvement projects, unnecessary training, and a confounding and fancy reporting system.

Leadership and Acceleration in the GLACIER of the Service Scorecard form critical arch stones. Leadership inspires employees to excel, and Acceleration drives improvement. Most business successes are headed by inspiring leadership, such as Steve Jobs at Apple, Bill Gates at Microsoft, Jeff Emmelt at General Electric, Bob Galvin at Motorola, Herb Kelleher at Southwest Airlines, Louis Gerstner at IBM, Warren Buffett at Berkshire Hathaway, Michael Eisner at Disney, and Lee Iacocca at Chrysler. On the other hand, many business failures, such as Enron Corporation, Tyco International, DeLorean Motor Company, TWA, and Arthur Andersen, can also be attributed to leadership failures. The corporate leadership makes or breaks the company at any state.

Simple analysis will show that if one strategy will ensure corporate success, it is acceleration in improvement. If every department, including design and development, continually improves significantly, then the corporation will do well. The strength of a company is determined by how fast and how much an organization can adapt to changing conditions. Continual improvement must be a habit. In some critical areas, inefficiency must be remedied and waste must be eliminated fast, as the profit margins become limited and prone to rapid deterioration due to intense global competition. Acceleration in performance improvement must become a major corporate initiative, mandating clearer accountability, faster improvement, and dramatic results. Acceleration facilitates growing profits.

Leadership

Service organizations are becoming more complex, more autonomous, and more interdependent in the changing Internet economy. Service organizations such as telephone service providers, banks, restaurants, airlines, education institutions, regulatory and compliance organizations, IT service providers, and R&D service providers have both global reach and local impact. In order to lead an organization with attributes such as local and global presence, in-house and outsourced services, human- and technology-based services, personal and infrastructure level options, and centralized and distributed systems, leadership must be able to do the following:

- Handle complexity while keeping it simple.
- Learn technology while inspiring people.
- Empower people while ensuring performance of the organization.

Due to this significant and critical latitude in the performance of an organization, the Service Scorecard includes the leadership element with guiding measurements such as employee recognition and profitability. Continually inspiring employees by having them actively participate in strategic as well as operations planning is now a more important aspect of leading an organization. For example, Colleen Barrett, president of Southwest Airlines, has said the following about the significance of stakeholders: employees first, customers second, and shareholders third. In service organizations, employees and their happiness matter, because the happier the employees, the more pleasantly they will serve customers. The leader of a service organization must be other-oriented instead of self-oriented to ingrain a service attitude in the organization.

The Leadership element is supported by the other elements of the scorecard to create synergy and achieve synchronization among various departments. The leadership role is critical in achieving sustained profitable growth. A decision by leadership may lead to action by all employees, resulting in a significant impact on the performance. Thus, the leadership decisions are weighted at 30 percent of the total forming the Service Performance Index (SPIn). Assigned weights are baseline weights and will vary depending on the business context.

One of the challenges in today's corporations is that the CEO is involved more in dealing with external aspects of the business, such as shareholders' concerns, Wall Street expectations, major individual investors, key customers' concerns, or external communication through various media channels. As a result, leaders know more about what is not going right and what they should say, rather than what they should do more or better. The Leadership element of the Service Scorecard ensures a certain level of engagement and ensures that critical activities are performed.

Typical leadership expectations are to establish a vision for the organization, ensure strategic planning and execution to realize desired business objectives, communicate to inform various stakeholders, ensure a sound financial bottom line and top line, monitor compliance to government regulation, and be available at critical opportunities to meet with employees, clients, or other stakeholders. Successful CEOs or leaders are fast learners, whether that learning is about new technology, new product designs, or new methodologies similar to Six Sigma, Lean Manufacturing, or Innovation. Every CEO or president is a very smart person. Questionable strategy and tunnel vision are what misdirect corporate resources and lead to unsatisfactory business performance.

Transformational and Transactional Leadership

Vast literature resources exist on the leadership topic. Some popular themes of leadership are the stewardship approach requiring a servant-leader paradigm, the empowerment paradigm providing enablers to get things done, and the learning organization approach. Leadership has been defined as a process, as a relationship providing influence and motivation of personality traits, as a system of processes, and as an instrument to achieve desired corporate goals. Most of these approaches, however, fail to take the situation or business context at hand into account. Some of these approaches are also idealistic in nature. Additionally, none of these approaches appears to have been tested empirically. The situational (that is, contingent) approach of leadership is the most relevant for the Service Scorecard.

The transformational approach of leadership considers the business context and includes transactions and relationship elements. Considering leadership styles as a continuum, the transformational style is on the far-left corner, the transactional style is in the middle, and the hands-off approach is on the far-right corner. The Service Scorecard measures the impact of leadership on employees and other stakeholders. In this section, the transformational approach to leadership, as described by Peter Northouse in his book *Leadership: Theory and Practice*, is examined. The Multifactor Leadership Questionnaire is based on the elements of transformational leadership. The questionnaire is divided into three broad leadership styles:

1. ***Transformational style***—Leadership showing transformational styles, including influencing, visioning, inspirational motivation, intellectual stimulation, and individualized consideration.

2. ***Transactional style***—Leadership providing rewards and placing checks and balances/corrections in place. Rewards and recognition are measured in the Service Scorecard.

3. ***Hands-off leadership***—Leadership places no rigid structure or guidance or rules in place.

Leadership Measurements

Current trends in globalization, service mix, technology advancements, the use of intellectual resources, and tough competition require continually rapid organizational changes that add other dimensions to the leadership job. Globalization demands working with multiple organizations, dealing with people with diverse backgrounds, and communicating with businesses having a variety of cultures, government policies, and laws. All of these factors add to the complexity of the organization and challenge the leader to look for optimal and multidimensional solutions. So many tasks and the complexity of working with such organizations require that the CEO stay focused on his task of bringing out the best in people everywhere.

While developing measurements, the challenge for the leadership is that there can be so many important measures that could be established. However, too many measurements for CEOs could lead to "runaway" CEOs, because they do have to deal with subtle aspects of the business. Selecting the two best measurements for the leadership must define roles clearly for the CEO. One measure is to inspire employees to do their best for producing outstanding results that create significant value for the organization through the CEO Award recognition. Employees or teams love to be recognized with the CEO Award for Exceptional Value. A trivial-looking aspect of the CEO Award is its publicity. The CEO Award must be publicized to create interest in employees to strive so that they identify areas for creating exceptional value.

Every employee wants to do a good job at work with the given tools, information, and knowledge (provided motivation exists). Bureaucracy and recognition for "waste savers" prevent employee engagements, especially in large organizations. Thus, CEO recognition of the employee provides the extra incentive for employees to strive for innovative, extraordinary performance. In smaller companies, employees are closer to the CEO or the president; however, in most larger organizations with a deep hierarchical layer, employees can not even think of seeing their CEO in person. An opportunity to be recognized by the CEO provides huge motivation to create significant value.

The second leadership measure for the Service Scorecard represents the CEO's commitment to create value for stakeholders. Thus, Return on Equity (ROE) has been identified to be the second measure for leadership. This requires CEOs to continually monitor the financial performance of the corporation to satisfy the fundamentals of the business for ensuring ROE. For some businesses ROE may not appear to be a suitable measurement; however, the organization may decide to replace ROE with a similar measurement. Each measurement has been weighted at 15 percent for its contribution to the Service Performance Index (SPIn). For the leadership element and measurements to work effectively, the CEO must own these measures of performance personally and participate actively to achieve business objectives.

Having a CEO responsible for financial performance is the ultimate measure of the leadership performance. There is a long list of financial measures that corporations utilize. Selecting one that is representative of the CEO's performance makes a difficult choice. ROE or an equivalent measure is a tangible and critical measure of the leadership's performance. Most corporations have a ROE measure in place already; however, they do not necessarily utilize it to monitor corporate performance.

Implementing Leadership Measurements

Leadership buy-in for implementing the necessary measurements is an imperative. No leader wants to be measured with the understanding that a leader is accountable for the overall performance of the company. By depending on the overall performance, the CEO is taking a chance of achieving desired business objectives without personally getting engaged. He must be willing to be held accountable for the necessary actions and expected outcomes. Many measurements can be used; however, selecting the two measurements, wherein the one is the input to the business performance and the other is the output of the business performance (ROE), makes sense for the Service Scorecard.

Initially, the CEO recognizing extraordinary performance may sound trivial. The intent is not to give awards; instead it is to inspire employees to give their best to the CEO's vision and to the company. Accordingly, appropriate resources must be allocated, and organizational responsibilities must be assigned. For the CEO recognition to work as intended, clearly defined criteria for recognition must be established and communicated to all employees. The recognition must be inclusive and fair to all employees; otherwise, it would create more discontent rather than fulfilling its intent to promote intellectual engagement of all employees.

Most important of all is the CEO's personal effort to achieve established goals for the two leadership measurements. Responsibility of the leadership measurements should not be delegated; instead the CEO must demonstrate personal passion and set an example of going after performance measurements. The CEO's staff responsible for other performance measurements would certainly follow the CEO's lead in planning, executing, and achieving the desired business objectives.

Planning for the leadership measurements can include input from stakeholders such as managers, employees, and customers, and a team must be formed to establish guidelines to gather information about exceptional successes, evaluate various successes, select successes for recognition, communicate those successes to the organization, and recognize individuals involved in creating the exceptional value.

Besides, aggressive goals must be set to install the culture of continually raising the bar higher, whether annually, quarterly, or monthly.

One of the major challenges to establishing meaningful leadership performance measurements is creating a culture of accountability all the way from the top to the floor. If goals are established they are meant to be achieved; if reviews are held they are meant to challenge the status quo; if actions are identified they are meant to be completed on time to deliver desired outcomes. If one department needs help from others, priorities must be aligned and help offered. Such is the culture in which everyone is working toward achieving business objectives, making decisions in the interest of the organization, and optimizing department processes with team spirit, thus minimizing interdepartmental conflicts.

A CEO is respected as a leader if a clear vision is communicated, employees are inspired, and the organization is creating value for customers, employees, and society. The previously stated two measures provide leading indications of the CEO's success.

Acceleration

If a company has only one measurement as a leading indicator of the corporate performance, that measurement is acceleration. Acceleration is defined as the rate of improvement. Corporations have been improving their performance for many years. Large OEMs demand price reduction from their suppliers at a rate of about 2 percent to 5 percent every year. Wal-Mart asks its suppliers to improve performance and reduce cost on an ongoing basis. To meet customer demands, suppliers must find a way to cut cost. Initiatives using Six Sigma or Lean Manufacturing are implemented to reduce scrap, eliminate waste, or streamline processes. However, competitive forces require that this rate of improvement be accelerated. Indeed, the Six Sigma methodology works optimally when improvement targets are aggressive, thus forcing involvement of all employees and executives.

The Acceleration element in the Service Scorecard has been incorporated to create a culture of relentless and dramatic improvement for keeping up with competition and changing customer demands.

Acceleration overcomes built-in organizational procrastination by forcing the middle management to take responsibility for rapid and dramatic improvement. Imagine the ability of a person to walk, jog, run, and race. Walking involves mostly the legs; jogging utilizes the stomach for retrieving energy; running involves the heart; and racing gets the head actively engaged. In a similar way, the hearts of people do not get involved unless we accelerate people to get involved to promote and realize improved performance.

For an organization to accelerate improvement, all employees must be synergized. In other words, when employees get intellectually involved, creativity sprouts, new ideas are born, and innovation occurs. Thus, it is critical for an organization to accelerate improvement to sustain profitable growth for overcoming the rate of inflation, increasing customer demands, higher employee compensation, and inefficiency in the newer processes.

The Acceleration element affects all other elements of the Service Scorecard as well as all aspects of an organization. Acceleration implies that each department head must establish aggressive goals for improvement, develop an action plan to achieve goals, monitor progress, and take necessary action to ensure progress as intended. One of the barriers to accelerating performance is the fear of failure that occurs due to setting arbitrarily aggressive goals, committing insufficient resources, and missing the established improvement target. Leadership in the organization must allow risk-taking, understand failures, and encourage aggressive goals. In the absence of such an environment, managers tend to set goals that are achievable and nonchallenging. As a result, organizations perform below their capability and miss the opportunity to improve corporate performance.

To establish aggressive goals, benchmarking must be performed to assess the market position and understand best-in-class performance levels. Considering the market position, internal inefficiencies, and waste of resources, managers can establish goals such that employees will be challenged to think creatively and do something different to reduce waste, gain competitive advantage, and improve corporate performance.

The Acceleration element illuminates the long-term commitment to continuous improvement. Business acceleration can be divided into the following categories, as shown in Figure 7.1:

- **Acceleration at the individual employee level**—Examples are employee performance and learning curves.

- **Acceleration at the team level or service group level or business unit level**—Examples are team performance indicators and service-time-to-market measures.

- **Acceleration at the process level**—Examples are process time and quality. These processes relate to core customer requirements.

- **Acceleration at the organization level**—Examples include improvement in corporate measures.

In his book *Accelerate: 20 Practical Lessons to Boost Business Momentum*, Dan Coughlin identified the importance of business acceleration based on his learning from various Fortune 500 and top private companies, including AT&T, Citigroup, Marriott, McDonald's, and Toyota. No rigorous test is provided of this concept, however.

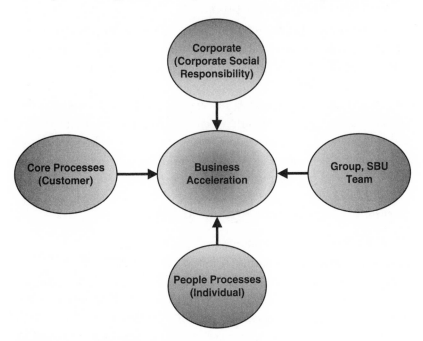

Figure 7.1   Acceleration defined

A common input of measuring acceleration in a company is the process of goal setting. Goal setting helps organizations focus on the results and outcomes and holds the party accountable for its actions. Clear expectations are set during the goal-setting process. The goals may be at the organizational level, process level, or business unit level. These goals may be objective or subjective, helping maintain or improve the performance, and at the process level or corporate level.

Measurements of Acceleration

Benefits of accelerating improvement are multifold. Due to the aggressive improvement goals, teamwork is required. It creates interdependence among departments and sensitizes them to each other's goals. Each department understands that acceleration in improvement is a corporate goal for everyone, so cooperation is critical and benefits are mutual. Acceleration promotes involvement of the customer for ensuring growth and exceptional service. Most important, once committed to accelerate improvement at an aggressive rate, the leadership and managers must both get passionately involved; otherwise, failure is imminent. Without the leadership involvement, a corporation cannot accelerate improvement.

Innovation is an outgrowth of acceleration in business performance. Normally, improvement and innovation are considered to contradict each other. Incremental improvement is all about consistency, whereas innovation is about disruption. When the improvement becomes dramatic, it requires innovation, as the new process must become consistent at the different level. Improvement can reduce inconsistency, whereas innovation can raise the bar. The typical goal for improvement must exceed the comfort level, forcing the new solution to be significantly different from others.

Implementing the Acceleration Measure

Being a nonconventional measure, practicing acceleration in improvement becomes the most challenging measure. The typical measure is the rate of improvement that is needed for each department. Besides being a new measure, another challenge is that this rate of improvement measure causes discomfort for managers, because it requires them to set an aggressive rate of improvement. Based on the market position, and internal opportunities for improvement, a typical rate for improvement may range from 30 percent to 70 percent in manufacturing processes and 15 percent to 30 percent in nonmanufacturing processes.

The improvement measures reduction in waste of both time and material. For example, if a manufacturing process is yielding 80 percent, the rate of improvement goal could be set between 30 percent and 70 percent of the 20 percent waste. Similarly, if a sales process is producing a certain level of sales or margins toward the established profitable targets, the improvement goal could be a 15 percent to 30 percent reduction in gap from the targets. Of course, internal and external, as well as controllable and uncontrollable, constraints must be considered for each process. The controllable constraints could be fixed, while the uncontrollable constraints are managed with some uncertainty using statistical analysis.

To implement the rate of improvement measure, each manager establishes a baseline for the key processes and submits a plan to achieve dramatic improvement that mandates redesigning the process for superior performance. If a process is running close to perfection, or a process has a significant performance loss, the latter gets the priority in setting the departmental goals. In addition, if a process is very critical to the success of the department, that process gets the priority in setting departmental goals. However, goals must be set such that they make each department operate better, faster, and more cost effectively. After the department identifies key processes and its baseline performance, each manager submits the improvement goal and a plan to improve the performance.

The improvement plan includes key tasks, departmental responsibility, critical assistance required from other departments, and estimated date of completion. The improvement plan must also include methods of reporting and communicating the departmental performance internally and externally to the department. The report may include posting trend charts on a bulletin board, for example.

Experience shows that many performance reports show the final goal and performance with respect to the final goal. In such cases the performance target will be missed during most of the year. Even if incremental improvement is realized in some months, it looks like failure and can discourage employees due to lack of recognition. Therefore, dividing the year-end goal into monthly goals, and tracking the process performance against these monthly goals to ensure continual progress, is recommended.

The plan for accelerating improvement must be developed with extensive cross-functional participation. Breakthrough thinking is incorporated at the planning stage by setting aggressive goals and assigning tasks requiring innovative approaches. Otherwise, low-hanging opportunities will show an initial improvement that will hit an impasse in the latter months. Changing course in later months becomes difficult due to initial successes. Thus, the department manager must commit to an innovative approach at the planning stages.

Implementing acceleration requires passion and enthusiasm from the department manager, a culture of employee participation at all levels, and deployment of all resources. It requires leadership, the use of technology, the intellectual engagement of employees, knowledge management, benchmarking, research, and idea management. The department manager plays a significant role by demanding the improvement, providing resources and guidance, and monitoring performance. If the monthly goals are not achieved, all brains must be brought into a huddle to determine remedial actions with a sense of urgency. There must be awareness that the department expects excellent—not acceptable—performance. The standards of excellence are being on target. Highlighting performance targets regularly sensitizes employees to their responsibilities and consequences.

Take Away

- Both the Leadership and Acceleration aspects of GLACIER in the Service Scorecard are critical to continuous and improving business performance.
- Leadership drives the performance and is the central piece of the Service Scorecard.
- Creating a culture of accountability is very important to institute measures for the leadership element.
- Acceleration drives rate of improvement and is driven by middle managers.
- Acceleration and leadership elements both require cross-functional participation and buy-in.

8

Collaboration

Collaboration is defined as a partnership with service value chain partners. Collaboration could be downstream, often described as with
suppliers or service chain partners, or it could be upstream, often described as with alliance partners. Collaboration could also be internal,
often among various business functions, or external, often among various business entities. Consider a service chain similar to a typical supply chain for a product. The (supply) service chain includes end
consumers, as they contribute toward the revenue of the whole value
chain. Various collaborators (that is, partners) provide value to end
consumers. Often this value is intangible and hard to define in the
service environment.

As service chains evolve, a few trends can be noted: fragmentation
and outsourcing, complexity reduction, and competition at the service
chain level. The service value chain is becoming more fragmented and
global in nature. As service firms focus on specific core competencies
and a particular customer segment, the firms tend to outsource business processes to other firms. Collaboration becomes increasingly important in this fragmented environment. Service providers also want
to reduce the complexity of the value chain processes and stay agile
and responsive to customer needs. Reduction in complexity is driven
in part due to the nature of services and customer participation in
service production. For example, Chase Bank has reduced the complexity of ATM transactions and made transactions simpler, more intuitive, and faster. Customers now set and save preferences, such as
the most common amounts withdrawn and the printing of a receipt.

The strategic importance of the collaborative service chain is
understood by recognizing the importance of the competitive landscape in a particular service sector. Similar to the manufacturing world,

competition is between service delivery chains and not between service firms. For example, the competition is not between Wal-Mart and Target; rather, the supply chain of Wal-Mart is competing with the supply chain of Target. Similarly, the service delivery chain of a financial institution competes with the service chain of its direct competitors.

Therefore, the focus of the Service Scorecard is on collaboration. Collaboration among service chain partners impacts other elements of the scorecard. For example, collaboration is understood to impact customer experience. In Larraine Segil's book *Measuring the Value of Partnering—How to Use Metrics to Plan, Develop, and Implement Successful Alliances*, she describes the importance of partnering. The book provides metrics at different stages of alliances and describes the role of each stakeholder.

An understanding of service chain dynamics is obtained by discussing the demand and supply side of the service chain. A service firm typically serves a particular customer segment. This particular customer segment has an expectation about variety, customization of services, quality of services, and availability. All of this "demand-side uncertainty" faced by the service provider needs to be matched by its supply side. Service firms build alliances, partnerships, outsourcing agreements, and joint venture partnerships to provide an appropriate level of responsiveness. Service firms also utilize the existing organization structure consisting of an internal collaborative infrastructure. The health of internal collaboration at a particular service firm impacts the time it takes to bring a new service to market. Good internal collaboration ideally melts away all organizational barriers within a firm, hence improving decision time and reducing time to market.

Drivers of Collaboration

Various forms of collaborations are possible—alliances, joint venture partnerships, and business process outsourcing. Figure 8.1 shows a pyramid of various strategic partnerships. A transaction-based partnership forms the very first level. At the top level, service innovation and end-to-end partnership are found, where two service firms work together in multiple areas, leading to service innovation and end-to-end service management. Generally speaking, collaboration is driven by the following strategic business decisions:

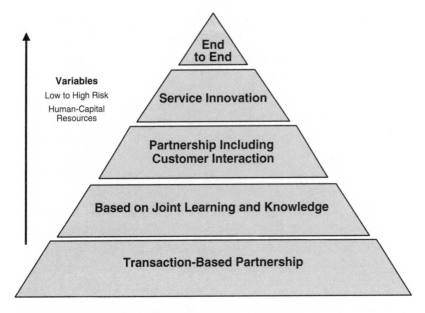

Figure 8.1   Pyramid of partnerships

1. **Market position of the service firm.** Market position for all partner firms could likely improve as a result of the partnership. An example is Amazon.com focusing on its core processes and working with UPS for delivering packages. Both UPS and Amazon.com improve their market positions as a result of their partnership. UPS provides supply chain solutions to Amazon and other firms, including inspection, warehousing, and return services. Some important considerations for this form of collaboration are the strategic position of the partner service firm, scale of operations and geographical reach, access to competitive technological advantage, and long-term strategic position.

2. **Cost reduction.** Often the reason for collaboration with partners is driven by the cost, because a service firm must focus on its core processes. An example could be a large multinational bank outsourcing check processing, loan processing, and other transaction processes to another provider. In this case, a business process is moved to an external organization, often referred to as business process outsourcing. The transaction processes could also be offshored, or moved to an overseas

office of the same service firm. For example, JPMorgan announced in 2005 that a third of its operational staff will be based in India by the year 2008. Goldman Sachs and UBS announced similar plans. JPMorgan cited the cost and quality benefits of these plans. These offshoring operations are often called captive business process outsourcing.

3. *Increased responsiveness.* A firm could form a partnership agreement to streamline its activities and stay responsive to customer demands. An example could be a large hotel chain forming a partnership with airline(s) to provide better service to its business customer segment. Customers could print check-in and boarding passes at their convenience within the confines of the hotel. Hotels could also provide luggage check-in services to some of their high-value customers.

4. *Growth.* Service firms need to grow to stay competitive in the marketplace. Growth could come through service innovation by tapping into new markets/customer segments. Partnerships, if used properly, help a firm grow. For example, Google, along with 33 mobile-headset makers, cellular carriers, and other partners, has started developing a new platform called Android. (Its phone is called the Gphone.) This new platform, likely to be provided free of charge, is projected to launch during the second half of 2008. This software paves the way for cheaper advanced mobile devices with capabilities of a personal computer. With Android, software makers can write applications that run on any user's phone regardless of the provider. Carriers traditionally have decided what applications to include within their own cellphones, setting rules and fees for software developers. With a transition to Android, T-Mobile USA wants to develop social networking applications to its devices as well. Applications would include the user's location, communication history, contact list, and "presence," a signal of whether someone's phone is on or off.

5. *Reduce time to market for new services.* For example, a service firm could outsource noncore or backroom processes and focus exclusively on core activities to reduce time to market for new services.

Recently, organizations have expressed discomfort with the strategy of single outsourcing to one partner. A long-term collaboration with one partner has its inherent risks. Many firms are exploring a strategy of multisourcing—that is, working with multiple sourcing partners. This way, firms do not get locked in with one particular service chain partner. Firms are still grappling with the challenges of managing multisource projects.

Collaboration health is impacted by various factors, such as the culture of a service firm, strategic considerations and alignment, and trust between partners. Establishing trust is one of the key considerations to a long-term partnership. A partner could become the competition. For example, Solectron or Celestica or Foxconn could become a competition to a large telecommunication provider. Manufacturers such as IBM, Cisco, Nortel, Palm, and Compaq (HP) have outsourced manufacturing to Solectron and Celestica. Trust considerations vary across the cultural landscape. For example, in some business cultures, trust considerations will override financial and economic and strategic considerations. Many Eastern business cultures, such as Chinese and Japanese cultures, place higher emphasis on trust factors. Establishing, sustaining, and measuring trust is a critical consideration for such a partnership.

A typical partnership relationship should focus on the following stakeholders:

- **Internal**
  - Management: Management needs to consider the definition of success, corporate objectives of the partnership, public perception of the partnership, and effect on brand value.
  - Employees: What is in it for us? How can we contribute? How can we learn and develop knowledge to do the job better the next time around? Employee buy-in is critical to the success of the process. Employees should participate during the design and development of the measurement system.

- **External**
  - Competition: What is the impact on market position and business proposition?
  - Partners: What is the best way to extract value from the relationship?

- Competition of partners: How can we work with each other if an opportunity arises?
- Customers: Customer experiences are directly impacted by collaboration. Customer participation creates an added challenge—a challenge that did not exist in a manufacturing-dominated world.

Measures of Collaboration

Measures for collaboration will depend on the long-term goals of the partnership. If the strategic goal is to reduce cost and improve productivity, the metrics will focus on the process side. If the strategic goal is to improve market position, the measures will focus on the related metrics. Longer-term partnerships will focus on trust development, communication, and learning aspects. Ideally, we should measure the *overall health, reach,* and *relevance* of the collaboration.

All measurements related to partnership could be divided into the following categories:

- **Outcome measures such as financial measures, return on investment, productivity, and effectiveness**—These measures are lagging and often functional indicators of the partnership. The approach is based on the transactional view of the partnership. Cross-functional and enterprisewide measures that truly represent collaboration must be included here.
- **Partners' attributes such as cultural differences**—Many of these measures are qualitative in nature and represent the difference between collaborating partners.
- **Relational attributes such as trust, cooperation, and values alignment**—These enterprisewide measures are based on a relational view of the partnership. These measures represent the strength of the relationship or health of the collaboration.
- **Relevance measure**—The relevance of the collaboration is often overlooked, and the focus of measurement tends to shift to other measures. However, the relevance and reach of collaboration are extremely important.

Literature on partnership focuses mostly on the benefits of the partnership and not much on the attributes of a successful partnership. As a result, the measures of partnerships are vague and have not been developed. Common metrics used to measure the partnership in a product-centric environment are cost, speed of delivery, and conformance or quality. A broader index called the Collaboration Index has been suggested to measure the strength of a partnership. The index consists of three different elements: information sharing and knowledge management, decision-making alignment, and incentive alignment. Information sharing represents the degree of collaboration. The extent of collaboration could also include measuring the extent of mutual cooperation, which leads to improved quality and mutual assistance in problem solving, which then leads to improved quality.

One obvious measurement, partner satisfaction, was the subject of a recent e-partnership study. The study found that more than 70 percent of firms surveyed did not measure partnership satisfaction! However, a majority of these firms also indicated the need to measure and track partnership satisfaction as an indicator. The study identified the importance of partnership management as an area of performance management. Very little about what drives partner satisfaction has been discussed so far. Factors such as the cooperative nature of the relationship, the understanding of mutual needs, managers' satisfaction, and open communication contribute to partner satisfaction. Partners and suppliers are considered passive players, and partners take the relationship as a given.

Another measure of the partnership relationship is trust between partners. The trust between partners is an important indicator of the strength of the partnership. Trust affects the performance outcome of a relationship. Performance outcomes could be in the form of time to completion, the financial outcome, or satisfaction. However, no common understanding of the way trust should be measured exists. Measurement of trust should consider the following dimensions:

- **Trust at multiple levels**—Trust should be considered at the various levels of organization and across cultural/geographical contexts. Trust between partners evolves as the relationship evolves.

- **Trust evolving with time**—The initial stage of trust could be based on purely transactional needs, followed by mutual learning and understanding. The final stage of trust evolution involves total internalization of each other's needs.

Similar to the evaluation of a supply chain, a service chain could be evaluated by measuring the surplus of the chain. Considering an integrated service chain with each step owned by one firm, one could calculate the total cost incurred. The surplus could be determined by calculating the difference between total revenue and total cost.

Supply chain performance is often measured using a model called the Supply Chain Operations Reference, or SCOR, approach. The model provides a strong process and technological approach but lacks the social and experience dimensions required for services. The SCOR approach identifies the Source, Make, Deliver, and Return processes as key processes. This model considers the flow of physical inventory (or product), information, and money. Active involvement of customers is not implicitly included in the model, however. The model also fails to include the demand side of the chain. Since the model is heavily process-driven, the direct application of the model to the service chain is not recommended. As mentioned previously, services need to consider the customers' viewpoint (driven by experience) as opposed to a process viewpoint (driven by the provider).

Collaboration and the Service Scorecard

Partnership directly affects customer retention as documented in the literature. Partners and service chain partners are often in touch with customers. As the service profit chain hypothesizes, employees' satisfaction drives the customer satisfaction. Similarly, employee satisfaction at the partner firms affects the customer satisfaction. Often, the partner firm is considered as an extension of the firm for customers. Customers do not see any difference between the partner firm and the firm itself.

The Service Scorecard places an unambiguous and clearly identifiable importance on the collaboration measure. A strategic partnership and collaboration could lead to faster new service introductions, added flexibility, and strengthened financial stability. In the Service Scorecard, the focus is on the reliability of the partner and the trust between partners. Reliability represents the tactical and execution orientation of the relationship. A service firm will often depend on its partner to provide a certain level of service quality. A reliable and dependable partner must be found for such collaboration. Trust represents the long-term perspective of the relationship.

A service delivery chain model is shown in Figure 8.2. The figure represents the operational view of a service chain showing service capacity, service inventory, service channels, and information. The design of these drivers is based on the demand facing a service chain.

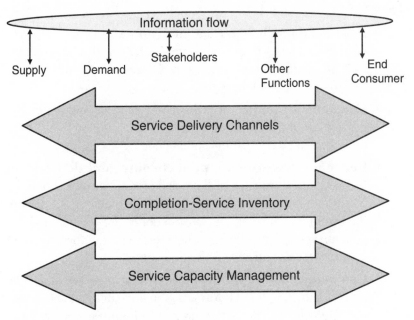

Figure 8.2 Pyramid of partnerships

Depending on the business drivers, the collaboration measurements fall into one of the following four categories:

1. *Customer-related metrics*—Customer retention, errors in dealing with customers, and add-on revenue per customer are included in this category.

2. *Efficiency metrics*—Measures representing volume and productivity fall into this category.

3. *Service Innovation metrics*—Measures bringing new ideas and new services to the market should be included in this category.

4. *Flexibility metrics*—Flexibility in terms of provided extra capacity and added customization fall into this category.

The degree of trust will directly dictate the degree and reach of collaboration. As the relationship between business partners improves, mutual learning is followed by bonding, which leads to a greater degree of trust. Various components of trust include the following:

- **Business domain expertise and reputation**—Available resources and skills to do the desired job. The firm should also have an established and proven track record that could be verified by an independent party.

- **Commonality and compatibility**—Reality should match the perception and shared vision to achieve common goals. Cultures should be compatible and aligned.

- **Reliability (consistency, predictability, and dependability)**—The performance of the collaborating partner should be consistent and predictable. Many of these elements are part of the customer expectations. Customers desire reliable and dependable service experience. Therefore, a partner firm needs to apply protocols and standards consistently.

- **Communication and information sharing**—Providing the correct and completed information in a meaningful and timely way. Utilizing collaborative tools and techniques enhances both internal and external collaboration. Many of these virtual online tools and techniques allow immediate sharing of information, podcasting, video chats, virtual presentations, and the formation of virtual communities. The information and knowledge management fields at the enterprise levels are complicated enough. When two service firms collaborate, new approaches to information sharing and knowledge management must be considered. The earlier approach to knowledge management was to capture all the knowledge at a depository and let others tap into this information depository. The new approach considers making connections based on skills and interests, or building virtual communities and letting individuals decide what information they want to share and reveal.

* **Responsiveness**—The capacity and willingness to cater to different needs as circumstances change.

As mentioned previously, trust is an important element of collaboration. However, monitoring and control mechanisms to balance the trust element must exist. The balance between trust and control creates an added level of confidence in the partnership.

Steps to a Successful Partnership

A successful partnership should provide measurable results to both parties. Here are some general actions you can take to achieve a successful partnership:

* Perform a strength, weakness, and gap analysis and prepare a long-term strategic plan. A first step is to identify the advantages of a partnership and whether a partnership is necessary to achieve required business objectives. Incorporate the strategic plan and likely changes in customer behavior into the plan.
* Identify partners' needs and goals. A firm needs to understand the partners' needs, culture, and goals to identify commonality of goals.
* Drill down the core objective (cost saving, improved market position, add-on revenue, added flexibility and an advantage due to improved new service offerings, shorter time to market). The drill down should provide a detailed analysis of the desired objective, set goals and standards, and identify responsibilities and identity change mechanisms. This exercise is similar to a typical project management process that identifies inherent risks and mitigating mechanisms.
* Rank-order opportunities and identify the alignment. Consider the operational aspects of the collaboration.
* Perform due diligence about the partner; that is, financial health, reputation, capabilities, resources, commitment, and value alignment.

- Jointly identify performance management indicators. Identify key risks and prepare mitigation strategies.
- Continuously monitor, improve, and manage the system. Communication is key to a successful win-win partnership. Key performance measures need to be monitored during the process.

Relationships with partners also experience evolution and maturity. For example, service firms are more concerned about cost and quality during the initial one to three years of the outsourcing relationship. As the relationship matures, firms expect flexibility, speed, and innovation in addition to productivity improvement. Partners need to continuously keep track of changing needs. In the long run, service firms expect a partner to contribute toward the profitable growth of the firm.

Cases

This section provides three specific cases where collaboration is used as a driver to achieve superior corporate performance.

A Call Center

An outsourced call center is a typical example of a cost-driven partnership agreement. Performance measures include the revenue/cost/total cost per call, the customer retention rate, the percent of downtime, the percent of overflow calls, and the accuracy of calls or errors. Total cost per call is usually calculated by taking the total cost for a particular period and dividing by the total number of calls received. A partner can enhance revenue by suggesting add-on services and by understanding customer needs. Call centers often get calls from customers to cancel or to terminate services. Depending on the skills and competence of the staff, the call center should be able to persuade some of these customers to continue with the service. A high-quality supplier will not only help enhance the revenue per call but also help improve the customer retention rate. The accuracy of orders and calls could be measured by callbacks or by measuring the accuracy of the order taken.

Starbucks

Starbucks has expanded internationally using a partnering model. Starbucks follows a rigorous partner selection process. Starbucks used alliance partners in the local market. The selection process includes an initial phase of checking the financial health and resources available with the firm. Cultural fit and alignment and value alignment are over-riding factors in the selection process. The process takes between 18 to 24 months. The company does not consider itself to be process-driven. Some of the metrics used to select partners are consistencies and alignment of values and beliefs and cultural fit.

Knowledge Process Outsourcing

The recent trend of service firms outsourcing business processes is a common example of a partnering relationship. Most metrics measuring the performance of an outsourcing partnership fall into the following four categories: process outcome, customer outcome, financial outcome, and quality outcome. Process measurement involves identifying key indicators and is an objective measure of productivity and efficiency. Customer output measures, or moment-of-truth measures for services, identify customer interaction measures. Examples of outcome metrics are the percent of customers retained, the add-on revenue per customer, and the profit per customer. Financial measures could be related to the collection rate or any related financial impact measurement. Quality measurement focuses on the accuracy of the transaction and experience. As services focus more on the experience and solution-centric view of the system, quality outcome measures gain an added importance. Service firms strive to transform a transaction with customers into an experience so that customer will keep coming back.

Drivers of outsourcing have also evolved. Firms are not outsourcing for simple cost-reduction reasons. The type of work being outsourced has also moved up the value chain. Knowledge Process Outsourcing, KPO, is expected to be the next wave of outsourcing. KPO requires advanced analytical, technical, and knowledge skills. A GlobalSourcingNow report states that the Global KPO industry is expected to reach USD 17 billion by the year 2010.

KPO is not simply an extension of business process outsourcing. KPO touches the global delivery service chain and is a part of the core processes of a service firm. Initially, the activities were mostly transaction-oriented. These days, it is common to outsource high-value-added activities such as research and development, market research, intellectual property research, equity research, financial modeling and valuation, media and animation, distance education, human resource services, financial services, medical transcription in healthcare, and legal services. For example, legal firms such as Jones Day and Kirkland & Ellis are outsourcing basic legal tasks. Kirkland & Ellis, a Chicago-based legal firm, used offshoring on clients' requests. Typical outsourced services are legal research/analysis, legal opinion, and contract drafting services.

As mentioned previously, appropriate monitoring and control mechanisms using a proper measurement system are needed. The switching cost to change a collaborating partner is huge for a particular service firm. The costs in terms of customer loss could easily add up due to missteps in the selection process.

Take Away

- Collaboration is an increasingly important measure of the Service Scorecard, primarily because many service firms must outsource important tasks so as to focus on their core competency or objective.

- Strategically forming partnerships can help the service firm grow, reduce time to market for new services, increase responsiveness, and improve market position.

- In the Service Scorecard, the focus is on the reliability of the partner and the trust between partners.

- A service firm will often depend on its partner to provide a certain level of service quality. A reliable and dependable partner must be found for such collaboration.

9

Innovation and Execution

In today's competitive global marketplace, employee engagement enables a service firm to tap its own resources for developing innovative services and solutions as well as sustaining business financial performance. The engagement, defined as the attitude of employees toward issues such as "Great Place to Work" or "Employer of Choice" or similar indices, is driven by socioeconomic factors, business practices in a particular geographical context, the culture of the firm, the position of an employee within a firm's decision-making hierarchy, and the size of the firm. Generally speaking, a large service firm will find it more challenging to engage all of its employees.

Based on the literature available, no common definition of employee engagement was found. The following specific factors or drivers of employee engagement are discussed in the literature: trust and integrity, nature of the job, relationship between individual performance and firm performance, professional/employee development, pride about the firm, coworkers and team members, and relationship with the manager. In a 2006 study by the Conference Board on Employee Engagement, the Board studied 24 firms, reviewed current literature, and discussed its implications. The Service Scorecard makes a distinction between *employee-led innovation* and *service innovation*. Service innovation is an all-encompassing innovation that includes employee-led innovation. The focus of the employee innovation element is limited to innovation led by the employee engagement. Service innovation, led by employees, customers, partners, and other stakeholders, is discussed in Chapter 10, "Retention and Growth," which describes the Growth element of the Service Scorecard.

Employee Engagement and Innovation

Employee engagement directly affects the financial performance of a service firm. Studies by Mark Huselid, Tower Perrin group, and Hewitt Associated have reaches similar conclusions. Traditionally, an employee engagement strategy is not considered a differentiating strategy. However, for a service firm in a competitive situation and with a high turnover, business requires senior managers to create and sustain a differentiated employee engagement strategy. Employee engagement and involvement directly affect employee turnover, employee satisfaction, and innovation at a service firm. Turnover at a firm possessing highly engaged employees is significantly lower compared to firms with disengaged employees.

The challenges of employee engagement could be discussed at three difference levels: strategic, tactical, and operational. The strategic level defines the perspective shared by the top management and the general direction of differentiation of the employee engagement strategy. The role of the workforce in executing the corporate strategy is part of this level. The tactical level includes various policies, processes, and metrics to take the employee engagement strategy to the next level. Workforce planning, development of the required culture by hiring the right type of employees, the metrics used to measure the effectiveness of workforce management, and the mix of full-time and part-time employees are part of the tactical level. The operational level includes day-to-day information exchange, knowledge management, and communication methods. A firm needs to work on all three levels of challenges to improve employee engagement effectiveness. The effectiveness of employee engagement goes beyond the human resources function and beyond a few simple measurements. This effectiveness leads to innovation and growth of a service firm. Eventually, a combination of strategic- and operational-level practices creates a differentiating business strategy.

Employees at service firms deal directly with the customers and need to be engaged positively. Customers usually have longer contacts with employees at service firms. Therefore, employee engagement is even more important in the service context, because it influences customer retention and behaviors. Employee engagement drives human capital when employees are considered as assets. Generally, employee engagement drives the following:

- **Relationships with customers**—Employees interface with customers during the service design and delivery process. The quality of the relationship depends on employee traits and their skill set. Employee traits such as reliability, empathy, energy, and general attitude contribute to the quality of this relationship, which, in turn, contributes to the financial performance of a service firm.

- **Intellectual capital and innovation**—The creativity of employees, and their risk-taking attitudes under the right circumstances, drives innovation. Intellectual capital at service firms is generally not in the form of patents or trademarks. The knowledge and information reside with the employees. A service firm should convert data and the available knowledge of employees into actionable information. The actionable information, combined with management insights, will lead to effective business intelligence. Business intelligence eventually helps business decisions, thus creating firm value. A distinction is made here between human asset and intellectual capital. Human asset, or human capital, is defined as capital that goes home with employees every day when the employee leaves the workplace. Intellectual capital is part of the intangible or tangible capital left behind after an employee has left the firm.

- **Firm culture and processes**—A firm culture includes a set of beliefs, values, and processes. A firm culture might encourage risk-taking behaviors and an entrepreneurship culture. A February 2007 working paper authored by Gerard Tellis, Jaideep Prabhu, and Rajesh Chandy identified the importance of firm culture. The working paper published by Marshall School of Business, *Innovation in Firms Across Nations: New Metrics and Drivers for Radical Innovation*, is based on the information from 759 public companies representing a broad economic spectrum. Specific cultural elements are future market orientation, tolerance for risk, and willingness to cannibalize.

For service firms, employee engagement has been known to affect customer retention and service innovation. The Service Profit Chain model, a framework discussed previously in the book, describes such a relationship, specifically the following points:

- Employee selection and internal quality drive employee satisfaction.
- Employee satisfaction drives productivity and value.
- Productivity and value affect customer satisfaction.
- Customer satisfaction drives customer loyalty.
- Customer loyalty drives a service firm's profitability and growth.

Hence, employee satisfaction and workforce management become critical at a service firm according to this framework.

Employee-Driven Innovation

In this section, we describe a few methodologies to calculate the value of human asset. These methodologies fall into three broad categories: the Accenture Human Capital Development Framework, the Human Economic Value Added (HEVA) approach, and the Return on Investment (ROI) approach.

Accenture Human Capital Development Framework

A conceptual model is shown in Figure 9.1. This framework has four tiers and could be used as a diagnostic assessment tool, as a recurring measurement activity, and as part of organization-wide transformation. Similarly, Saratoga Institute breaks down the human capital financial index into three categories: Revenue, Cost, and Profit. Hence, the Human Capital Revenue Index, the Human Capital Cost Index, and the Human Capital Profit Index are three major indicators to focus on while managing human assets.

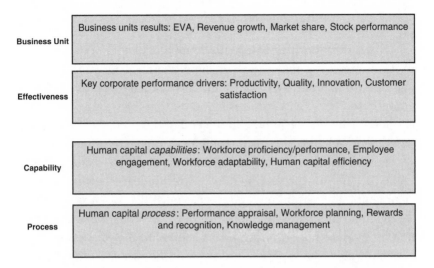

Figure 9.1 The Accenture Human Capital Development Framework

Human Economic Value Added Model

Stern Stewart popularized the Economic Value Added concept. The concept could be modified and applied to human capital asset management. The idea is to identify the true performance of managers and to measure the extent of value created above and beyond usual expenses and cost of capital. In other words, are we receiving returns that are more than the returns received simply by investing in the financial aspect? Human Economic Value Added, or HEVA, is defined as net operating profit after tax minus the cost of capital.

The objective of HEVA is to measure the true economic value added by the actions of employees and management. A company generating typical financial returns will have a HEVA of zero. HEVA measures the value above and beyond these typical financial returns. The HEVA number shows the true value generated after all expenses, taxes, and the cost of capital have been subtracted. HEVA can be converted into a standard human capital number by dividing HEVA by the number of full-time equivalents. Therefore,

HEVA = (net operating profit after tax × cost of capital) / FTEs

Return on Investment Model

The Return on Investment (ROI) methodology forces managers to justify various employee engagement decisions. Organizations using the ROI methodology move from providing human resource programs based on activity to focusing on bottom-line results. This shift is evident from the beginning to the end of the process. The activity-based approach describes many traditional human resource functions in years past. The results-based approach is needed to ensure that programs begin with the end in mind—with a clear, specific business alignment. The attention and focus must be on accountability throughout the process, as all stakeholders are brought into the equation. A measurement of success must exist, and that success must be communicated to a variety of groups with the results summarized in an overall scorecard. Some progressive HR departments recognize the need for ROI and are persistent in making progress on this issue.

In a specific situation, it becomes a reasonable task to assign monetary values to these measures. The benefits are then compared to the monetary value of a particular program to develop the ROI. Firms use ROI methodology to keep track of investments in training, development, and other workforce initiatives. Two metrics are often used to measure the ROI: benefit/cost ratio and ROI. The benefit/cost ratio (BCR) is the monetary benefits of the HR program or intervention divided by the costs. In formula form, it is as follows:

**BCR = HR program monetary benefits /
HR program costs**

The ROI uses the *net* benefits divided by costs. The net benefits are the program benefits minus the costs. The ROI in percentage form is as follows:

**ROI (%) = net HR program benefits * 100 /
HR program costs**

An example is presented to illustrate the difference between these two metrics. Consider an absenteeism reduction program producing savings of $200,000 with a cost of $100,000. Therefore, the benefit/cost ratio is as follows:

BCR = $200,000 / $100,000 = $2.0

As this calculation shows, for every $1 invested, $2.0 in monetary benefits is returned. In this example, net benefits are $200,000 × $100,000 = $100,000. Thus, the ROI would be as follows:

ROI = 100,000 * 100/100,000 = 100%

This means that for every $1 invested in the program, there is a return of $1.00 in net benefits, after the $1 is recovered. The benefits are usually expressed as annual benefits for short-term programs, representing the amount saved or gained for a complete year after the program has been implemented. Although the benefits may continue after the first year, the impact usually diminishes and is omitted from calculations in short-term situations. For long-term projects, the benefits are spread over several years. The timing of the benefits stream should be determined before the impact study begins, as part of the planning process.

In the 2006 report "Key Trends in Human Capital—A Global Perspective," 2006, Saratoga Institute (now part of PricewaterhouseCoopers) uses similar metrics to measure the effectiveness of human capital. The metric is a comparative metric of value added by full-time employees:

value added = (revenue × nonwage cost) / (number of FTEs * average remuneration)

Eventually, customer relationships, intellectual capital, and firm culture affect both the top-line and bottom-line growth of a service firm. The previously mentioned methods and models quantify human capital and return values at a service firm.

Innovation Measures

The first step to determine the measures needed is to examine those currently in use. The following list represents measures cited in more than a dozen current studies on human capital measurement. (This list is adapted from *Investing in Your Company's Human Capital: Strategies to Avoid Spending Too Little—or Too Much*, by J. Phillips, AMACON, 2005.) Some of the measures presented in this list evolved from the beginnings of "personnel administration" to what is today known as human resources or human capital management.

These are simple measures that were tracked during the field's infancy, such as absenteeism and turnover, and are still tracked today. Although these measures have existed for some time, they are still important for understanding the nature, scope, and progress of human capital. The measures represent a balance of the old manufacturing-heavy economy and the new knowledge-based organizations.

- **Recruitment**—Recruitment sourcing and effectiveness, recruiting efficiency, length taken to recruit an employee
- **Employee Profile/Capability**—Experience, knowledge, competencies, educational level, demographics, diversity
- **Innovation and Creativity**—Number of suggestions per employee, new services per employee, revenue from new services
- **Human Capital Investment**—Total human capital investment, hours of training per employee, training cost
- **Productivity/Attitude**—Unit/gross productivity, satisfaction, engagement
- **Employee Relations/Workforce Stability**—Absenteeism, work/life balance, turnover, length of employment, employee benefit, compensation

Several measures are industry-specific. For example, safety and health measurements may be an important issue where employees are routinely at risk for an accident, injuries, and illnesses. The previous list provides various human capital drivers under various categories. Service and white-collar businesses, such as financial services and software companies, would not necessarily list these measures as a priority. They include other measures that are critical to developing and emerging industries, such as innovation, leadership, and competencies.

At a typical service firm, the cost of human capital is usually more than 50 percent of revenue and can be even higher for a professional service firm. The major organizational asset includes employee skill, knowledge, and competency. These assets that drive innovation and growth can also move to another firm and are not easy to retain. In spite of the importance of this element, very few firms report measurements of human asset in corporate financial reports. Some firms report measures such as revenue per employee. However, this measure is a simplistic and lagging measure. Some firms might consider not disclosing these measures publicly to have a competitive advantage. Ideally, a firm's reporting should focus on the following elements, as proposed by R. Kasselman in a thesis titled *Human Capital Framework for Inclusion in Company Annual Reports* (University of Pretoria, 2006):

- Increasing operating margin: Reduce cost of employee recruiting, administration cost, improve execution
- Increasing revenue: Improve impact on customers, improve employee performance
- Improving asset effectiveness

We include employee ideas, employee involvement/engagement, and employee satisfaction as measures of employee innovation. The employee ideas measure provides a leading indication about the pipeline of innovation at a particular service firm. Number of ideas implemented is another measure that could be considered. It is about new ideas submitted per employee per year. Employee satisfaction is another leading indicator. Lower satisfaction will likely lead to higher employee turnover.

Along with co-author Jerry Porras in the book *Built to Last* (1994), James C. Collins explored the deep reasons behind long-term corporate success stories in the United States. The authors asked the fundamental question "What makes the truly exceptional companies different from other companies?" Throughout their research, the importance of people was evident in every aspect. These companies practice what they preach when it comes to the role of employees in the organization. Table 9.1 represents most of the core ideologies of these visionary companies. The researchers did not merely paraphrase the company's most recent missions, visions, and values, but they tried to find out from various sources the historical consistency of their ideologies through multiple generations of key executives. These values, missions, and philosophies highlight the importance of people and their contributions as the basis for companies that are built to last.

A diagnostic tool to measure the gaps and a workforce scorecard are available in the book *The Workforce Scorecard: Managing Human Capital to Execute Strategy* (Huselid, Becker, and Beatty, 2005).

TABLE 9.1 Ideologies of Visionary Companies (Collins & Porras, 1994)

Company	Ideology
American Express	Heroic customer service
	Worldwide reliability of services
	Encouragement of individual initiative
Citicorp	Autonomy and entrepreneurship (via decentralization)
	Aggressiveness and self-confidence
IBM	Give full consideration to the individual employee
	Spend a lot of time making customers happy
	Seek superiority in all we undertake
Marriott	Pay attention to details
	Friendly service and excellent value
	People are #1–treat them well, expect a lot, and the rest will follow
	Work hard, yet keep it fun
	Continual self-improvement
Nordstrom	Empowered employees, recognize outstanding employees
	Service to the customer above all else
	Continuous improvement, never being satisfied
	Excellence in reputation, being part of something special
Walt Disney	Strong tradition of service innovation
	No cynicism allowed
	Fanatical attention to consistency and detail

IBM

IBM has transformed itself from a product-focused firm to a solution/service-based firm. IBM utilizes the adaptive workforce principle to match worldwide demands. Information is collected in a dynamic fashion about the capability available at IBM and the needs of various projects. IBM is a global firm that needs to assemble a project team within a very short period. The team often requires skills not available locally. The principles are similar to the supply chain issue faced by a product firm. Such a system could be called an "on-demand workforce."

Verizon

Based on publicly available literature, Verizon implemented the HR Scorecard. Communicating the scorecard to employees was a major part of the process. Executives held roadshows, implemented various tools and techniques to communicate the scorecard's intent and its relationship to business results, and considered feedback received from the employees.

Execution

Operational execution enhances process performance in terms of value and responsiveness. Operational excellence is about improving productivity and efficiency and, hence, reducing the cost of doing business by providing incremental improvement to the processes. The improvement is driven by customer requirements and cost drivers. Operational excellence also provides a standard methodology and a common corporatewide language. The Execution element of the Service Scorecard has two dimensions: executing the operations strategy or what is required, and improving the responsiveness of execution. The use of various operational improvement methodologies is relatively new in the service sector. The lack of use of these methodologies could be attributed to the mindset of managers and a mentality that services are intangible. (Thus, no standard methodology should be applied.) Accuracy and responsiveness are two measures that are used for the baseline SPIn model.

Importance of Execution has been identified by Larry Bossidy and Ram Charan in their book *Execution: The Discipline of Getting Things Done*. Leaders need to be engaged at all times and focus on people, strategy, and operations. Right people with right strategy using the operational principle will bring sustainable growth to a firm. Following the principle of Execution is paramount because the majority of effort is spent in executing a strategic change. Execution also differentiates high performers from others. Approximately 90 percent of the necessary effort is spent in executing a change strategy. Importance of Execution should be looked at in the context of management style. Let us consider total time as consisting of two elements—time to arrive at a decision and time to execute a decision. The first part will be shorter if the decision-making process is authoritative and top-down. On the other hand, the time to execute this type of decision will be longer. A consensus-based and participative decision-making process will take longer to arrive at a decision. However, the time to execute such a change decision will be quicker because the process was participative.

Some service firms have applied these methodologies and reaped the benefits. Some service firms have adopted methodologies such as Six Sigma, ISO 9000, or the process audit. An international standard such as ISO 9000 emphasizes internal quality and focuses on process management. The year 2000 version of ISO 9001 includes the customer view explicitly and, therefore, is gaining more traction, even within the service sector. The improved version suggests the importance of monitoring customer satisfaction to identify the outcome of performance improvement after ISO processes are implemented.

Service firms can learn much from the use of ISO 9000-type standards adopted by manufacturing firms. One way to understand the use of such a standard is by categorizing all services into either front-room-heavy or back-room-heavy systems. *Front room* refers to customer contact and customer view, and *back room* refers to activities that are out of view of the customers. Back-room-heavy services are sometimes referred to as the "production-line approach of services," the "service factory approach," or "service industrialization." Front-room and back-room terminology is based on the concept of service blueprinting.

Although services signify intangible offerings, the consumers demand reliability. Reliability builds trust contributing to customer loyalty. Reliability depends on reduction of variability. Service firms face additional challenges in variability management. Managers at manufacturing firms worry about variations during the production process and all variations occurring internally.

Some of the challenges related to operational excellence for managers are measurement of productivity and reduction of complexity. As discussed earlier in the book, *measuring* productivity at service firms is a challenging task. Compared to a manufacturing assembly-line environment, these processes are slower. Service processes are often labor-intensive and time-consuming. In addition, most of these processes have a wait time. For example, the theoretical time taken to process a mortgage loan application is less than 24 hours, considering the needed theoretical time for steps such as a credit check, employment verification, and collateral verification and underwriting. However, the real time could be in days or weeks.

In the language of lean principles, service systems have huge waste. Waste can be in terms of wait times, servers sitting idle, and redundant process steps. On the other hand, if we compare productivity gains in the manufacturing and service sectors, the service sector lags behind the manufacturing sector in productivity gains. Reasons could be attributed to a lack of understanding about service processes, variety and customization in service systems, and involvement of the customer in service design and production.

Implementing Execution Measures

Service industrialization has its own limitation and fails to consider customer intimacy aspects. The service industrialization concept was discussed in the early 1970s, but services have failed to gain an advantage with regard to this concept. One reason could be that service industrialization focuses exclusively on processes and activities and fails to consider "experience and customer intimacy" aspects. Standard services with little variety will be more amenable to such a process-focused concept. We argue for an "industrialized intimacy" concept that considers customers as an integral part of the system. The extent of self-services is a managerial driver to reduce cost and improve productivity. However, the right type of activities should be available for self-service. All self-service should lead to at least one of the following outcomes: reduced cost, increased customer satisfaction, increased customization, reduced service time, and improved quality.

Information technology firms use maturity models as indicators of business process excellence. Maturity models, which are evolutionary in nature, provide guidelines for IT service organizations. The disciplined approach of maturity models results in the implementation of various process approaches companywide.

Service Blueprinting

A service blueprint is based on the concept of customer visibility and the view of the customer. Service blueprinting redraws a process map in terms of what is visible and what is not visible to customers. Back-room operations are not visible to customers and are usually easier to standardize. Service blueprinting still has standard terminology and symbols. Some firms draw a separate blueprint for a service recovery system. We usually require a separate service blueprint for a particular segment of customers. A cross-functional team is desirable when drawing a service blueprint to represent a balanced front- and back-room perspective. A service blueprint can be used to identify opportunities for productivity/efficiency improvement.

Service Recovery

Service recovery, a process of managing service defects, is an important aspect of execution. Services could have defects due to various reasons: wrong customer segment, instructions now followed by front-line employees, the intent being lost in the design translation process, and customers not being ready for services. Some measures that could be used to measure the effectiveness of a service recovery process are number of complaints, percent of customer complaining, easiness of complaint process, and time taken to resolve a typical complaint.

Little's Law

Traditionally, the efficiency and effectiveness of a service system can be measured by process time, wait time, and work-in-process inventory. Little's Law relates flow-through time to work-in-progress inventory and flow rate or throughput. Flow time is the ratio of inventory and flow rate. Flow rate should be equal to demand in an ideal pull-based demand scenario. Inventory and flow time are proportional to each other, indicating that reducing inventory will reduce the flow rate. Inventory in this case can include customers who are waiting in line or are being served. This simple relationship helps improve the system by focusing on efficiency metrics such as total time (including wait time).

Six Sigma for Services

Applying Six Sigma methodology only for transaction-type services represents traditional thinking. Six Sigma thinking can be applied at the process level (process Sigma level), at the corporate level (Corporate Sigma level), and at the functional level (Six Sigma pricing). Successful service firms have reduced service complexity by breaking down the experience into discrete steps and by providing the required customer intimacy. For example, Hard Rock Café has very clear metrics from the beginning of the experience of seating at the table to providing dessert and the bill. The key is to understand the customer's needs, provide solutions to the needs, and measure performance by applying process-based thinking.

At the end of this chapter, we provide templates to implement the same steps. Five steps of the Six Sigma for Services methodology are presented in these templates: Define, Measure, Analyze, Innovate, and Embed. The step of Improve has been replaced with the Innovation step, and the final step of Embed replaces the traditional Control step.

Outsourcing as a Business Strategy

Outsourcing is widely used by service firms to stay competitive in the marketplace. A recent Gartner report projects the Business Processing Outsourcing (BPO) market to grow to $173 billion in 2007 with an annual compound growth rate of 9.5 percent. The first wave of outsourcing included only discrete steps, followed by the outsourcing of the whole process. A majority of outsourcing has occurred for the back-room processes. Business Process Outsourcing is witnessing a paradigm shift. Earlier, BPO was meant for cost reduction in transaction-intensive back-office processes. Business Process Outsourcing is now considered as a management decision-making tool to achieve tactical and strategic advantage by contributing speedy time-to-market turnaround, a cost advantage, and a focus on core competencies. The strategy has one or more of the following objectives: cost reduction, speedy time to market, operational flexibility, reduction in the working capital requirement, increased transparency, reduction of operational risk, and increased access to new technology and tools.

Execution in Service Scorecard

Service Scorecard considers *accuracy* and *responsiveness* as two measures of execution. Accuracy and reliability are critical to the service delivery process considering that the system often includes customers as coproducers. Consider a healthcare setting and the flow of patient information from one shift to the next shift. The information should be accurate, timely, and reliable. Similarly, a financial institution needs to provide accurate information about transactions.

Because customers are coproducers in most service production systems, additional variations are introduced due to the fact that customers are now involved in the process. In short, customer-introduced variability is added variability that needs to be managed by managers at service firms. Any standardization effort needs to take this difference into account. Firms also seek to have systems and methodology in place, enabling managers to execute the processes correctly. Service recovery instances or service defects also become visible when some of these methods are used. In short, accuracy becomes paramount to a successful customer experience.

A service firm should also provide *responsiveness*. The degree of responsiveness refers to meeting the customer demands in terms of variety of services, on-demand availability (24/7 availability, online availability), degree of customization, and a prompt service recovery. A service provided needs to manage all possible customer contact methods or service delivery channels to minimize cost and improve productivity. Priceline.com, eBay, Web check-in for airlines, online tracking of a package by FedEx, self-service check-in counters at airports, and self-service counters at grocery stores are successful examples. Consider a service delivery system facing demand uncertainty from the customer side. An emergency room at a hospital is a prime example of such a system. The emergency room faces an uncertain demand in terms of how many patients will show up, when they will show up, and what type of response they might require. An emergency room still has to be responsive to this demand situation by having additional staff at hand, service capacity, various delivery methods to deal with patient flows, and a way to handle information needs.

Typical hospital executives want to have high patient satisfaction, shorter patient stays at the facility, higher throughput of patients, and higher revenue/profits. A recent report discusses the installation of self-service do-it kiosks at the Emergency Room at Parkland Memorial Hospital, Dallas, Texas. The ER facility, handling about 300 patients a day, has reduced its wait time after installing the system. Patients take about eight minutes to enter the information. Seriously ill or wounded patients still go through the line faster. After the information is entered, the information pops up at the nurse's touchscreen. Patients with chest pains, stroke symptoms, or other serious and worrisome complaints get priority. The system is an example of using industrialized customer intimacy. The Emergency Room represents a service system with very high variability. ER providers have to embrace this variability or complexity and try to institute processes that can streamline the healthcare process and still maintain the responsiveness.

Ritz-Carlton Hotel

The Ritz-Carlton Hotel is extensively discussed in the literature. The Ritz-Carlton uses an information system that takes customer preferences into account and helps customize services while at the same time reducing cost. The system preferences reduce the time taken to make the reservation the next time around, and customers feel that services are customized to their needs.

Call Center

Similarly, the call center of a service should strive to provide solutions at the first point of contact. A recent article in *Call Center Magazine* describes customer-centric metrics at a typical call center. The top seven metrics were identified. These metrics are call resolution, service level/response time, adherence to the schedule, forecasting accuracy, self-service accessibility, quality of contact, and customer satisfaction. Call resolution, no doubt, is one of the key metrics. The usual definition of First Call Resolution (FCR) is whether a follow-up call was made or whether the call was transferred. Some call centers use customer feedback to measure FCR value. These values usually are in the range of 67 percent for a typical firm to 86 percent for an elite top performer.

A consulting firm, Service Quality Measurement Group, conducted a study that shows that on average, customer satisfaction drops by 15 percent with each callback a customer makes to resolve the same issue. FCR improvement is also positively related to customer satisfaction. Self-service is another aspect of the measurement and has been applied to a multitude of services. However, some questions to consider here are (a) whether self-service is enhancing customer experience and (b) whether customers are still coming back to the call center to resolve the issue or to get the information.

Banks and Insurance

General Electric applied Six Sigma methodology to a process in both the manufacturing and the service contexts. GE Financial adopted Six Sigma principles and benefited from its application. Other financial institutions also applied similar principles to reduce the cycle time for a loan origination by focusing on bottlenecks and waste reduction. These days, almost all large banks and financial institutions use these methodologies to stay competitive and enhance customer satisfaction. Some services where the methodology is applied are the mortgage industry, the wire transfer business, and the insurance sector. Bank One has similarly applied Six Sigma principles to streamline processes and reduce cost.

Bank of America recently acquired FleetBoston Financial Corp. The combined entity is going through IT integration and consolidation between the two banks. These cost-saving efforts are contributing to a $1.85 billion pretax saving for the bank. Bank of America also acquired MBNA Corp. recently and is combining the credit card portfolios of these two institutions. The effort is likely going to take approximately one million work-hours to finish and is supposed to generate $850 million in after-tax cost savings in year 2007.

IKEA

IKEA considers all cost implications of a new product design even before the product comes into market. Component commonality reduces cost by reducing the inventory holding cost. Supply chain and product packaging implications are also considered in terms of overall cost. The product should be modular, easily packaged in a flatbed, and stackable.

Take Away

- Employee engagement drives service innovation.
- The service innovation topic needs further study and clarity.
- Service innovation measures such as number of ideas per employees per year should be included in the Service Scorecard.
- Execution differentiates high performers from the pack.
- Execution measures providing an indication of accuracy, timeliness, and service recovery should be included in the Service Scorecard.

Five Steps of Six Sigma for Services Methodology

Define Phase

(Reference: Goel et al., Six Sigma for Transactions and Service)

Project Title:	**Project Leader:**
Team Members:	**Project Start:**

Estimated Project Selection Parameters: Probability of Success (P) _____
Cost (C) _____, Time (T) _____, Savings (S) _____, Project Index (PI) _____

Project Description:

Project Goal and Objectives:

Customer(s):

Customer Critical Requirement (based on House of quality or similar analysis):

Project Scope

Resources Required and Their Source(s)

Figure 9.2

Stakeholder Analysis:

⬇Stakeholder ⇨	Customer	Mgmt.	Employees	Quality	Supplier
Support					
Passionately Committed					
Supportive					
Compliant					
Neutral					
Opposed					
Hostile					
Not Needed					

Legend: X = Present level of commitment; O = Required level of commitment

---

Customer Requirements:

Assumed and Unspoken:

Spoken and Measurable:

Love To, but Unspoken:

Critical to Quality (Operation) Requirements:

Degree of Customer Participation and Co-production Desired:

Figure 9.3

Service Blueprinting Analysis

Critical back-room operations
- 1
- 2
- 3
- 4

Critical front-line operations
- 1
- 2
- 3
- 4

Process Map:

#	Activity	Process Time	Wait Time	Ops.	Information	Insp.	Cycle Time	Qual. (L/M/H)	Value Ops. (Y/N)	

All times are in minutes

Figure 9.4

Measure Phase

Project Title:	Project Leader:
Team Members:	Project Start:

Estimated Project Selection Parameters: Probability of Success (P) _____
Cost (C) _____, Time (T) _____, Savings (S) _____, Project Index (PI) _____

Project Descriptive Statistics:
Zone of Tolerance (if no descriptive statistics available):

Measurements	Quantifiable?	Average(Standard Deviation)	Comments

Cost of Quality

Back-Room Failure Items	Front-Line Failure Items	Appraisal Items	Prevention Items	Summary	Cost
				Internal	
				External	
				Appraisal	
				Prevention	
				Total	

Figure 9.5

Performance Measures (Use columns as appropriate)					
Measurement	Quantifiable?	Cpk	DPU	DPMO	Sigma

Figure 9.6

Analyze Phase

Failure Mode and Effects Analysis for Identifying Potential Causes

Process	Potential Failure Mode	Potential Effects of Failure Mode	S e v.	Potential Causes of Failure Mode	O c c.	Current Process Controls	D e t.	R P N

Figure 9.7

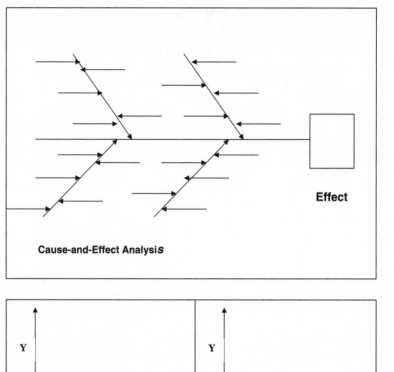

Cause-and-Effect Analysis

Effect

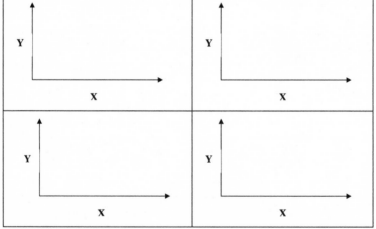

Visual Regression Analysis

Observations:

Figure 9.8

Innovate Phase

Project Title:	Project Leader:
Team Members:	Project Start:

Estimated Project Selection Parameters: Probability of Success (P) _____
Cost (C) _____, Time (T) _____, Savings (S) _____, Project Index (PI) _____

A.I.#	Improvement Action Item	Responsibility	Committed Date of Completion
1			
2			
3			
4			

Mind Map Analysis

Breakthrough Process Check:

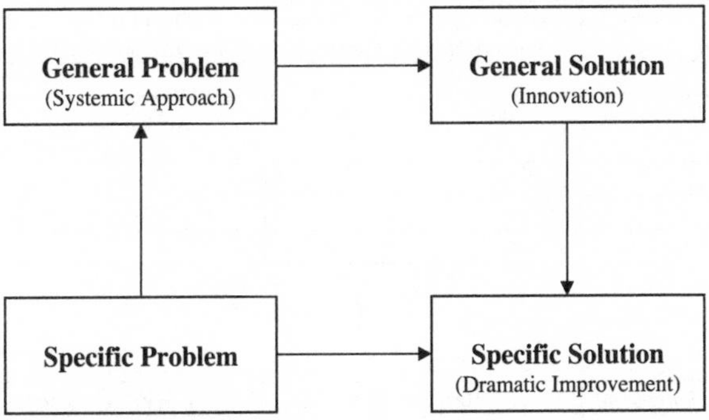

General Problem
(Systemic Approach)

General Solution
(Innovation)

Specific Problem

Specific Solution
(Dramatic Improvement)

Percent Improvement Realized:

New DPU _____

New DPMO _____

New Sigma Level _____

Figure 9.9

Embed Phase

Project Title:	Project Leader:
Team Members:	Project Start:

Estimated Project Selection Parameters: Probability of Success (P) _____
Cost (C) _____, Time (T) _____, Savings (S) _____, Project Index (PI) _____

NEW SIPOC DIAGRAM

NEW SERVICE BLUEPRINT

Critical Input Process Parameters for Control	Critical In-Process Process Parameters for Control	Critical Output Process Parameters for Control

Critical Risk Factors	Plan for Managing Critical Risk Factors
1	
2	
3	
4	

Figure 9.10

Commitment to Six Sigma Initiative

Commitment	Results Achieved	Comments

Management Review Actions

Figure 9.11

10

Retention and Growth

Customer retention is an important aspect of any service business. The present literature has a plethora of information about the ways to measure customer satisfaction. Customers are the raison d'être for any for-profit firm. At a majority of the service firms, customers rank above any other shareholders. However, customer management has more often been an art. Customer metrics are often not correlated with the corporate performance metrics and are not that well defined. Managers most often rely on financial metrics.

Customer satisfaction, retention, customer equity, and lifetime value are some of the commonly used metrics. All of these metrics could also be classified as observable (or behavioral) and unobservable (perceptual) measures. Unobservable constructs, such as service quality, perception of the service, and intention to buy a service, are more important for a service firm. Customer loyalty and retention are observable constructs and usually are measured in terms of customer equity or lifetime value of a customer. Successful management of these behaviors should result in financial gains for a service firm.

Customer satisfaction and service quality are the most common unobservable measures used by service firms. Customer satisfaction is the customers' perception or judgment about whether the service has exceeded, met, or fallen short of the expectations. Satisfaction is usually an overall perception rather than evaluation of individual processes or transactions. Survey methodology is the most common method to measure customer satisfaction. Marketing research textbooks have detailed descriptions of the survey methodology.

In certain cases, however, customers may not articulate their preferences or may not know their needs. In these cases, firms, especially in service sectors, use methodology based on the principles of anthropology and ethnography. These techniques take knowledge from fields such as clinical psychology, cognitive neuroscience, and sociology. One such patented technique called ZMET (the Zaltman Metaphor Elicitation Technique) combines such principles and identifies perceived personal relevant mental models. The technique involves conducting in-depth interviews with customers and mapping the mental model. The exercise of mapping the mental models is similar to a mind-mapping exercise.

Customers do not think in terms of processes but perceive the whole service as an experience. Customers also think in terms of satisfying the need and do not think in terms of products or services. The most common approach to measuring the quality of a service is ServQual, a methodology developed in the 1980s. The ServQual model identifies gaps in service along different service quality dimensions. The driver is the difference between customer perception and customer expectations of the service delivered.

Customer Solutions and Customer Retention

A service firm not only needs to provide a service to its customers, but it also must provide a solution to customer needs leading to a memorable experience. The paradigm of processes to service to solution to experience is an important one to understand for a service firm, because customers do not think in terms of discrete steps or process activities. Customers need solutions and experiences. An example of managing an experience includes a theme park right at the center of the Mall of America in Minneapolis, Minnesota. Another example is providing video games, news, Internet services, and movies during a long flight on an airplane.

A customer-centric view is a key success factor in the competitive marketplace. The customers are at the center of understanding the needs of the market. Firms that fail to understand their customers' needs are doomed for failure. A customer-centric view requires that a firm map customer needs and demands an ongoing dialogue with the customers. Customer needs could be implicit or explicit. Implicit needs are in terms of features of the service, and explicit needs could be considered benefits or the value to customers.

Customer needs result in expectations. The expectations of customers also consider previous experience with similar services and any word-of-mouth or communication by the service provider. At the "moment of truth" or at the time of delivery of the service, customers compare expectations with the perception of the service delivered.

A solution perspective takes the view that customers have needs and need solutions to satisfy those needs. As described by Mohanbir Sawhney in *The Service-Dominant Logic of Marketing—Dialogue, Debate, and Directions*, a product-centric view can no longer sustain long-term competitive advantage. Solution needs are specific to a particular segment of customers. Some of the metrics that are relevant in a solution-centric view are the share of customer spending and segment profitability/revenue.

One tool that helps identify the need of customers is customer activity mapping. Activity mapping describes how customers select, buy, and consume services. Customer experience mapping or activity blueprinting describes the whole experience in discrete steps. Each step clearly identifies the value added and should be analyzed for the purpose of providing differentiated solutions.

As we acknowledge customers as cocreators of value in a service context, we need to consider the importance of this particular element. Because customers participate, create, and consume services, firms need to continuously identify the latent need of customers. Service firms also engage customers during the process of service innovation. As firms become customer-need focused, the firm is more likely to retain customers leading to sustainable profit.

Retention Measures

The purpose of the customer metrics is to focus on firm profitability and growth. A firm incurs customer-related costs to acquire and retain a particular customer. These costs include acquisition cost, operating cost, and customer retention costs. On the revenue side, a firm gets base revenue, future revenue, and some price premium from early adopters. A higher loyalty and retention will lead to reduced acquisition costs and perhaps higher revenue if a firm is able to cross-sell other services to its existing customers. The net effect is higher profit.

A differentiation should be between loyalty and retention. The customer loyalty is "earned" and proves customers are truly satisfied and have received a high quality of service. Retention shows that customers have repurchased from the same firm but does not give any indication about the true satisfaction of customers. Loyalty could be "bought" by providing some incentives such as coupons, promotions, or some special deals for existing customers. This section describes typical customer retention metrics.

Customer Satisfaction

Customer satisfaction is the most common measure used at a firm level and at the national level. At a macro level, we have seen the development of a satisfaction index, such as the American Customer Satisfaction Index (ACSI) and the Swedish Customer Satisfaction Index (SCSI). The SCSI, established in 1989, was the first national customer satisfaction index. ACSI was introduced in 1994. It is supposed to represent the economy as a whole and provides firm-level and sector-level satisfaction indicators. Scores of individual service firms relative to the sector average indicate the strength or weakness of a particular firm's strategy. For example, the Southwest consistently beats the industry average score.

Net Promoters Index

Frederick Reichheld proposed a metric called the "Net Promoters Index" and suggested that this is the *only* index a firm needs to grow. The hypothesis behind using one number is that "the only path to profitable growth may lie in a company's ability to get loyal customers to become, in effect, its marketing department." The basic idea is that a firm should grow the size of promoters and reduce the size of detractors. The index is defined as the percentage of respondents answering a 9 or 10 on a 0–10 willingness-to-recommend scale minus the percentage of respondents answering 0–6. A typical net promoters score is between 10 percent and 20 percent for most firms. The index is simple, is easy to measure, and has gained some traction among practitioners. Firms that have used this index are General Electric, *The Wall Street Journal*, Intuit, and Symantec.

Existing customers should be acting as the marketing department, promoting the image of the company, and in turn bringing in more business. Many companies, especially service firms such as an airline, car-rental company, and Internet service provider, grow based on word-of-mouth recommendations. A firm needs only to know answers to basic questions, and the customer survey should reflect this simplicity of intent. Firms have started using the Net Promoters Score as one important score to tie compensation and other rewards throughout the organization. The usual practice of making the number transparent throughout the organization and working on improving the number should be followed. However, because we know that one particular number cannot predict the performance of a firm, the theoretical basis for this index has been questioned and has yet to be proven.

Customer Equity and Lifetime Value Models

Customers are considered assets just like any other tangible/intangible assets. Considering that customers are financial assets, firms should measure, analyze, and improve the customer equity component. Customer Equity and Lifetime Value are similar concepts. Lifetime Value (LTV) is defined as "net present value of future streams of contributions to firm profit expected from the customers." Without considering the time value of money, the lifetime value is simply equal to total customer revenue times percent margin times total number of loyal years. Some of the decisions made during the calculation include pricing policies, extent of service provided, and add-on services provided.

Focusing on a metric such as Customer Lifetime Value is important for a firm, because this metric provides long-term focus and directly relates to the firm profit. One implicit assumption of the model is that it is indeed possible to accurately predict future profitability of the customers. With time, in reality, customers might be misclassified. Therefore, a service firm needs to manage the Lifetime Value model dynamically and continuously update the numbers. While calculating the Lifetime Value of a customer, one needs to identify the time horizon or customer life cycle, the forecasting method, the source of customer data, and supported managerial decisions. LTV should include direct contributions by the customers as well as indirect contributions, such as recommending the services to others and providing ideas for new services.

Customer equity can be broken into the following three categories: Acquisition Equity, Retention Equity, and Add-On Selling Equity. The equity calculation method is shown in Figure 10.1. Calculation methods are still evolving, and no general agreement exists about the time horizon to use in projecting sales and other data, the time periods to measure, and the customer cohorts of subsegments to use. As shown in these equations, the rates, expenditure and margins of acquisition, retention, and add-on selling are included in the calculations. Margins and expenditures are per customer.

Total customer equity per customer is the sum of acquisition, retention, and add-on selling equities. One basic assumption of customer equity calculations is that no discount factor is considered. Another basic assumption is that retention rate, expenditure, and margins are constant throughout the life cycle. Some of these assumptions can be relaxed, and calculations may be modified accordingly.

As proposed by Blattberg, Getz, and Thomas in book titled *Customer Equity*, customer equity could also be considered as a flow, and the Customer Equity Flow statement could be prepared to help managers make better decisions. The Customer Equity Flow statement considers the dynamic nature of retention rates and changes in the buying patterns of customers. Changes to numbers could be made from period to period to reflect the numbers close to reality.

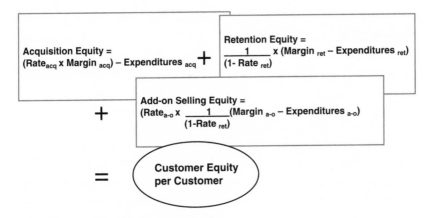

Figure 10.1   Customer equity model

Implementing Retention Measures

Satisfaction leading to loyalty logic is much more applicable in the service context, where customers are often coproducers, and delivery takes place at the choice of the customer. Loyalty could likely have a negative impact on a firm's financial performance for a product-centric firm. For a service firm, however, the impact is positive. Service firms need to "earn" the loyalty of customers. Product firms often bring down prices to retain customers. This logic was tested using three-year data, and services do tend to show a stronger affinity toward the satisfaction-loyalty-profit argument. Customer referrals and intangible recommendations should make a greater difference for service firms. Product quality is tangible and can easily be communicated to customers. Typical metrics will include growth in business with existing customers, number of new customers with referrals from existing customers, customer satisfaction, customer equity, or net promoter index.

Wachovia Corporation

Wachovia Corporation ranks high in the ACSI ranking of customer satisfaction. The team is now calculating household customer equity for each of its households. Wachovia has more than 13 million customers. Wachovia wants to optimize customer contact. A ten-member team is using advanced statistical analysis and multilevel modeling techniques to analyze available data. The information is used to make managerial decisions to achieve superior performance.

Sprint

Sprint is the third-largest wireless service provider in the U.S. On June 25, 2007, Sprint fired about 1,000 of its customers by sending mass cancellation letters. The call volume from these customers represented around 40 to 50 times the average call volume from customers. This mass cancellation provides an example of customer equity and customer management calculations and taking a drastic measure to "cull its customer base." The decision was likely based on customer equity. Perhaps, customer equity for these customers was negative. The long-term consequences of such a decision are still not clear.

British Airways

British Airways, one of the largest global airlines, is considered to be among those with the best customer service. The airline provides an easy way to complain using various available channels. For example, an e-mail could be used to categorize the type of issue under in-flight, baggage, airport, or corporate policy issues. Often, firms fail to respond to complaints, and customers either keep quiet and move away or tell others about the bad service, causing loss of customer goodwill.

Growth

A service firm could grow by acquiring new customers, entering into new markets using existing services, creating and delivering new services, and selling more services to existing customers. However, the most important and sustainable way to grow a service business is by creating and delivering new services. In this section, growth by service innovation is examined. Innovation could be in the form of new services or a new solution to existing customer needs.

Creating a new solution is as important as creating new services. Customers require an end-to-end solution to satisfy their needs. Customers do not need a product or a service per se. Understanding customer needs is a challenge for service firms due to its intangibility and other characteristics of services. The solution paradigm has been adopted by many firms recently. Some firms recently adopting a solution-based paradigm are IBM, Ericsson, General Electric, and Cargill.

Differences between the solution-centric paradigm and the product-centric paradigm are highlighted in Table 10.1. Solution (service) innovation is based on creating solutions for a particular segment of customers. The front-facing organization is based on the needs of the customer, and the back-end organization could be based on the capability of the organization. In a ground-breaking article titled "Evolving to a New Dominant Logic for Marketing," published in the Journal of Marketing (2004), S.L. Vargo and R.F. Lusch described Service Dominant Logic. Service Dominant Logic considers customer needs and provides a solution.

TABLE 10.1   Innovation in the Solution and Service Environment

Development Step	New Product Development	New Service/Solution Development
Opportunity Identification	Feature-based Find customers for products	Experience and activity focus Customer solutions Reduce complexity
Design and Development	Concurrent engineering Design for assembly Design for manufacturability	Collaborative design Design for flexibility Design for reliability Design for repeatability
Testing and Improving	Product prototyping and testing In-house testing	Prototype using experiences Testing with customers and partners
Implementation	Pricing Distribution channels SKU	Coproduction incentives Learn as implementation happens
Key Performance Indices (KPIs)	Product revenue Profit Market share	Customer experience Repeatability

Innovation in a service environment is a bit different compared to managing innovation at a product-centric firm. Differences between innovations in these two contexts are still debated. Service firms typically do not have a department called Research and Development and hardly ever apply for a patent for the intellectual property. Innovation is driven by employee engagement, customer engagement, business practices, and the human-resource-management practices of a firm.

As discussed in the previous chapters, the following four views dominate the service innovation literature:

- **Assimilation approach**—The process of innovation is similar in both manufacturing and service settings. Concepts and tools derived from the manufacturing setting are applicable to the service context. Innovation in transaction-based services could be explained using this approach.

- **Demarcation approach**—Service innovation is inherently different from innovation in the manufacturing setting because of intangibility and customer participation in the production process. The approach broadly defines service innovation as an improvement in the delivery system and the customization of services to satisfy the needs of different customer segments. Innovation in experience-based services could be explained using this approach.

- **Traditional view**—Innovation in services is not an interesting topic and services are relatively unprogressive. This view considers service firms to be dependent on suppliers or service-chain partners, as suppliers control innovation inputs. According to this view, a service firm does not have an important role to play.

- **Synthesis approach**—This approach combines the demarcation approach while applying existing tools and concepts to the service setting. This approach makes the most sense.

The appropriateness of the innovation approach will also depend on the subsector of the service firm and the nature of the offerings. The three main service sectors discussed in the literature are the supplier-dominated, production-intensive, and specialized service sectors.

Special characteristics of new service development, NSD, are discussed in the literature and are important to note. NSD innovation may not be recognized, new services can be imitated by and from competitors, termination of NSD projects tends to be easy, NSD is considered a trial-and-error process, there are no natural occasions for review, and a problem with communication may arise; thus, frontline coworkers should be involved. With these characteristics in place, it is easy to say that service firms do not innovate by use of "formal methods" like those used in the manufacturing sector. NSD tends to be an ad hoc process. Thus, NSD is easy to imitate by the competition, and improvements will most always be on a trial-and-error basis.

Authors J.P.J. de Jong, A. Bruins, W. Dolfsma, and J. Meijaard have explored service firm innovation in the business sector. The academic environment and existing literature have yet to fully integrate service innovation into their domains. The field itself is relatively new, and hardly any courses are offered that focus exclusively on service innovation. To understand service innovation, understanding the nature of services is crucial. The classical differences between products and services are discussed widely in the literature: Services are intangible, services are produced and consumed simultaneously, services are heterogeneous, and services cannot be stored.

The intangibility and simultaneous production and consumption aspects of services create an added challenge in terms of defining the value of innovation and the impact on customer behavior. Because customers experience the service and do not look at it as a collection of processes, a firm needs to study the experience aspect upfront. An example is provided by a large bank that introduced an innovative, fast, and efficient ATM. The ATM was superior to previous models and provided a faster service. However, the ATM was totally silent. The bank wanted to study the impact on customer experience and was puzzled when examining customer reaction. Customers faced an ATM that was totally *silent* and were, in a way, afraid that the machine was idle and not doing anything. In the end, the bank had to add an artificial sound effect to make the machine look as though something was happening to provide a comfort factor to its customers. Demand-driven innovation and consumer participation is much more critical for innovation in services.

Service innovation could also be described using the value chain concept. Value is added by the delivery interface, technological options, delivery system, and delivery concept. Hence, four dimensions of innovation in services could be described: the service concept, client interface, service delivery system, and technological options. Service innovation can happen along any of those four dimensions. The innovation is more often nontechnological in nature. The service concept adapts to an existing market environment, including competitive reactions and offerings.

Client interface (or client service delivery channels) is defined as being service offerings that are marketed and produced in a client-specific way. Various delivery channels are provided for customer convenience, and an appropriate pricing scheme is devised for the same purpose. The service delivery system is the third part of service innovation and is the "internal organizational arrangements that have to be managed to allow service workers to perform their job properly." Service delivery includes service capacity at various points in the system, delivery channels management, information management, and various aspects of service inventory. Service inventory or access policies were discussed in Chapter 2, "Performance Challenges in the Service Sector."

The final dimension of service innovations is the technological option. The technological options dimension refers to the development and implementation of new forms of technology and related reconfigurations so that service concepts and processes can interface with customers. New technology options could include new software, improvements in existing concepts and technologies, or anything that has to deal with the improvement of technology overall. A conceptual model of service innovation is shown in Figure 10.2. Services are inherently unique.

Strategy service innovation, or business model service innovation, touches customers directly and includes providing the total solution by including additional services, thus creating new markets and new customer segments. This type of service innovation includes the way a service markets to its customers and how it delivers the services. An example is provided in Figure 10.3.

Service Characteristics

Intangibility	**Forms of innovation**
Heterogeneity	• New business model
Inseparability	• Process
Perishability	• Operations
	• Experience
Information need	• Market
	• On demand

Service Performance

Customer experience, value
Process quality
Strategic value
Market performance
Profitability performance

Innovation Process

Involvement of customer/partners
Customer characteristics

Figure 10.2   A conceptual model of service innovation

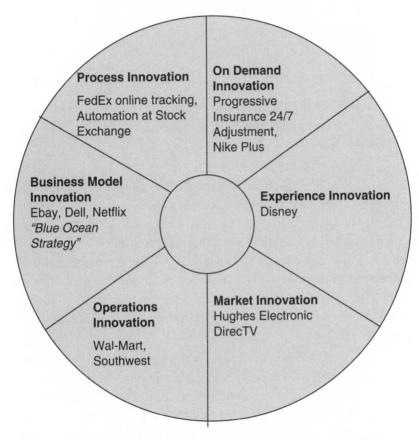

Process Innovation
FedEx online tracking, Automation at Stock Exchange

On Demand Innovation
Progressive Insurance 24/7 Adjustment, Nike Plus

Business Model Innovation
Ebay, Dell, Netflix
"Blue Ocean Strategy"

Experience Innovation
Disney

Operations Innovation
Wal-Mart, Southwest

Market Innovation
Hughes Electronic DirecTV

Figure 10.3   The elements of strategy innovation, adapted from Robert Tucker in *Driving Growth Through Innovation* (2002)

Figure 10.3 shows new distribution methods used by Dell and Amazon.com using this direct model. The method bypasses retailers and wholesalers. Firms such as eBay and Priceline.com build new markets by providing unique ways to satisfy customer needs. Similarly, Wal-Mart enter into Wal-Mart.com and Hughes Electronics providing DirecTV are other dimensions of strategic service innovation. Southwest Airlines is yet another dimension of this unique business model, which includes utilizing the following services:

- A point-to-point direct service
- No seat assignments
- One type of aircraft
- Direct-to-customer online and live (phone) booking systems.

On-demand innovation is provided by firms to customize the service provided and makes use of the service inventory approach described previously.

Innovation will affect bottom-line or top-line growth depending on the degree of impact on the organization and its customers. The impact could be radical, substantial, and/or incremental. Examples of incremental impact are a hotel providing an automated check-in/out using an ATM-like machine, a retailer providing automated approval for checks and age checks, and an airline providing more legroom for passengers in economy class. Incremental innovation can easily be copied by other service firms. However, incremental innovation should be considered an essential part of the continuous improvement process.

Substantial and breakthrough innovations provide a first-mover with competitive advantage by providing unique services and/or solutions to its customers. A successful service firm should have a comprehensive and enterprisewide innovation program. The innovation process should involve all stakeholders and should be measured using leading indicators.

A service firm needs a well-defined innovation strategy that everybody understands and that has been institutionalized firmwide. A best practice firm should also hire, train, develop, and retain an effective workforce that has the flexibility and necessary empowerment to bring innovative ideas to the market.

Idea Management for Service Innovation

As discussed in *Ideas Are Free,* by Allan Robinson and Dean Schroeder, a firm named Wainwright found that idea-generating employees helped the culture of the company as well as the company's performance. Service innovation aspects and human resource aspects are intricately related to the corporate performance. High-performing firms have a deeply rooted innovation culture as well as happy employees. The management of Wainright found that when they trusted employees more, the employees formulated better ideas and generated them more often. By 1994, using these total quality management techniques led Wainwright Industries to win the Malcolm Baldrige National Quality Award. Since then, the company has continued to experience success. In 2002, Wainwright averaged 65 implemented ideas per employee. Because the employees were able to act on their ideas, many of these new visions by employees were implemented by the company.

The book also describes how in the late 1980s, Japanese companies were getting many more ideas through their employees than companies in the United States were getting from their employees. Japanese companies did not have to pay out heavily in rewards for those ideas, either. U.S. companies were paying out 200 times what Japanese companies were, and U.S. companies were getting less than three-hundredths of the number of ideas. In 1989, Japan was averaging 37.4 ideas per employee, while the U.S. was averaging only 0.12 ideas per employee. Japan also had a participation rate of 77.6 percent, while the U.S. had a participation rate of 9 percent. The average reward for idea generation in Japan was $2.83; in the U.S. the reward was $602.

Throughout the 1990s the U.S. companies used benchmarking to attain greater results in idea generation. They learned and utilized Japan's reward system; because of this they were getting more ideas and paying less for them. The explanation for why the employee steps forward (while not getting rewarded) is pretty straightforward. Employees naturally want to make their job easier, so when employees see a problem in front of them, they want to fix it.

The only way for this system to work is if the management welcomes proposals from the employees about problems they find. If the management is willing to listen, being heard is enough reward for the employee. The truth is most people step forward with ideas because they want to do so. Even if the ideas are small ones, their importance is not undermined. Small ideas are often just as valuable as "home run" ideas. Employees want to see their ideas being utilized, and they also appreciate a little public display of praise.

Managers need to create a supportive environment for employees to share their ideas. Managers can use coaching or mentors when trying to get employees active in generating ideas. Most important, managers need to help develop employee ideas and let the employees know that their ideas are valued by the company. The management needs to get employees excited to participate in generating ideas. Wal-Mart does this by using "pep rallies" before their morning shifts to pep up their employees and get them excited to serve the customers. That same environment needs to be created when employers are trying to get employees to participate.

The book *Ideas are Free* describes the metrics that are used to measure idea performance. This system measures the quantity of ideas, where they come from, and the speed at which they are processed. The quantities of ideas are measured by time using weeks, months, or years. The book makes references to seasonal effects on the number of ideas generated. For example, during a new product or service launch, idea generation by employees may experience a spike. Problems could easily arise because the new product or service is in its early stages; the kinks in any system always need to be worked out. Few systems are impervious to errors when they are first implemented. Because of this tendency, employees generate a greater number of ideas during these periods.

If idea generation is low, there may be a morale problem or something deterring employees from speaking up. This will decrease the number of ideas generated. Source metrics measure where ideas are coming from. This metric is usually measured by quarters; it is measured by the percentage of people in a given unit. For example, if you have 300 employees, and your company is generating a lot of ideas, where do those ideas come from? Are they coming from 10 employees or all 300? If only 10 people are generating all those ideas, what are their supervisors doing to get them to generate so many? What are other supervisors doing wrong? The source metric can answer these questions.

Knowing how to promote employee ideas will become a core competency for managers and will be the difference between effective and ineffective managers. Ideas are free, and they have the power to liberate employees and transform a company. Without the support of the service firm's leadership, it is very difficult for new services development to take hold and have a corporate culture that supports it.

Implementing Growth in Service Scorecard

Considering growth through service innovation as a process, we could consider metrics at three different levels: input metrics such as number of ideas per employees as discussed in the employee innovation section in Chapter 9, "Innovation and Execution"; process velocity metrics tracking the employee responsiveness to ideas; and output metrics such as revenue/profit growth from new services. For example, when an employee has an idea, how long does it take to get heard, and how long does it take to get the idea implemented? A company that is very responsive will likely have more employees who want to participate. We consider percent of revenue from new services to be a relevant metric. By using this metric in combination with other metrics, companies and managers can stay informed about how their employees are doing in generating ideas. Typical metrics could include one or some combination of the following: revenue (profit) from existing customers with existing products, revenue (profit) from existing customers with new products, revenue (profit) from new customers with existing products, revenue (profit) from new customers with new products, or number of new customers added.

Growth drives profitability and the growth of a firm. Innovative services allow a firm to charge a price premium. Generally speaking, service innovation could take place at three levels: the process level, the service offering level, and the strategic level. New services innovation provides new solutions, new services, or offerings to customers, thus driving the top-line growth and, hence, the profit. New processes usually drive the cost or productivity side of the equation by making a firm more effective, hence driving the bottom-line productivity. Process innovation is about execution excellence, usually involves back offices, and is usually not visible to customers. Front-office process innovation should improve customers' perception of the service. Examples of front-office process innovation could be FedEx providing an online tracking facility for a package or a bank providing online wire-transfer capability to its customers.

Therefore, one of the prerequisites for new service development is the service firm's culture and leadership. The main parts of an NSD firm's culture are the management support, an open culture, internal communications, trust in employees, and the autonomy of the co-workers. Culture also involves hiring the right type of employees. Innovative service firms generally look for the following characteristics when hiring an employee:

- **Resourcefulness and problem-solving abilities**—Whether the person can experiment and find a solution to the problem and not be worried about making mistakes; and whether the person can discover the necessary information and gather necessary resources and make things happen, or whether the person waits for things to happen.

- **Possessing an open mind and varied interests**—Whether the person has a spongelike attitude toward absorbing new information and thrives in an environment where steep learning takes place; and whether the person is an explorer and a "world traveler" who reads on a variety of topics.

- **Strength of character**—Whether the person has a strong work ethic, and whether the person is disciplined and self-motivated.

- **Creativity**—Whether the person is creative.

Appropriate metrics should also be used to manage service innovation. We propose two types of metrics to manage such a process. First, a metric about revenue share from new services should be considered. Second, a metric showing the velocity and amount of flow of innovative ideas throughout the system, such as launch rate, commercial success rate, and time to market, should be used.

Progressive

One prime example of various forms of service innovation is the insurance firm Progressive, which implemented a fast-claim process that allows its clients to settle claims on the spot. Other insurance firms take weeks or days just to have the whole incident reported. Progressive also provides quotes from its competition on its Web site. Various pilot studies are taking place using new ideas.

American Airlines

American Airlines uses a suggestion management system called "IdeaAAs" that allows employees to provide ideas and be appropriately rewarded. In a typical year, the company receives about 17,000 ideas. Eight thousand of those ideas could be considered seriously, and about one-quarter of those might be implemented.

Take Away

- Various customer retention measures are in use by service firms. Examples are net promoters scores, customer equity/lifetime value, and customer satisfaction.
- Growth of a service firm is driven by customer retention and business innovation.
- Growth from new services is an important indicator of the growth potential.

Part III

Practicing Service Scorecard

11

Implementation of the Service Scorecard

Service businesses are similar to manufacturing businesses in that they have the common business objective of making money and achieving growth. Successful service businesses have implemented scorecards. Banks, airlines, hospitals, and restaurants all deploy some form of scorecard. Some organizations have an elaborate set of measurements; others have sketchy ones at best. The Service Scorecard provides an initial and complete framework of a business scorecard that allows organizations to relate their measurements to the financial performance.

In a service organization, the following scenarios may exist:

1. There is already an existing performance measurement system that is considered to be satisfactory.

2. The Balanced Scorecard is being used in a limited fashion in a department or two.

3. Most employees are unaware of the scorecards being used by executives.

4. Measurement systems are not being used at all.

5. Employees already feel overwhelmed with putting out fires, and implementing a scorecard will be considered additional work.

6. Business performance is marginal at best, but executives feel they know what to do.

7. Other struggles or strategies are more important than having a good scorecard to monitor progress and ensure success.

8. The value proposition of implementing a good scorecard is not clearly understood.

Considering these situations, a company must look at implementing the Service Scorecard as an opportunity to improve the measurement system, establish an intelligent relationship with corporate financials, and use a holistic measurement model both for the alignment of resources and as a tool to accelerate business performance. With the Service Scorecard, one must be able to answer questions about the current performance, identify areas for improvement, and discern estimated future performance. The important aspect of the scorecard is its ability to aggregate the multidisciplined measurement-based information, and then transform it into business intelligence that can be used to lead the organization in the direction of sustained profitable growth.

To implement a service scorecard, the value proposition and the effort associated with its implementation must be clearly understood. Companies do need a measurement system to ensure profitable growth; however, without leadership support and organizationwide implementation, full benefits of the Service Scorecard cannot be realized. For a service business to be successful, all departments must be aligned and accelerated using the Service Scorecard.

Approach to Implementing the Service Scorecard

Each company implements its scorecard in a slightly different way depending on the leadership style, corporate culture, business strategy, and performance objectives. Certain steps, however, are recommended to implement the Service Scorecard effectively. The implementation begins with the leadership commitment and ends with the ability to (a) predict corporate performance in the coming months and (b) adjust the business processes proactively to ensure realization of business objectives.

The following steps can be helpful in implementing the Service Scorecard to achieve business objectives:

1. Committing to the fundamental business strategy of Sustained Profitable Growth.

2. Achieving executive understanding of the Service Scorecard and its elements.

3. Getting leadership endorsement of the Service Scorecard.

4. Having strategic and organizational alignment.

5. Planning for the Service Scorecard:

   a. Prepare for implementing the scorecard.

   b. Determine the service scorecard measurements.

   c. Determine the data source.

   d. Establish goals for each measurement.

   e. Leverage the technology.

6. Training for using the Service Scorecard.

7. Validating and adjusting the measurements.

8. Institutionalizing the Service Scorecard:

   a. Organizationwide deployment.

   b. Data analysis and communication.

   c. Critical executive review:

      i. Review operations and financial performance.

      ii. Review performance against strategic goals.

   d. Actions for improving performance.

9. Renewing and reigniting the organization.

Committing to the Fundamental Business Strategy of Sustained Profitable Growth

Most financial structures and stakeholders expect quick return on investment. Wall Street analysts expect quarterly performance to write about. Thus, the bottom line rides over the top line, and executives take actions to make the expected bottom line. This stride to achieve the profit sometimes inspires executives to make short-term decisions that may prove to be detrimental in the longer term. In other words, decisions to make money may stifle corporate creativity and thus revenue growth.

Businesses need both profit and growth, even though sometimes profit and growth appear to be contradictory. Thus, the first critical decision for corporate leadership is to strive for sustained profitable growth (SPG) rather than just to make money. After the leadership commits to SPG, focus changes from action to thoughtful action. To affect the corporate profit, leadership normally focuses on cost reduction, whereas to drive growth, leadership looks into significant investment.

When profitable growth becomes the objective, however, the leadership considers all parts of the business, all assets, and all opportunities for improving the performance. For example, a typical strategy to cut cost is to squeeze out the suppliers by 3 percent. Those who follow such a strategy, however, fail to recognize that in the longer term, the quality of supplies will eventually determine the quality of the organization, customer satisfaction, and retention. Departing customers, a shrinking business due to cost-cutting, and negatively growing revenue are signs of short-sighted leadership leading to a downward spiral of business death through mergers and acquisition or insolvency.

4P Model of Process Management for Services

One of the main challenges in service businesses is the process management, which is a building block of a business. A service business is a collection of service processes. Practicing sound process management principles for delivering excellent customer service and ensuring overall business performance are requirements. The recently published 4P model of process management (Gupta, July 2006) presents a sound process management model that will ensure excellence at every step of the service. As shown in Figure 11.1, the 4P model stands for Prepare, Perform, Perfect, and Progress.

The 4P model of process management is an actionable method of achieving desired results. In process management, either failures occur or too much verification of performance happens, which implies that either clearly defined targets are nonexistent, or not enough preparation has happened to deliver the desired service. In the absence of performance targets, we look for acceptable performance.

4P Model of Process Management

Prepare
(To do well)

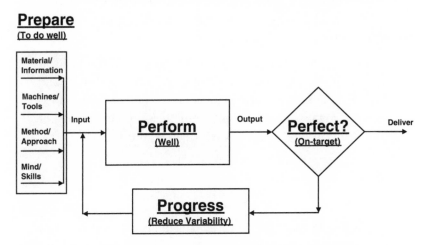

Figure 11.1   The 4P model of process management for services

Acceptable and excellent performance levels are starkly different. Acceptable performance demonstrates the minimal performance to survive, whereas excellence represents maximal performance to be the leader. To be the market leader, one needs to strive for excellence and define clear targets. Processes designed for a target performance will result in more consistent and improving performance in comparison to processes designed within acceptable operating range (which are normally suboptimized and leave much room for variation and failures). The target must be a point value rather than a range, because the target value becomes a criterion for the process design.

Preparation represents doing the homework and ensuring availability of everything needed to perform various process activities well. Root cause analysis highlights the few specific items needed to complete a task well. The four items are material or information, machine or tools, methods or approach, and skills or training. For a service process to produce desired results, the necessary customer information, process information, and input data (if necessary) or raw material must be present. Machine or tools include widgets, software programs, computers, or a hammer. Method or approach represents a process design captured by a defined and documented, step-by-step procedure to produce the target performance. Finally, skills or training represents the competency level to minimize people-dependent inconsistency. The following comments represent experiences with the 4P model of process management:

"The 4P's methodology is clearly a successor to the brilliant developments of Shewhart, Deming, Ishikawa, Juran, and Taguchi. I am particularly persuaded by the emphasis on excellence obtained by meeting a target. Mere compliance or conformity to specifications is no substitute for true excellence."

Scott Tonk,Consultant

"Using the 4P model of process management at a process, our manpower requirements were decreased approximately 2124 WIP hours or 1.22 man-years. The time saved was applied to more productive endeavors. The government or military, despite public perception, constantly looks for savings in time, money, personnel, and process. Therefore, forward-thinking individuals with concepts/processes ultimately saving the taxpayer money are welcome."

George Stemler,University of Military Intelligence

"The 4P model has helped our Service Delivery area in creating and defining our procedures. Although we are still evolving the approach, the 4P model forces us to determine the skills/materials to execute the step; define the necessary steps from an established beginning and end (scope); and set the required measurements to identify success (performance measurements). Answering all of these questions/needs provides us with an efficient process. We envision the benefits will continue in reducing questions from users unfamiliar with a certain procedure and continuous process improvement, as we're capturing metrics on critical points of the process."

ISO 9001 Management Representative, A Marketing Services Company

One of the main benefits of using the 4P model of process management is that it points to the design of the process for achieving the target performance rather than blaming people for performing below par. The authors' experience shows that a process designed and operated to its target will have about a 50 percent less error rate on the average than the process operated to lower and upper specification limits for producing acceptable process output.

Executive Understanding of the Service Scorecard and its Elements

To look at the entire organization and its resources to realize the business strategy of sustained profitable growth, the leadership must understand the intent and elements of the Service Scorecard. Recognizing interrelationships of various elements of the Service Scorecard, a simple but purposeful understanding of each element must be developed. For example, leadership must seek answers to questions such as these:

1. Can I fit the Service Scorecard framework to my business?
2. How will my company practice various elements of the Service Scorecard?
3. Will my company need to modify the Service Scorecard?
4. What measurements are critical to my business?
5. Do I adapt the Service Scorecard measurements to my organization?
6. How will I use the Service Performance Index to identify opportunities and enhance the performance of my organization?
7. What problems should I expect in implementing the Service Scorecard?
8. How much will it cost me to implement the Service Scorecard, and what will be the return on investment?
9. Who will I designate as the Service Scorecard champion?

After answering various questions about implementing a sound measurement system such as the Service Scorecard, leadership can focus on sustaining the profitable growth. This requires considering growth strategies through innovation or employee engagement, and profit improvement tactics such as waste reduction and process improvement. With a clear understanding of (a) the value-stream to profit and growth and (b) corresponding measures built into the Service Scorecard framework, leadership must commit and endorse establishing a framework for performance measurements.

Leadership Endorsement of the Service Scorecard

Endorsing the Service Scorecard for a corporate performance measurement system implies becoming a passionate user of the scorecard for identifying opportunities for both improving the performance and predicting future performance. Leadership expectation of the necessary measurements will filter down to the mid-level management as well as to the process owners. The best endorsement of the Service Scorecard is communicating business performance with employees throughout the corporation, and sensitizing employees to the Service Scorecard measurements.

Enthusiastically reporting the corporate performance, formally (or informally) measuring performance against goals, and rewarding superior performance in various elements (or measurement) of the Service Scorecard are good ways to demonstrate leadership commitment to the Service Scorecard. Most important, the leadership must expect significant improvement that is reported through Service Scorecard measurements and corresponding aggressive goals for improvement. Finally, providing necessary support to realize return on investment is critical to ensure successful implementation of the Service Scorecard.

Strategic and Organizational Alignment

After the leadership's endorsement and the champion's appointment, the next step is to align the scorecard with the strategic objectives and map it to the organization structure. Effective organizational alignment depends on objectives using the scorecard, which is considered successful if it leads to profitable growth, as shown in Figure 11.2. To that effect, an organization must align with the strategic intent in terms of marketing and sales for growth; customer relationships management; executive, operations, and partnership management; service acquisition and innovation; and excellence management. Modifications to these categories can occur, such as marketing and sales for market research and growth, customer relationships for sustaining the business, operations incorporating sourcing partnerships, service acquisition and innovation needed to introduce new service products, and excellence management replacing quality management. To benefit from the Service Scorecard, innovation, excellence, partnerships, and market research are critical pieces for success.

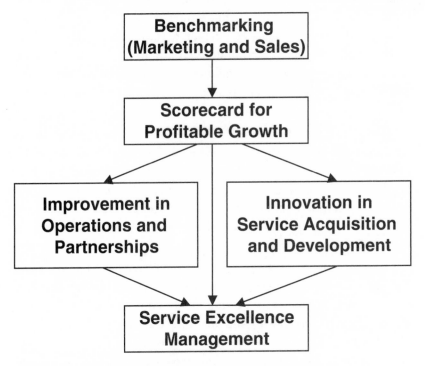

Figure 11.2   Strategic alignment factors

Planning for the Service Scorecard

Planning for implementing the Service Scorecard requires good preparation: identifying stakeholders, determining applicable process measurements aggregating into service scorecard measurements, and setting relevant goals for improvement. In addition, data accuracy and use of technology must also be considered to ensure ease of data collection and timeliness of measurements to initiate improvement actions.

Prepare for Implementing the Service Scorecard

After the leadership and the employees understand the Service Scorecard, preparation for implementing it includes getting necessary IT technology and software, developing a methodology for reporting business performance, discovering trends or areas for improvement, and preparing a preliminary action plan to implement it. The preliminary action plan must incorporate the employee feedback obtained from the employee awareness training. A person of the executive rank is needed to take an overall responsibility for implementing the scorecard.

The scorecard champion first listens to various stakeholders for their main points, needs, and wish list. The input from across the organization can be used in utilizing the Service Scorecard, identifying key service processes, and establishing effective measures of performance. For implementing the Service Scorecard effectively, the champion may utilize the action plan template, as shown in Figure 11.3.

In preparing to implement the Service Scorecard, a company can look into the required necessary information regarding expectations, barriers, information and reporting needs, communication methods, and tools and technology for implementing the scorecard. In addition, a methodology for effectively using the scorecard, including interpretation of data, frequency of review, incentives for success, consequences and corrective actions for questionable performance, and training required for employees and leadership to understand the scorecard, should be examined.

Scorecard Element:		Element Owner:	
Performance Target:			
Objective:			

AI #	Action	Responsibility	Committed Completion Date	Critical Resource Required

Figure 11.3   Action plan to implement the Service Scorecard

Determine the Service Scorecard Measurements

The Service Scorecard has ten executive-level measurements to determine the Service Performance Index (SPIn) and to identify improvement opportunities for sustaining the profitable growth. However, to arrive at the ten top-level measurements, an organization needs several process-level measurements for key processes.

Key process areas are those that perform below excellence level or are critical to meeting business objectives. Some processes such as sales are directly specified as an element in the Service Scorecard. However, collaboration or execution may include multiple processes or multiple partners. To minimize the complexity and burden of measurements, start with key processes or key partners, while monitoring the remaining processes or suppliers sporadically. In an IT corporation, for example, key processes could be requirements gathering, system design and architecture, project management, or product release (which could be more critical than the task of coding itself).

After key processes are identified, a set of questions can be asked to determine process-level measurements. The questions to be answered are as listed here:

1. What is the purpose of a process?
2. What is the expected output of the process?

3. What are critical aspects (inputs, activities, or output) of the process?

4. How will one verify the critical aspect of the process?

Answers to the last question will reveal necessary process measures. Examples of process measures are shown in Table 11.1. These process measures will vary from one organization to another organization based on their priorities. A key process in one organization may not be the key process in another organization due to its performance. If a process is robust and its performance is superior, such that it does not need to be monitored as rigorously as others, it may not have to be used in determining the SPIn (unless it is directly related to the Service Scorecard elements).

For example, to ensure revenue growth, an organization must look into all possibilities for increasing sales. The new sales can be for existing products or new services, and to existing customers or new customers. Knowing that higher margins can be possible from new products, a company should simply not focus on selling existing services to current or new customers at high discounts. To grow revenue on a sustained basis, having a revenue target for new services is critical. As a result, the measure will drive the need for new services, thus requiring an internal focus on innovation. Instilling an innovation culture is good for an organization in the long term, rather than simply finding a way to get revenue at any cost for existing services. An effective measurement leads to process-level activity for impacting the business performance positively.

At the activity level, we can track the number of orders processed, number of visits made to the potential customers for new services, marketing or advertising budget, customer reviews of the service, or the branding effectiveness. A clearly determined measurement ensures that the area needing improvement can easily be identified for specific action items.

While implementing the Service Scorecard, a corporation will typically find many of the scorecard measurements that are in place to be disconnected. In other words, the measurements may be there but not utilized in a proactive manner. These measurements are used to describe the history rather than predict the future performance.

TABLE 11.1   Example of Process Measurements

Element	SPIn Measurements	Process Measurements
Growth	Revenue Growth	Revenue from existing customers with existing products
		Revenue from existing customers with new products
		Revenue from new customers with existing products
		Revenue from new customers with new products
		Number of new customers added
Leadership	Employee Recognition Return on Net Assets	Percent of employees recognized by CEO for their exceptional contribution to profitable growth
		Employee surveys
		Profit margin from existing products
		Profit margin from new products
		Net income or EBITDA
Acceleration	Rate of Improvement	Management of performance against aggressive improvement goals
		Number of major improvement projects completed
		Reduction in recurring problems
		Reduction in customer complaints
		Reduction in credits received from suppliers
Collaboration	Reliability of Partners Trust	Quality performance of partners
		On-time performance of partners
		Partnership performance index
		Cost per transaction
		Total person-effort per transaction
		System utilization
Innovation	Employee Ideas (C)	Number of new ideas submitted per employee
	Employee Satisfaction (D)	Number of new ideas implemented per employee
	Employee Involvement (R)	Value of new business generated/cost saving by the new ideas
		Employee satisfaction index
		Annual employee turnover

TABLE 11.1   Example of Process Measurements

Element	SPIn Measurements	Process Measurements
Execution	Accuracy	Process sigma level
	Responsiveness	On-time service delivery
Retention	Customer Loyalty (Equity)	Growth in business with existing customers
	Net Promoter Index	Number of new customers with referrals from existing customers

The Service Scorecard highlights linkages among various measurements and identifies missing measurements. Only when relevant measurements are aggregated can the "big" picture of the business, and major areas for strategic adjustments, be identified. When a new measurement has to be established to complete the Service Scorecard, it may take some effort in committing, planning, and preparing for it, as well as overcoming initial barriers, monitoring it, and creating value.

The Service Performance Index is a weighted sum of all the elements, and hence it is robust in terms of minor variation/error in the measurement of the different elements. One can derive value from the Service Scorecard by monitoring trends, to predict performance, and initiating operational correctives to realize strategic business objectives. When the Service Scorecard is working, customers must be receiving better service, and the organization should be achieving sustained profitable growth.

Address Information Issues

When a good measurement system is being implemented, one of the major challenges is getting good data. Some organizations collect too much irrelevant data, whereas others have too little. Some organizations have no data, whereas others have questionable data. The quality of data is one of the biggest challenges of any organization. Another problem with implementing a measurement system is the analysis and use of the data. Many corporations have identified right measurements, collect good data, and publish several reports.

However, no analysis occurs, no follow-up action takes place, and thus no improvement happens. Eventually the measurement system is erroneously blamed for lack of improvement.

When establishing process measurements, a company should look into ease of collecting and analyzing data. Actually, performing backward analysis—that is, determining the type of analysis to be used and reports to be published to establish data collection methods—is sometimes preferable. Collected data must be utilized, communicated, and acted on to be useful. Otherwise, data collection methods start becoming less reliable, because the people collecting the data realize that no one cares for the data and thus adopt a "why bother?" attitude.

After the data to be collected is identified, the collection methods must make the data collection easier for people. When data collection requires a significant effort, employees start collecting less data. Therefore, the data collection method still must make the actual task easier through analysis and improvement actions.

A company can look at the value proposition of data collection using the following equation:

Data-Value Index = (potential benefit of data collection / cost of data collection) × probability of realizing benefits

For people to be convinced of the value of data collection, the minimal probability of realizing benefits must be .7; thus, the data value index must exceed a value of approximately 1.5.

Establish Goals for Each Measurement

Before establishing goals for individual measurements, the organization must establish an overall strategy for improvement. External benchmarking will determine the market position of the company and the gap, if it exists, with the competition. In addition to external benchmarking, the business opportunity analysis will determine internal opportunities for reducing waste of time or resources. With a combination of the market position and internal opportunity, the organization can establish an overall rate of improvement, which then can be translated into departmental or process improvement goals.

If a company has committed to Six Sigma–like initiatives, which require a lot of improvement quickly, that commitment must be considered in establishing the rate of improvement goals. Normally, companies set goals for their fiscal year by improving the starting baseline by a certain percentage. The new year-end goal then must be broken down into several monthly goals to sustain the improvement over the entire year, instead of expecting a sudden improvement at the end of the year, which rarely happens.

Goals for various measurements are revisited every year for the coming year. One of the challenges is that if a measurement shows significant improvement in one year or two years, then how can managers show improvement in the third year? To overcome such a challenge, the leadership must continually look for new opportunities. If the improvement in a measure of process performance is achieved to the virtual perfection level, the focus must shift to another process and another opportunity and thus a different measure. Unless the business is sustaining profitable growth year after year, and running flawlessly, plenty of opportunities for improvement will exist. After the target performance is realized, processes are monitored at a reduced frequency.

Leverage Technology

Information technology offers a new capability to accelerate execution of business strategies. Today technology is everywhere, and we are so dependent on technology that we cannot believe that the world existed without it at one time. Technology is the sign of progress, giving human beings time to do something *better.* Technology is now quite an integral part of the service industry in spite of the human interactions with customers.

Today's technology makes the data collection process very efficient. Technology can automate the data collection and processing in real time. Data can be easily displayed in various forms in colorful gauges and dashboards. The dashboard or data display methods can help in analyzing and interpreting the information, as well as in making decisions.

Technology sometimes can be a liability as well. Too much dependency on technology renders people helpless. Thus, continual engagement of employees in absorbing the information, internalizing the knowledge, and developing intelligence for being prepared must be maintained to make the best decisions at any given time. In the absence of available technology, the newly gained business intelligence must perpetuate improvement for sustained profitable growth.

Train for Using the Service Scorecard

Most people know what they are supposed to do, about one-third of people know how well they do, and only 1 person in 20 knows how much he has improved in the past 12 months. Thus, implementing the Service Scorecard for driving improvement is a change and must be managed accordingly. One of the main activities in managing change is to provide education. Employees must understand the intent, categories, measurements, and methodology to implement the Service Scorecard. Building harmony among various departments, a common language and common goals for improvement requires teamwork.

Resistance to accepting aggressive goals for improvement may become an issue with some managers. Agreeing to achieve a lot of improvement requires commitment to think and do things differently. As a result, the leadership must commit to risk-taking, recognizing successes, and demanding a lot of improvement by doing things differently, which includes redesigning processes frequently.

Employee training should also include employee incentives for achieving dramatic improvement. Sharing savings and celebrating successes are great ways to inspire bigger successes. Enlisting employee ideas throughout the improvement journey can be accomplished during the training. Some team activities can be developed, and fun activities can be planned for allowing employees to think freely. After all, happy employees keep customers happy and create more value for the company.

Validate and Adjust the Measurements

Measuring a performance level using two different measurement systems will yield two different results. In such an instance, the system is not necessarily presenting two different values. The absolute value of a measurement is less significant than its relevance. Thus, to ensure that the Service Scorecard measurements relate to the actual business performance, an initial validation must be performed. The validation can be through regression analysis between financial outcomes and operational measures, and through identification of areas for improvement. As a result of the validation activities, it is possible to fine-tune various measurements, evaluate goals, overcome barriers, review effectiveness of data collection methods, and calibrate SPIn for its relationship to profit and growth.

After validation of the Service Scorecard, the measurement system can be tested over three months for a dry run before its formal release. All elements of the Service Scorecard must be implemented to maximize its benefits. In the absence of one or two categories, the puzzle will be incomplete and follow-up actions will be misleading. Recognizing that the Service Scorecard categories are interdependent is crucial. Critical aspects of the business must be implemented in synchronization to produce resonant results.

Institutionalize the Service Scorecard

The value of the Service Scorecard must be planned through companywide implementation. The organization may have multiple profit and loss centers and be a large organization, a not-for-profit organization, or simply a complex organization. The Service Scorecard can be institutionalized after its initial validation through the leadership commitment to the performance-driven learning organization, the intellectual contribution of employees, and the fundamental strategy of sustaining profitable growth. If these aspects are traded for short-term benefits such as profit only, the organization will be on a downward spiral of cutting costs and causing organizational instability.

Continual deployment of a measurement system depends on its usefulness to executives and employees. A scorecard cannot be designed only for executives without its empowering application to employees. A well-implemented scorecard will challenge and empower employees to excel and produce significant value for the organization. This requires analyzing the data in real time, communicating the results, interpreting the data, and taking necessary actions with a sense of urgency. Without actions, improvement will not be achieved and benefits will not be shared; thus, stakeholders will not perceive any value being added to the company. Data start to appear questionable when (a) employees feel their effort in data collection is not being valued and (b) executives are not taking actions based on the scorecard indicators. After a group of stakeholders starts losing interest in the measurement system, it starts falling apart, eventually looking like a burden and thus rendering it useless and abandoned.

Service Scorecard performance must be reviewed by department managers for operations and financial performance together, as well as by executives for maintaining the scorecard's strategic suitability to the organization. The departmental review of the performance can be based on the regular reports published by the scorecard owner or by the system. Process owners must review the data daily, department managers must review the data weekly, and executives must review the data monthly. In a departmental review, the management is looking for deviations from the target performance and remedying the causes quickly. The executive review, on the other hand, involves all department managers and is looking for questionable interdepartmental performance and performing remedial actions.

Many times opportunities are identified through the scorecard; however, remedial actions are taken without understanding the causative relationship between the process and its outcomes. Thus, managers and employees must receive training to get to the root cause of the problem quickly. Training in statistical analysis—specifically, statistical thinking—may be very helpful in interpreting the variation or inconsistencies correctly, and thus preventing panicky reactions or overcorrections. The overreaction sometimes is just as responsible as no action for making the scorecard fail.

Renew and Reignite the Organization

Implementation of the Service Scorecard is a strategic initiative that must be implemented with passion for creating value and a high return on investment. After the initial implementation, the stability of the process and/or lack of improvement lead to managerial boredom. The leadership starts diluting the significance of the measurement system and questioning its usefulness. In such an environment, sustaining any initiative over the longer term becomes nearly impossible. Therefore, the Service Scorecard must be revisited every year for organizational renewal and reignited for employee power.

Renewal activities may include new measurements as necessary in some categories of the scorecard, simplification of departmental reporting, modification of criteria for recognition, or simple communication with employees. The corporate performance measurement system must be designed such that it (a) encourages change rather than stagnation, (b) promotes risk-taking rather than process preservation, and (c) challenges for growth rather than leaning for profit. Reigniting employee power requires the CEO or equivalent leader to engage, drive, and demand worthwhile performance from employees. Worth can be assessed in terms of societal recognition, visibility, financial incentives, or excitement of newness. Changing the application of the Service Scorecard is a critical aspect of sustaining its usefulness, its excitement, and its profitable growth.

Take Away

- The most important elements of successful implementation of the Service Scorecard are top leadership commitment and alignment with business goals.
- A model such as the 4P model provides an actionable agenda to the implementation.
- Planning for the Service Scorecard consists of steps including preparing for the implementation, solving information issues, leveraging technology, adjusting measurement and continuous renewal, and institutionalizing the scorecard.

12

Integration of Service Scorecard and Improvement Initiatives

Organizations have multiple initiatives sponsored by key individuals disconnected from the business objectives, because it is difficult to develop synergy at the executive level. You might wonder how corporations can hire the best people at the executive level, yet cannot figure out how to run the business to achieve sustained profitable results. Corporations will have service initiatives, HR initiatives, operations initiatives, measurement initiatives, quality initiatives, Six Sigma initiatives in some departments, or software initiatives, such as Capability Maturity Model (CMMI), Information Technology Infrastructure Library (ITIL), and TickIT as an ISO 9001-like management system. You can see that people in different silos are busy climbing the wall, but cannot get out of silos. It appears that if the business scorecard can be used to harmonize various priorities and initiatives, organizations will be able to achieve better results without so many initiatives.

Each service organization has its industry-specific standards, international standards, improvement methodologies, and large-customer-driven standards to deploy, some for benefits and others for bureaucracy. Instead of the organization gaining efficiency, inefficiency creeps in without warning. After a year or two of deployment, the managers who launched these initiatives get recognized, promoted, and transferred to another department before the initiative produces results. The next manager starts the next initiative to make the change in leadership felt. The cycle of initiatives continues every two or three years, and waste perpetuates. As a result, most of the managers inadvertently avoid implementing a good scorecard.

Implementing a holistic and effective business scorecard requires the commitment at C-level. Either the CEO or the CFO must make a decision to implement a business scorecard that would harmonize resources, synergize improvement initiatives, optimize the performance, and create the culture of ownership. Figure 12.1 shows assimilation of sample methodologies that organizations deploy. As shown in the figure, the leadership is at the core of the organization, creating and implementing a service scorecard to assess overall business performance, establishing process-level metrics, deploying improvement methodology, and ingraining the management system to sustain performance. Some organizations deploy management systems and metrics, including the Balanced Scorecard, but are unable to link them to activities to be performed due to fragmentation and conflicting priorities.

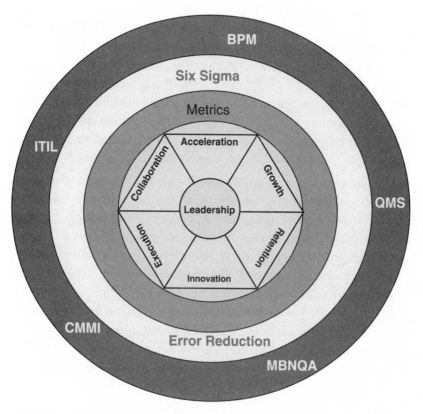

Figure 12.1   The Service Scorecard and methodologies

For example, in the software industry many organizations have been trying to improve the software quality using numerous methodologies. These methodologies are derivatives of some known methodologies from other industries proposed by some organizations dominated by individuals with conflicting interests. One or two large organizations may deploy a methodology due to a relationship with the "individual" and suddenly it is touted as an industry standard. Having been involved with quality and standardization, one can see that ISO 9004-3, Management System for Software, and TickIT, though good systems, have been canned because software groups were still part of a larger organization, so executive-level decisions to adopt the methodologies could not be made. However, one software methodology, CMMI, has survived in the software industry because it has directly touched the software professions. The challenge with CMMI is that it was first developed as an assessment methodology to drive improvements in the software industry. This was difficult to achieve in the U.S. after expensive audits. However, it has became a common practice in the software industry. The CMMI was primarily developed for the software development environment. Now, another methodology, ITIL, is being deployed in the software industry for nondevelopment areas such as delivery and service. Looking from outside, the CMMI stages are stages of the process definition, development, and documentation that should not be fragmented and instead must be deployed in one stroke, process by process. Similarly, the ITIL is promoting the process definition, development, and documentation in the areas excluded by the CMMI. Regardless of the methodology deployment, software products still offer disclaimers instead of warranties demonstrating the effectiveness of the methodologies.

The experience with the software industry quality initiatives and performance teaches us that it is good to reuse existing knowledge developed in matured industries and adapt to the new industries rather than reinventing the wheel. No matter what, every business is a collection of processes that include material or information, method or approach, machine or tools, and people with skills. Service businesses are no exception to this basic tenet of business. Service organizations do have processes too, such as sales, marketing, operations, management, quality, purchasing, and so forth. True, there are exceptions such as having little physical inventory in service businesses, but the differences cannot override the similarities, which are too numerous to ignore. Therefore, leadership in the service businesses may look into the sound service scorecard to drive business processes toward overriding business strategy of sustained profitable growth. And the basic process management methods are not affected by industry. Organizations must attempt to deploy minimum methodologies and measurements to reduce friction among processes and forces required to overcome the friction. Unnecessary forces cause extra work and, thus, waste of resources, affecting profit margins.

Performance Initiatives

Businesses continually discover new performance improvement initiatives. New performance initiatives result from academic research, industry practices, global standardization, and a desire to strive for perfection. Key performance improvement initiatives considered in this chapter include ISO 9001, Process Management for Excellence, Lean thinking, and Six Sigma. Many industry-specific performance improvement initiatives are derived from these key initiatives.

ISO 9001—Quality Management System

Since the release of the ISO 9000 standards in 1987, about nine hundred thousand companies have achieved registration in just over 20 years. The ISO 9000 standards series was easily accepted due to its flexibility in implementation, simplicity of requirements, and, of course, market demand or competitive reasons.

The new ISO 9001:2000 version has considered input from various sources about the effectiveness of the standard in general (Gupta, 2006; ISO 9001:2000 Standards). Focus has shifted from documentation to a process-based model for effectiveness. The emphasis has changed from focusing on procedures to focusing on methods to collect, analyze, and act on data. The requirements have been reorganized and regrouped based on the process model.

According to the process model, any activity, or set of activities, that uses resources to transform inputs to outputs can be considered a process. For a company to effectively implement a quality management system, it needs to identify and manage various processes and their interactions. The output of one process is an input to another process. To implement a companywide quality management system, the company must implement process management at each process (function or subsystem) level.

The success or failure of any initiative in an organization depends on the leadership. The responsibility of "top" management has been more clearly defined and documented in ISO 9001:2000. Following is a list of requirements in the ISO 9001 system that can be applied equally well to a service business:

Quality Management System

- General requirements
- Documentation requirements

Management Responsibility

- Management commitment
- Customer focus
- Quality policy
- Planning
- Responsibility, authority, and communication
- Management review

Resource Management

- General
- Provision of resources
- Human resources

Product Realization

- Planning of product realization
- Customer-related processes
- Design and development
- Purchasing
- Production and service provision
- Control of monitoring and measuring devices

Measurement, analysis, and improvement

- General
- Monitoring and measurement
- Control of nonconforming product
- Analysis of data
- Improvement

To implement a quality or business management system according to the ISO 9001 standards, an organization must establish a business process flow, identify key processes, and establish measures of effectiveness. After the measures of effectiveness have been identified to measure the process performance, organizations must establish performance targets and improvement goals. The results must be periodically reviewed by the management for ensuring success and shared with employees to ensure their involvement. The Service Scorecard can be a good framework for identifying key performance measures.

The 4P Model for Process Excellence

ISO 9001 standards have been evolving from being a documented system to being an effective quality management system. The ISO 9001:2000 version incorporated the process thinking using the PDCA (Plan, Do, Check, Act) model. However, it has been a challenge to implement PDCA due to lack of specificity, and thus practicing the process thinking. Besides, "Check" has been misinterpreted to mean checking or verification against specification limits, leading to the concept of acceptability. When the output turned out to be unacceptable against predefined limits, root cause analysis was conducted using the Ishikawa chart. However, the problems recurred. Data collected was mostly attribute type, which led to limited information, thus providing little information for continuous improvement. As a result, corporations utilized tons of inspection, testing, and verification to ensure quality. We have learned that inspections are marginal at best because they always leave some opportunities for escaping defects or rejecting acceptable output. Most of the rejects occur due to process inputs identified using the root cause analysis.

The 4P (Preparation, Perform, Perfect and Progress) model offers a better implementation of the PDCA concept, or the process thinking. The "Preparation" implies doing homework, or setting up a process to achieve excellence. For example, if a maintenance technician is scheduled to service a process, the technician must prepare for the service by ensuring that all the tools or supplies are collected, or necessary information such as work order is gathered. Preparation is a critical element of managing a process for excellence. Without good preparation, rejects occur, and the target is missed. "Perform" implies doing things well, instead of just doing it. During the Perform phase, any critical process step must be identified, measured, and monitored against specified target values. "Perfect" represents verification of performance against a specified performance target. Initially, aiming for a target performance may appear to be an impossible task; however, the process must be designed through inputs and activities such that the output lands at or close to the target value. This implies purposely centering the process, which keeps the process output away from the lower and upper specification limits, implying lower failures, thus the cost of failures.

Performing to produce output aimed at a target does result in some variation around the target, which is likely to be well within the specification limits, leading to virtually no rejection. However, the process is still analyzed for variation from the target, and adjustments are made to progress toward the target. In case the variation is excessive, detailed root-cause analysis, or a process capability study, may be required to reduce the undesired variation.

Figure 12.2 shows the 4P model representing aspects of process management for achieving excellence. One of the main benefits of implementing the 4P model is the attitude changing from "acceptability" to "excellence." With the current implementation of PDCA, the process output is assessed against limits. "Zero" defect may represent a fully acceptable performance; however, it may not represent excellence. Testing or verifying against limits leads to continual acceptable performance, thus missing the opportunity to achieve excellence. The excellent process output will lead to better profit margins than the acceptable process output due to the reduced cost of appraisals.

4P Model of Process Management

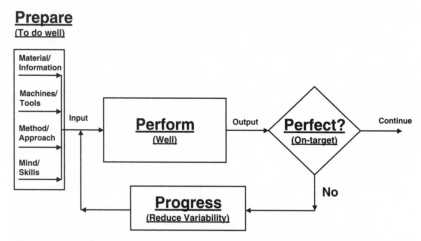

Figure 12.2   Process management for process excellence model

The 4P model has been proven to be helpful in identifying measures of effectiveness at the process level and the system level. Measures of effectiveness can be established at the input, in-process, or output stages of a process. Thus, while deploying the Service Scorecard, the 4P model can be used at the process level to establish meaningful measures for sustaining excellence.

Lean for Streamlining Processes

"Lean" thinking begins with a concept of identifying activities necessary to add value to the intended service, be that serving hamburger at a fast-food restaurant, or serving a patient in an intensive care unit. These value-added activities must be performed efficiently and effectively. Lean is about minimizing waste of material, time, person-hours, skills, or time available for service in order to build a rhythm of service operations, thus minimizing service interruptions.

Creating a rhythm requires balancing demand and supply. To manage demand, customer needs are understood better; and to manage supply, just-in-time deliveries are planned. Typically, demand is difficult to control, and supply can be mandated at some extra cost.

However, the benefits outweigh the cost. Thus, the supply and demand are balanced to some practical level and sustained. There are various tools that are used to map, streamline, improve, balance, and sustain the lean principle to have the shortest, straightest, and simplest flow of information, material, or the patient.

The currently known Lean principles have been derived from the Toyota Production System (TPS), which is a system geared to achieve perfection. Employee participation is critical to the success of lean methodology. As the waste is reduced, employees are redeployed to more value-add activities to support business strategy of sustained profitable growth. Lean was meant to be implemented in "growing" times, rather than in times of cost cutting.

Lean minimizes changes, fluctuations in the flow of material, use of wrong tools or equipment, hidden operations, deviations, and immediate reactions to unacceptable activities or outcomes. Lean emphasizes planned and leveled workload. Lean when combined with Six Sigma overcomes disruptions to implementing Lean and speeds up the Six Sigma implementation. The practical combination of Lean and Six Sigma leads to significant reduction in waste of material, streamlines process, and reduces errors to virtual perfection. In other words, Lean and Six Sigma together create a rhythm that produces virtually perfect service outputs.

Muda is a term for waste in service operations. There are seven types of waste: overproduction, inventory, extra processing steps, motion, defects, waiting, and transportation. In the case of the service industry, overproduction may imply excess capacity or extra services; inventory may imply too many supplies; extra processing means too many reviews or checks; motion implies actual movement of the material or personnel, defects means simply errors or mistakes; waiting time means the time customer waits for receiving services; and transportation waste implies required customer travel time to get the service.

Measuring Lean performance has been a challenge. On the one hand, Lean measures include service rate, customer perceived quality, lead time, internal quality, inventory levels, and delivery performance. In addition to the operational measures, financials are monitored. One controversial measure is the number of employees laid off, which is not a positive and productive measure at all. The Service Scorecard has built-in operational measures such as critical relationships with suppliers for keeping minimal inventory, service cycle time variances, service error rates, and employee participations through Collaboration, Execution, and Innovation elements.

Six Sigma for Perfecting Processes

Six Sigma was developed in the environment of extreme competition in new industries and poor economic conditions, and survival was at stake. Seeds of Six Sigma were sown in 1981 by the leadership of Motorola, when they decided to do something different to continue to stay in business profitably. The original methodology consisted of six steps that easily suit service operations:

1. Define your services.
2. Know your customers and their critical needs.
3. Identify your critical needs to meet customers' critical needs well.
4. Establish a process of doing your work consistently.
5. Error-proof your process and eliminate waste.
6. Measure and analyze your performance. If it's not perfect, improve your process.

The success of the initial implementation of Six Sigma at several companies led experts to package Six Sigma into a robust approach that included the DMAIC (Define, Measure, Analyze, Improve, and Control) methodology, application of methodology through projects, and standardized training programs such as Black Belt or Green Belt, and roles as Champion, and Sponsors.

One of the distinct and visible aspects of a successful Six Sigma campaign has been the visibility of the chief executive. The leader must be the Six Sigma crusader; this role cannot be delegated to a vice-president or subordinate. Six Sigma must be implemented as a business strategy to improve profits and achieve growth with the help of improved capacity and employee-driven innovation.

DMAIC is the most visible aspect of Six Sigma today. Most Six Sigma classes focus on the DMAIC methodology and tools associated with it. The discipline of DMAIC, and rigor in each phase, does yield improvement. However, two important aspects of Six Sigma have been overlooked. The most important aspect of Six Sigma is to dramatically improve performance with a sense of urgency. Dramatic improvement demands doing things in a different way that is very empowering to employees and brings out their creative contributions to produce significant results. The second aspect overlooked during implementation of Six Sigma initiatives is the measures of Six Sigma.

The three commonly used measurements are DPU (defects/errors per unit), DPMO (defects per million opportunities), and Sigma level. The DPU is a unit or the output-level measurement, DPMO is the process-level measurement, and Sigma is a business-level measurement. Sigma level provides a common theme for the organization and requires a lot of improvement to show a positive change. Organizations monitor their error rate and process Sigma levels; however, they are reluctant to measure their corporate Sigma level to assess effectiveness of the Six Sigma initiative. Given the extent of investment in Six Sigma, it is critical to ensure that the Sigma level improves to continually impact the bottom line positively. Otherwise, as the bottom line fluctuates, commitment to Six Sigma varies.

For the leadership to be engaged in the Six Sigma initiative, it must learn about Six Sigma: the understanding of intent of the methodology, key tools associated with various phases of DMAIC, and any organizational bottlenecks. Table 12.1 identifies key Six Sigma tools recommended for executives. The table includes the Business Scorecard to understand the performance of the entire organization to drive the financials instead of the other way around, the financials driving the organization.

Service Scorecard combines the intent of Six Sigma and elements of the Business Scorecard. The intent of Six Sigma to improve quickly is seen through the acceleration element, which is executed through the Rate of Improvement measurement. The Service Performance Index (SPIn) can be used to determine the Sigma level for driving improvement across the corporation. (Gupta, 2006).

TABLE 12.1 Executive Six Sigma tools

Tool/Concept	Description
Employee Recognition	Process of recognizing exceptional improvement activities and employees
Process Thinking	Understanding business is a collection of processes, and the process must be designed for virtual perfection
Business Scorecard	An organizational performance measurement system balanced for growth and profitability
Six Sigma Overview	Understanding of Intent, Impact, DMAIC, and Requirements
Pareto Principle	A graphical tool to prioritize commitments based on added value
Cause and Effect Analysis	Understanding causative relationship between performance and processes
Rate of Improvement	Differences between incremental and dramatic improvement, and commitment to dramatic improvement through innovative thinking

Gupta, *Six Sigma Performance Handbook*, 2004

Service Innovation for New Solutions

Services have become a dominant part of the economy. Similar to the product innovations, service innovations do occur; however, some of them occur at the activity level or at the interaction level. Today, services account for most of the advanced economies in terms of wealth, employment, and creativity. Similar to product innovations, where innovations are tangible, service innovations are more procedural solutions, or activity-based processes. Well-known business model innovations are more applicable to service innovations. Thus, one must look into types of service innovations that can occur. Outcome-based classification of innovation, such as incremental, radical, or breakthrough, tends to present innovation as an art. However, the activity-based classifications of innovation such as fundamental, platform, derivatives, or variations are more prone to developing a repeatable process of innovation. The following represents service-related innovations that can occur:

Innovation Type	=> Service Innovations	=> Innovative Services
Fundamental	Business model innovations	Concepts
Platform	Unique services	Services/solutions
Derivatives	Cost-driven services	Procedures
Variations	Minor changes in service offerings	Activities

For example, consider Dell's model of service innovation. Dell develops a new concept of delivering customized PC solutions. The model creates a new service that grows. Dell introduces derivative services for various products. Where possible, Dell offers various configurations based on customer needs.

Innovation Type	Dell	FedEx
Fundamental	Business model	Business model
Platform	Custom computers	Fast delivery
Derivatives	Other products (printers)	Other locations (Kinko's)
Variations	Custom configurations	Custom packaging/ duration

In both cases, Dell and FedEx start with a fundamental business innovation and create a new platform. In both industries derivatives came about in the form of more products by Dell, or more competitors replicating the platform. Compaq or HP later had a business model similar to Dell and caused Dell to revert to innovation to preserve its competitive edge. Dell has institutionalized a strong idea management system to innovate new solutions.

Figure 12.3 demonstrates how fundamental, platform, derivative, and variation innovations align with the well-known S-curve. All innovations move from fundamental to variation and repeat the cycle. However, variation innovation occurs with a lot of ideas, which eventually lead to another fundamental innovation. So variation innovation feeds into the new fundamental innovations.

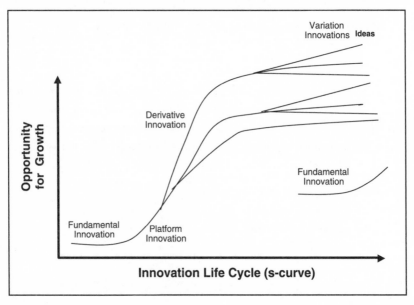

Figure 12.3   Types of innovation

To institutionalize service innovation, an idea management process must be established. Beyond the initial skepticism about the idea management, organizations must commit to engage employees intellectually. Thus, excellence in idea management must become an imperative for developing innovative services. One of the advantages of being in the service business versus the product business is that interaction with the customer is more frequent and intimate. Thus, it is more suitable for variation and derivative type innovations that are somewhat easier and faster to realize compared to platform or fundamental innovations.

Measuring innovation effectively is a daunting task. Various measures have been suggested and attempts have been made to create magical measures of innovation without adequate understanding of the innovation process. An organization attempting to develop measures of innovation initially must clearly state its objectives. Given the presence of a glut of measurements with no use in most organizations, an addition of nice-to-know measures is often perceived as "additional" work and not received well within the organization. The following steps help establish innovation measures:

1. Define the purpose of innovation in the organization.
2. Establish expected innovation deliverables (basic and specific) and their contribution to business performance, including growth and profitability.
3. Determine the measures of success of key innovation deliverables.

The initial measures must be CEO recognition (for inspiring innovation), employee ideas (for involving more brains), and revenue growth (to ensure economic benefits). These three measures are relatively easy to implement, represent elements of the innovation process, have potential to drive improvement in the innovation process, and may help predict the mastery of the innovation in a business. Table 12.2 shows how the three measures of innovation can be aggregated into in a Business Innovation Index (Gupta, www. realinnovation.com, 2007).

TABLE 12.2   Initial Business Innovation Index (BIN)

Measures	Initial Monthly Goal	Monthly Score (% of goal accomplished)	Measure Weight
CEO recognition for significant, unique value creation (CRE)	0.5% of employees per month	= (% of employees ° 100) / .5	30%
Number of innovative ideas per employee (IPE)	1 idea per employee	= (average number of ideas per employee °100) / 1	40%
Revenue growth—% of sales for innovation (MRG)	2.5% of annual sales	= (% revenue growth ° 100) / 2.5	30%
Business Innovation Index (BIN)		= (.3 ° CRE) + (.4 ° IPE) + (.3 ° MRG)	

What would a BIN look like in the real world? Table 12.3 shows an example of a company of 1,000 employees with an annual revenue of $80 million.

TABLE 12.3   Example of BIN Measures

Measures	Company Data	Company Goals	Company Score	Weighted Score
CEO recognition for significantly unique value creation	Number of employees recognized = 2	5 employees recognized per month	$= (2/5) °$ $100 = 40\%$	$= .3 ° 40 =$ 12
Number of innovative ideas per employee	Number of ideas for the month = 40	1,000 ideas per month	$= (40/1000)$ $° 100 = 4\%$	$= .4 ° 4 =$ 1.6
Revenue growth (% of sales for innovation)	$1M for innovative solutions	$2M revenue for new products	$= (1/2) °$ $100 = 50\%$	$= .3 ° 50 =$ 15
Business Innovation Index (BIN)				$= 28.6\%$

This example shows that the BIN is 28.6 percent, which can be improved by involving employees more through soliciting their ideas, encouraging more employees to develop breakthrough innovation solutions, and having a sales team hit the road for higher sales of new products or services. Businesses can establish goals based on their industry position and knowledge to make them meaningful. As the organization advances in the innovation process and matures their innovation process, they can select additional meaningful measures at input, activity, and output levels and revise the Business Innovation Index for its suitability to the organization.

Utilizing Service Scorecard to Synergize Improvement Initiatives

We have observed that many improvement initiatives fade out after initial spike due to lack of effective and direct measures. Leadership monitors improvement initiatives through financial measurements, which most of the time do not have direct bearing on the improvement initiative. Management Systems, Lean, Six Sigma, or

Innovation initiatives do require direct measurements, which must be required for determining the corporate performance. Without an expectation for measurements of the improvement initiatives, sustaining the initiative becomes a challenge.

The Service Scorecard requires acceleration and innovation for driving the improvement and innovation initiatives. The rates of improvement, employee recognition, employee ideas, and revenue growth are excellent measures for monitoring the various improvement initiatives. Figure 12.4 shows how various improvement initiatives for the software industry can be integrated toward achieving business performance. Eventually, a business scorecard is implemented to merge various initiatives, staying focused on the fundamental strategy of achieving sustained profitable growth.

	BIMS Elements	Reference Standards			
				Certifications	$
N **E** **E** **D** **S**	BIMS	ISO 9000 Layout	**I** **S** **O** **9** **0** **0** **0**	**C** **M** **M** **I**	Service Scorecard
	Leadership	MBNQA Category I			
	Operations	Company methodologies			
	Support	ITIL			
	Assessment	CMMI IT Relevance			
	Improvement	Six Sigma/Methodology			
	Excellence	MBNQA/Benchmarking			
	Innovation	Employee Involvement			

Figure 12.4   Relationship between the Service Scorecard and IT improvement initiatives

Take Away

- The Service Scorecard complements other similar initiatives such as ISO 9000, Six Sigma, Lean methods, and 4P methodology.
- The ultimate objective of the scorecard and these methodologies is to provide a solution to customer needs.
- Many initiative fails due to the lack of effective measures.

13

Service Scorecard Validation

To have efficacy, the Service Scorecard must have statistical validation. A rigorous statistical analysis of various scorecard frameworks provides higher confidence to the Service Scorecard users and justifies their commitment to the Service Scorecard. This chapter deals with various academic concepts and simplified statistical analysis. On the other hand, this chapter should not be considered a rigorous review on validation of various frameworks. The validation is divided into the following five sections:

1. Six Sigma Business Scorecard Experience
2. Research Roundtable on Service Measurement
3. Validation of Individual Service Scorecard Elements
4. Validation of Similar Methodologies and Frameworks
5. Validation of the Service Scorecard

Each type of validation represents different facets of the validation process. For example, the Research Roundtable provides a peer-group validation, and validation of individual elements provides confidence in the basic architecture of the scorecard. While validating the Service Scorecard, keep in mind that the individual measures are *not* being validated; rather, the validation is of both the individual elements and the whole framework.

Six Sigma Business Scorecard Experience

The Service Scorecard is an adaptation of the Six Sigma Business Scorecard. The Six Sigma Business Scorecard (SSBS) consists of seven elements and ten measurements, which are aggregated into one index, called the Business Performance Index (BPIn). The index provides an indication of the overall health of the organization and identifies opportunities for improvement. Unique measurements in the Six Sigma Business Scorecard (SSBS) include CEO Recognition of Employees for exceptional performance, Employee Recommendations, and Rate of Improvement. Firms usually do not report these measurements in the public domain. The SSBS has received excellent reviews from corporations and from reviewers. An extensive and rigorous statistical study is underway to validate the SSBS using the publicly available data. Preliminary validation was published in the book *Six Sigma Business Scorecard* by Praveen Gupta.

The BPIn measurements were applied to the Dow 30 companies using the Six Sigma Business Scorecard. The BPIn values vary between 53.6 and 84.3.

Research Roundtable on Service Measurement (Boston)

The (First) Research Roundtable on Service Performance Measurement was held in Waltham, Massachusetts, November 30 and December 1, 2007. Approximately fifty participants representing industries, academia, and consulting firms took part in this highly interactive research roundtable cum workshop. The participation was by invitation only and represented participants from the United States, Norway, Holland, Italy, and Mexico. Both authors were invited and participated on both days.

Key findings of the roundtable are highlighted here. The summary is based on the preliminary report prepared by Dean Spitzer, organizer of the research roundtable. The objective was to gain an understanding of the measurement system (or framework) requirements for service firms, identify key success factors in measuring services, and build a community of like-minded researchers.

1. Identify issues in the measurement of services. The following categories emerged: externally driven financials, difficulty in defining customer value, leaders measuring fragments and not

integrated business performance, distrust of people, "siloed" measurement, negative context of measurement, manufacturing mindset, lack of meaningful benchmarks, and lack of transparent measurement. The common understanding was the deficiency of measurement of intangibles, even though intangibles create value to customers in services.

2. Participants identified the most important measures under the "functional," "cross-functional," and "enterprise" categories. The challenge was to generate cross-functional and enterprise-wide measures.

3. Participants identified critical success factors for a measurement system for services. The factors were grouped into the following categories: user ownership, senior leadership commitment, measures that enable learning, and integrative holistic system design.

4. Eight small groups worked on frameworks that each group presented to the large group.

The roundtable tended to drift into discussion about a general measurement system without bringing specificity to service firms. A few unique characteristics of services, such as intangibility and, hence, value are hard to define, and higher variability and importance of employees were mentioned. However, an in-depth examination of the uniqueness of services was not discussed at length. Some of the specific comments that surfaced during these framework working groups were these:

- Engagement of employees—need to "trust the measures and trust the people."
- Mental models drive, questions and questions drive measurements. We should be asking the right questions in the right frame of mind.
- Need for more exploratory/emergent measurement.
- Measurement in services needs to be as much about learning and improvement as monitoring and control.
- Importance of "perception measurement" in services must be stressed. Current methods are inadequate.
- The employee is the first customer of a services organization.

- Higher variability is present in services. New frameworks need to accept and understand this added variability.

- Measurement must take an ecosystem view; measurement is not systemic; and more "whole system thinking" must be present in performance measurement.

- A measurement framework needs to be presented as a heuristic cycle; it must be developed and refined iteratively. Some participants viewed it as a hologram or a spiral.

Validation of Individual Service Scorecard Elements

This section provides validation of individual elements of the Service Scorecard. Table 13.1 provides a summary of individual elements of the Service Scorecard and related articles or books.

Leadership and Firm Performance

Leadership is considered to impact corporate performance. Frameworks such as the Baldrige award have identified the importance of leadership. The concept of leadership has evolved over time and is not completely understood, however, as mentioned in previous chapters. The complexity and lack of understanding of the leadership concepts make it difficult to prove the causal link between leadership and corporate performance using rigorous statistical techniques.

Current understanding of leadership states that leaders diagnose and understand the "situation" and take appropriate actions by adopting certain types of measures. A study by David A. Waldman and associates (2001) compared the transactional leadership style, or operating within the existing system to strengthen existing systems and structures, and the transformational leadership style, or providing clear vision and motivation to employees. Another study by Emmanuel Ogbonna and Lloyd C. Harris (2000) studied the impact of leadership on the corporate performance and found it is affected by the culture at a particular firm.

TABLE 13.1   Elements of the Service Scorecard

Elements	Books, Articles	Books, Articles
Growth	*Driving Growth through Innovation*, Robert B Tucker, Berrett-Koehler Publishers, San Francisco, 2002	*Ideas Are Free: How the Idea Revolution Is Liberating People and Transforming Organizations*, Alan G Robinson and Dean Schroeder, Berrett-Koehler Publishers, 2006
Leadership	*The Leadership Scorecard*, Jack J. Phillips and Lynn Schmidt, Elsevier Butterworth-Heinemann, Oxford, UK, 2004	
Acceleration	*Accelerate: 20 Practical Lessons to Boost Business Momentum*, Dan Coughlin, Kaplan Business, 2007	*Six Sigma for Transactions and Service*, Goel, P. et. al, McGraw-Hill, New York, 2005
Collaboration	"Measuring the Value of Partnering: How to Use Metrics to Plan, Develop, and Implement Successful Alliances," AMACOM, Chicago, 2004	
Innovation (Employee Engagement)	"The Workforce Scorecard: Managing Human Capital to Execute Strategy," Mark A Huselid, Brian E. Becker and Richard W Beaty, Harvard Business School Press, 2005	*New Service Development: Creating Memorable Experiences*, Eds James A Fitzsimmons and Mona J. Fitzsimmons, Sage Publications, 2000
Execution	*Execution: The Discipline of Getting Things Done*, Larry Bossidy and Ram Charan, Crown Business, 2002	
Retention	"Customer Equity: Building and Managing Relationships As Valuable Assets," Robert C. Blattberg, Gary Getz and Jacquelyn S. Thomas, Harvard Business School Press, 2001	

The Leadership Scorecard by Jack Phillips and Lynn Schmidt (2004) provides a scorecard methodology for leadership. The following seven types of information could be reported showing the results of leadership development:

1. Indicators presenting the volume and reach of the program, for example, number and variety of programs, percent of employee participation, hours of training per employee, investment in leadership program, length of time a leadership position is open, and so on.

2. Satisfaction with the development program

3. Learning from the program

4. Application of the skills and competencies in real job situations

5. Business impacts of applying newly gained skills and knowledge

6. Return on investment

7. Intangible benefits

Acceleration and Execution Impact on Firm Performance

Martell and Carroll (1995) studied more than 100 firms and the impact of goal setting on firm performance. Goal setting was the most consistent predictor of the corporate performance. Terpstra and Rozell (1994) concluded that firms with clear goal-setting processes are more profitable.

The Execution element of the Service Scorecard is about productivity and execution efficiency at a firm's process level and at its system level. Service firms use many methodologies, such as Six Sigma and ISO 9000, based on execution principles. A recent study by Foster in 2007 examines the impact of Six Sigma implementation on the long-term financial and operational outcomes. Annual reports of years 1996–1998 were studied using "content analysis" for Six Sigma mention and possible implementation. A four-year time tag, sufficient for the results of any quality initiative to be accomplished, was used to compare financial and operational data.

In total, 138 firms were used as a sample, including 24 Baldrige firms, 23 ISO firms, and a random control group from the Fortune 500. Six Sigma impacted free cash flow, EBIDTA, and assert turnover of these firms but did not seem to impact return on asset, return on investment, or firm growth. In other words, Six Sigma impacted the productivity of the firm. Firms with low asset turnover tend to get more benefit from Six Sigma as opposed to firms with high asset turnover.

Some data might have been influenced by 9/11 and other events. Also, the study did not differentiate between the methodology commitment level of a tool pusher and a world-class award winner. A new methodology, Six Sigma for Services, used Innovation as a step in the DMAIE methodology, replacing "I" for the Improvement step. The inherent weakness of productivity improvement is balanced by making service innovation part of the methodology.

Collaboration and Firm Performance

Collaboration with service chain partners could take many forms. A service firm could work with many partners or a few partners. Service chain partners could potentially impact customer satisfaction and moment-of-truth experience, market expansion, cost savings, and change in time to market, enhancing overall service chain management and improving learning and knowledge management.

Various aspects of collaboration need to be considered while discussing its impact on firm performance. The first major step is partner selection. How (sourcing or service chain) partner selection affects firm performance is an important research topic. A Harvard Business School study by MacBeth and Ferguson (1994) suggested that a key driver to the decline of U.S. manufacturing firms' competitiveness in the global marketplace is underinvestment in intangibles such as supplier/partner relationships. Various benefits of supplier partnership are mentioned in the literature. These benefits include cost saving, economy of scale, joint development, improved communication, and shared risks. Some of these benefits tend to show only after a period of two to three years.

The importance of collaboration with partners in the service context has been discussed; little, however, has been reported. Kalwani and Narayandas studied the impact of partnership in the manufacturing context. Long-term partnership improves profitability by reducing the discretionary expenses, SG & A, and overhead cost.

Innovation and Firm Performance

Innovation is driven by employee engagement. A study by Mark Huselid, *High Performance Work Practices*, shows a relationship between work practices and company performance. Firms utilizing so-called "high-performance work practices" tend to have lower employee turnover and higher overall productivity. This study's authors concluded that when a one-third improvement in high-performance work practices occurs (over the average firm in a particular sector), the shareholder value of the firm would increase by about 10 percent to 15 percent. Specifically, the impact of one standard deviation in high-performance work practices affects the corporate performance in the following ways: (a) approximately $27,000 increase in sales/revenue, (b) approximately $18,000 increase in market value, and (c) $3,800 increase in profit per employee.

High-performance work practices also act as a differentiating strategy providing a competitive advantage. A Tower Perrin study quantified the impact of employee engagement on firm performance. The finding indicated that a 5 percent total increase in employee engagement results in a 0.7 percent increase in operating margin. Hewitt conducted a longitudinal study over a period of five years; it demonstrated a causal link between employee engagement and the financial performance of a firm.

A recent article on Human Sigma in the Harvard Business Review claims to measure the effectiveness of the employee-customer encounter. The study occurred at service firms and shows the importance of engaged employees and engaged customers. Service firms with engaged employees and (emotionally) engaged customers tend to be 3.4 times more effective compared with the baseline group. A methodology to calculate this score is provided in the study.

Human Sigma scores are broadly distributed in six categories. For example, reduced turnover itself saves costs. Some of the costs related to turnover are the recruitment/selection cost, initial training/orientation cost, on-the-job learning and development cost, lost productivity cost, and job exit cost. The total of these costs could be around 50 percent of the total per-year salary cost (for a fast-food restaurant, frontline employee) or 150 percent to 200 percent of the total per-year salary cost (for a specialist or an engineer/manager).

Customer Retention and Firm Performance

Many studies indicate the impact of customer loyalty measurements on firm performance. Only a few of the key studies are examined here. Additional support for ACSI measurement is presented in other sections.

A recent academic study by Keiningham (2007) compared the Net Promoters Index to other benchmarks such as ACSI. The Net Promoters Index was adopted by a few firms and is touted to be the only number needed to manage firm growth. The study refutes this assertion using thorough analyses.

Based on a thorough literature review, the Net Promoters Index has not been rigorously validated using statistical tools. The index does have its usefulness, as indicated by its word-of-mouth popularity. In addition, the index is related to the growth seen in the previous time period. The index is based on a "recommend likelihood" survey. The study by Keiningham (2007) refutes two assertions, namely that the Net Promoters Index is superior to other indices, and that ACSI and growth are unrelated.

Eventually, customer loyalty, as measured by overall satisfaction and the likelihood to choose again, recommend, and purchase again, should predict the corporate performance. One of these elements alone will not be sufficient to predict the corporate performance.

Growth and Firm Performance

Impacts of innovation have been extensively studied in the manufacturing context. However, very little information is available on the impact of service innovation on firm performance. The reasons could be manifold. First, the difference between product innovation and process innovation is not so distinct. Services include the intangible component and involvement of the human element. The nature of service innovation is under-researched and is not well understood. Innovation does take place in services, however, and innovation does drive the growth of the firm.

A study by Daniel Prajogo (2006) shows no significant difference between product and process innovation in product and service firms. One hundred ninety-four managers (92 managers from service firms) from product and service contexts were surveyed. Process innovation showed a stronger relationship with corporate performance (defined as sales growth, market share, and profitability) for the product firm. Four measures of innovation were used: the number of innovations, the speed of innovation, the level of innovativeness (that is, novelty, newness), and the level of strategic aggressiveness in adopting or generating innovation (including being "first" in the market).

The impact of innovation on corporate innovation is supported from the study. Because most service innovations are incremental and easily copied by the competitors, the competitive advantage time span is relatively short. Therefore, the impact on corporate performance may not be as prominent as in the manufacturing sector, where one could protect innovation using intellectual property protection rights.

Validation of Similar Methodologies and Frameworks

In this section, we discuss the validation of existing methodologies. Only a select few methodologies that are similar in intent are discussed.

Malcolm Baldrige National Quality Award Framework Validation

The Malcolm Baldrige National Quality Award includes five categories: manufacturing, service, small business, healthcare, and education. The evaluation process consists of four stages: (1) independent review, (2) consensus review, (3) site visit review, and (4) final selection step of award winners. The criteria used to judge each application consist of the organization's excellence in these seven categories: (1) leadership, (2) strategic planning, (3) customer and market focus, (4) measurement, analysis, and knowledge management, (5) human resources focus, (6) process management, and (7) results. Each applicant receives approximately 200 hours of review, and those who proceed to stage 3, the site review, receive significantly more feedback. Each applicant also receives a detailed feedback report, analyzing the strengths and opportunities of the organization in comparison to those of its competitors.

We will discuss three types of studies in this regard. Some evidence on the validation is anecdotal and some evidence is statistical. Whether the Baldrige award codifies the principles of quality management (Garvin) or not (Cosby and Deming) is debated. Weights assigned in this approach are consensus opinions of experts. The first study was a stock market performance study. The second study uses Structural Equation Modeling to validate the framework by Wilson and Collier and Flynn and Saladin. The third set of studies is sector-specific for the automotive and healthcare sectors. Data from 220 hospitals were used to validate the criteria. Since its inception in 1988, the Baldrige National Quality Award framework has been modified twice, in 1992 and 1997.

The foundation of the framework has remained the same, but weights were reassigned and categories were redefined and renamed. From 1988 to 2007, 72 awards have been given, including two-time recipients such as the Ritz-Carlton. Flynn and Saladin used the 1997 framework, but Wilson and Collier used the 1992 framework of the award.

The current framework has two triads. The first triad includes leadership, strategic planning, and customer focus; and the second triad includes process management, HR development, and measurement and business results. Both of these triads are supported by information and analysis. Key findings of these two studies are presented here. Leadership is the most important driver of the performance. Process management is twice as important in predicting customer satisfaction and focus as it is in predicting financial performance.

The previously mentioned studies focus mostly on the manufacturing context and specifically on the automotive sector. In one study, plant managers at the business unity level were surveyed. Causal models explain around 46 percent of the variance in customer satisfaction and approximately 39 percent of the variance in financial performance. The only validation study by Meyer and Collier concerning services relates to healthcare services. The framework was adapted to the healthcare context and is very specific to the healthcare sector. In this case, the role of leadership directly impacted financial performance.

The stock market study comparing Baldrige winners with the S&P 500 firms provided important information regarding the performance of these firms. Baldrige winners outperformed the S&P 500 by more than 2.6 to 1. The study was done by the Commerce Department's National Institute of Standards and Technology (NIST). The study was abandoned later for unexplained reasons.

ACSI and Firm Performance

The American Customer Satisfaction Index (ACSI) measures customer satisfaction. The index measures the overall customer satisfaction using survey measures by assessing an overall rating of satisfaction, measuring the degree to which performance falls short of or exceeds the expectation, and measuring the rating relative to the ideal service. The ACSI is considered a measure of the quality of economic output nationwide. The ACSI uses a 100-point scale to determine the customer satisfaction for more than 200 companies and federal and local agencies. The ACSI is a rating that is received quarterly. The ACSI has 43 categories that range from airlines to wireless telephone services to "all others," including smaller to mid-size firms.

The ACSI is supposed to predict firm performance in the following period, because customer satisfaction affects the firm performance. Customers are considered assets of the firm, and any change in satisfaction levels directly affects the sales and profit of the firm. It does not appear that any independent validation of the ACSI framework has been performed. All the information that proves the existence of the correlation is part of the ACSI group, and the Michigan School of Business conducts a majority of the research. Data are provided by ACSI-related organizations.

An MI School of Business study showed correlation between the ACSI score and corporate earnings. A change in ACSI score indicates a change in earnings in the following period. The ACSI score correlates with the consumer spending growth. Firms with higher ACSI scores also have higher Market Value Added to their shareholders than those with lower ACSI scores (www.theacsi.org). About one-third of spending growth can be explained with the ACSI, however. Other factors also contribute to spending growth. Existing research by Fornell and Stephan (2002), covering the years 1995 to 2001, indicates that the ACSI explains 38 percent of spending growth.

Service Profit Chain and Firm Performance

The Service Profit Chain framework links employee satisfaction with customer satisfaction. Customer satisfaction drives the profit of the service firm. The central element of the framework is the "satisfaction mirror" that reflects the employee satisfaction/dissatisfaction into the mirror. Employee dissatisfaction leads to poor service, because dissatisfaction reflects in the transaction with customers. The framework has multiple interrelated linkages. The framework as a whole has not been rigorously tested in one organization over a long period thus far. An article by Silvestro and Cross (2000) claimed that the set of studies used to validate the Service Profit Chain took place at separate organizations. The framework might be explaining some intuitive linkages. Gallup utilizes an adaptation of this framework called the Gallup Path to Business Performance.

Another example mentioned to claim the validity of this framework is the case of Sears, Roebuck and Co. Sears studied the employee-customer linkage. The impact of the Service Profit Chain is complicated by other factors such as leadership, appropriate culture, and business environment. Recent development at Sears with news of a loss in consecutive quarters in the year 2007 is such an example. ACNielsen is another example of the proof of this framework. Employee satisfaction improved, leading to improved return on equity and income. The success is considered to be an outcome of the application of this framework.

ServQual and Firm Performance

The basic assumption of the ServQual model is that customers can evaluate the quality of service by comparing their expectations to the perception of the service delivered. Customers have preconceived notions of the expectation. The model is generic, however, and is considered to be much more valuable to services with low customer contact, low customization, and a lower need for professional judgment. The framework is also suitable for a competitive market where customers have formed expectations. In a highly professional situation such as medical and legal services, customers will not have an idea about the true quality of services even after the service is rendered. Some of the tangible factors could be used as proxy to the quality of service.

The ServQual model has been applied in various situations. The model is a valuable tool to diagnose gaps in customer-centric quality in a competitive market.

Balanced Scorecard and Firm Performance

The first-generation Balanced Scorecard did not incorporate causality into the scorecard. The second-generation Balanced Scorecard incorporates causality elements and is called the "strategy linkage model." The third-generation Balanced Scorecard incorporates "destination statements" in helping in the goal-setting process.

The Balanced Scorecard approach is very popular with U.S. firms and much less popular in many other parts of the world. For example, Tableau de Bord, which literally means "Dashboard" and has been used for many decades, is much more popular with French firms. Various reasons, including management styles and social dynamics, are provided to explain this phenomenon. The Balanced Scorecard works exclusively and is based on a top-down performance management approach.

Hanne Nerreklit (2000) suggested that reasoning among different perspectives of the Balanced Scorecard is circular and no cause-and-effect relationship exists. The different perspectives are interdependent and have a logical relationship, however. Zahirul Hoque and Wendy James studied 66 Australian manufacturing firms. The study suggests that a greater use of the Balanced Scorecard is associated with higher firm performance for these manufacturing firms.

EFQM and Firm Performance

The EFQM Excellence Award is Europe's most prestigious award for organizational excellence. EFQM and has been awarded to Europe's best-performing companies and not-for-profit organizations since 1992. The award is the highest form of recognition an organization can receive, because it comes from its own peers. Top executives from leading businesses and public service organizations study and visit the candidates and, after a grueling examination, select the few outstanding achievers. The assessment is divided into two major categories: enablers (500 points) and results (500 points). Leadership drives policy and strategy, partnership focus, people, and resource and process focus, which, in turn, drive business results. Studies have pointed out the complexity in the EFQM model and simplifications have been suggested.

CMMI and Firm Performance

Capability maturity models provide a structured approach for IT firms to achieve process and project management excellence. The capability maturity model–based improvements are reported online at the Web site http://www.sei.cmu.edu/cmmi/results.html. A sample of 25 organizations is available so far. Median values are as follows: cost, 20 percent; productivity, 62 percent; quality, 50 percent; customer satisfaction, 14 percent; and return on investment, 4.7:1. Results have been qualified by the statement that these results many not be repeatable at other organizations.

Validation of the Service Scorecard

This section sets a long-term agenda for a rigorous validation of the Service Scorecard.

Agenda for the Validation of the Integrated Service Scorecard Framework

The validation of a framework has different meanings for a practitioner and for an academician. A practitioner needs an easy-to-use framework that can be applied to real-life situations. An academician needs to validate the framework using rigorous statistical techniques.

Real-world validation includes finding service firms that are implementing elements of the Service Scorecard, directly or indirectly. Some of these firms are discussed in Chapter 14, "Best Practices." Finding sample service corporations that have sustaining profitable growth is important; then identifying key success factors for the implementation of the Service Scorecard is needed. Collecting measurements and corporate performance information from these firms is the next step.

The Service Performance Index (SPIn), values should be calculated for top performers in the service sector. Some measurements incorporated in the Service Scorecard are not readily available; in that case, SPIn values cannot be calculated. SPIn measures should include only causal factors and should not include any financial measures.

Validation in academic work is much more rigorous than a simple depiction of the relationship shown in Figure 13.1. Validation requires in-depth and advanced statistical techniques. Rigorous examination includes collecting extensive data from service firms using a valid survey instrument. The survey results are then analyzed for construct validity and internal consistency.

The next step is to perform a path analysis and exploratory factor analysis. A measurement model and valid constructs are developed in this process. The measurement model will validate the general theory. The specific direction of causality will also be confirmed. A two-step structural equation approach will be used to analyze these data, which will provide information about the critical few drivers and the relative importance/weight of individual elements.

This chapter does not provide statistical validation of the Service Scorecard. Differences abound based on the business context. For example, a service firm focused on service transaction and cost will have different measurements than a service firm focusing on customer experience.

Similarly, transaction-driven firms will find Execution and Acceleration and Collaboration drivers to be more important. Customer (intimacy) experience-driven service firms will find employee Innovation, customer Retention, and Growth drivers to be more important.

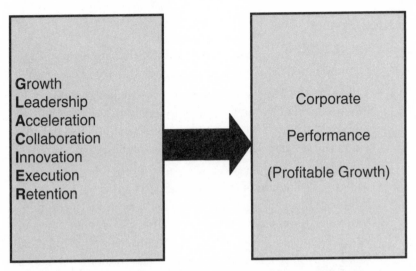

Figure 13.1 Causal relationship between Service Scorecard and corporate performance

A detailed step-by-step approach has, however, been set in motion to validate the scorecard. Individual element validation, peer expert validation at the research roundtable, and Six Sigma Business Scorecard validation provide initial confidence and important steps in this direction. Contextual factors such as the size of the service firm, variety of services provided, and market position of the service firm might impact the way the Service Scorecard is implemented.

Based on the preceding analysis, the service firms that achieve profitable growth have the following elements in common:

- Leadership encourages and rewards employee engagement. Leadership is the central driver for corporate performance.
- The firm is focused on treating its employees well and at the same time is focused on customer intimacy.
- The firm selects its partners carefully.
- The firm has focused on service innovation for growth.
- Managers are focused on accelerating the performance and the execution of the strategy.

Take Away

- Validation of the Service Scorecard is critical to its acceptance and implementation in firms throughout the service sector.

- Validating the Service Scorecard proves challenging due to the inherent difficulty in valuating intangibles. In addition, the higher variability and greater importance of employees inherent in the services sector makes validation difficult (but not impossible).

- Although validation of the Service Scorecard is not provided in this chapter, a game plan for doing so is provided. In addition, a thorough examination of research attempts at validating individual elements of the Service Scorecard, as well as validation that has been performed on similar measurement systems, are delineated.

14

Best Practices

The Service Scorecard offers a holistic framework for measuring service operations performance and provides leading indicators for ensuring sustained profitable growth. With this being a new framework, one must wonder if there are companies that have implemented the Service Scorecard. Had it been implemented fully, it would not be an innovative framework for corporate performance. However, there are companies that have implemented aspects of the Service Scorecard well and realized benefits. Imagine if a company implemented best practices throughout its operations. An aggregate of best practices will have a cumulative effect and accelerate improvement, thus raising the bar of business performance.

One of the distinctive features of the Service Scorecard is that it considers the organization as a system. The performance of this system is managed for profitable growth. Profit and growth are sometimes considered conflicting strategies when running a business. However, experience shows that successful companies do manage to sustain profitable growth. Such companies grow profitably over a long period. For example, Southwest Airlines has a history of growing profitably for a long time. Procter & Gamble within the manufacturing industry does the same. So there exists a need for implementation of the Service Scorecard to spur profitable growth similar to that of Southwest or Procter & Gamble. To realize this profitable growth, a concurrent strategy for growth continuance must be executed throughout the corporation for achieving profitable growth quarter after quarter.

To identify best practices, Fortune's most admired companies were examined, and a sample of companies known for their leadership practices was selected. The following sections provide the utility of

various elements of the Service Scorecard. Again, the Service Scorecard elements are described in the order of the letters in the GLAC-
IER acronym.

Growth

International Business Machines (IBM)

IBM is known for its mainframe (personal) computers and related
products. In the early 1990s, its revenue was hovering around the low
$60 billion range, a decline from 1990 of $69 billion. The breakdown
of its revenue was among Hardware (51 percent), Software (17 percent), Services (14 percent), Maintenance (12 percent), and Rentals
and Financing (6 percent).

In 2006, the IBM revenue was over $91 billion, which was distrib-
uted among Services (52 percent), Hardware (25 percent), Software
(20 percent), and Financing (3 percent). The Maintenance segment
has disappeared from IBM's portfolio, and the Services segment has
increased from 14 percent to 52 percent. Of course, the nature of the
Services business has changed as well, from IT services alone to business consulting services. The Services segment has grown by 270 percent, while the Hardware segment has reduced by over 50 percent.
This is a fundamental change in IBM's business model. Besides, the
shift in focus from hardware to service is also a fair representation of
the growth of the service sector in general.

Louis Gerstner is credited for changing IBM's strategic direction
from manufacturing to service. Instead of dividing IBM into Baby
Blues (similar to Baby Bells in the telecommunications industry), Gerstner identified IT and Business Services as the growth opportunities
for IBM. Today, Global Services is a crucial component of IBM solutions to its clients. Global Services include technology services and
business services. The technology services segment includes infrastructure and value through IBM's global scale, automation, and standardization. The Business Services segment includes professional
services for delivering business value and innovation in addition to
consulting integration and application management services.

eBay

eBay has become an innovative platform to do business and make money. eBay has started a different brand of entrepreneurship to build communities inspired by opportunity. Millions of people visit eBay to trade their antique, excess, and undesired items through auction for bidding. According to the eBay Web site, "On any given day, there are millions of items available through auction-style and fixed-price trading. With millions of buyers and sellers worldwide, eBay offers localized sites in the following markets."

In the third quarter of 1997, eBay reported revenue of $1.5 million, and eight years later the third-quarter revenue increased to $1.10 billion. eBay accomplished this growth through new verticals in countries, languages, or industries, and acquisitions of such companies as PayPal and Skype. Currently, eBay has 233.4 million registered users (up from 192.9 million a year earlier) and 82.9 million active users (up from 75.4 million a year earlier).

Besides eBay, there are several service companies, including Starbucks, Southwest Airlines, Amazon.com, Expedia, Apple, and Google, that have achieved significant growth over the years.

Leadership

Q Interactive

Q Interactive, founded in 1995, is an online marketing services provider for advertisers and publishers. Every year, more than 1,500 leading brands rely on Q Interactive to generate quality results. Q Interactive operates an extensive advertising network with more than 1,000 high-traffic partner sites, including Weather.com and About.com, as well as its own savings and shopping sites, including CoolSavings.com. Q Interactive services include online lead generation and e-mail. Q Interactive employs about 200 employees with revenue of about $150 million and CAGR of 35 percent in 2007.

Q Interactive contacts 10 to 15 million consumers in a month who want to hear from advertisers in the pharmaceutical, retail, finance, and direct marketing industries. Q Interactive sends about 30 to 40 million e-mails everyday.

Matt Wise, CEO of Q Interactive, believes in employee owner-ship and accountability for performance. During an interview regard-ing the reward system, Wise said that he strongly believes in CEO awards, and the criteria for rewards include continual interaction with employees and recognition for employee excellence and superior per-formance.

The Q Interactive Rewards and Recognition program serves to highlight the excellence that exists in all areas and job functions across the company. The recognition program consists of three awards:

1. On-the-spot recognition
2. Monthly or quarterly recognition
3. Annual corporate recognition

The on-the-spot recognition is given at the time of achievement. The recognition includes a note on the company letterhead and a small reward in terms of movie tickets, lunches, or team outings. Monthly or quarterly awards include the Cheers for Peers award, Q Rock, and Service Recognition. The Cheers for Peers awards recog-nize outstanding achievement in a given quarter for invaluable contri-butions with a significant impact on the company. Winners are announced in the quarterly company meeting and presented with a gift card. The Q Rock award is a foam rock passed around for recog-nizing individual contribution for two weeks. The Service Recognition rewards employee dedication and commitment to Q Interactive. The Annual Corporate Recognition includes Manager of the Year and Em-ployee of the Year awards. The CEO announces these awards at the annual company meeting or the holiday party.

In most of these awards, the CEO is involved in presenting the award in person, or recognizing the individual through a card, or even participating in selecting the award winners. The annual awards may appear to be formal CEO awards, but the other awards also include the CEO's participation. The Q Interactive approach to recognizing employees for superior performance and contribution is facilitated by the CEO's approach to interacting with employees, as well as by for-mal recognition at annual meetings.

Southwest Airlines

At Southwest people are recognized continually, including through the awarding of the Star of the Month award to many employees for extraordinary things. Stars of the Month meet with the chief executive officer. Interestingly, the extraordinary acts do not necessarily have to do with Southwest Airlines; instead, recognition could be for setting examples of superior service in the community. The employees are also featured in Southwest Airlines' *Spirit* magazine. Southwest Airlines has won five consecutive "Triple Crowns" distinctions, in the years 1992, 1993, 1994, 1995, and 1996, for the best performance in areas of baggage handling, fewest customer complaints, and best on-time performance.

Southwest Airlines provides consistent return on equity to its shareholders by following a strategy of point-to-point service, one type of aircraft, using secondary airports, faster turnaround, and providing no-frills services. Southwest Airlines has provided superior return on equity in its 36 years of history by following this strategy. In the years 2006 and 2005, Southwest provided average returns on stockholders' equity of 7.6 percent and 7.9 percent, respectively.

Another service firm that has achieved consistent return on equity is Berkshire Hathaway.

Acceleration

Infosys Technologies

Seven people established Infosys in 1981 with about $250 as seed capital. Today the company has offices in dozens of countries and revenue of about $5 billion, and it has earned a long list of awards worldwide. Infosys provides IT-related business solutions, including business and technology consulting, custom software development, and business process outsourcing.

To achieve sustained profitable growth, the Infosys leadership has defined the corporate vision, mission, and values. Its vision implies being a globally respected corporation in providing business solutions. Its mission is to achieve its objectives in an environment of fairness, honesty, and courtesy. The values include customer delight, leadership by example, integrity and transparency, fairness, and pursuit of excellence. To achieve excellence, Infosys leadership constantly strives to improve operations, teams, and solutions.

To achieve excellence in execution, the corporate strategy is flowed down to Unit Business Plans, where strategy is articulated in multiple forums such as the Board meeting, Annual Strategy meeting, Analyst meeting, and so on, as well as internal discussions. The draft corporate strategy map is developed and discussed with internal and external boards, as well as unit heads, for their approval. The corporate strategy map is published to the Board, Unit Leadership, Client Facing Group, Delivery, and Clients.

The corporate strategy map is translated into a business unit strategy map and a unit business plan. Each business unit develops its scorecard ensuring functional alignment and coverage leading to goals. Each unit head and senior managers then own a goal sheet that is reviewed in operations and business review, as well as the performance assessment.

Business objectives exist for values and ethics, financial performance, client and market focus, operational excellence, talent management, and scale infrastructure. The business objectives are flowed down into Infosys performance measures and goals. For example, objectives specific to operational excellence include new business ideas, intellectual property, customer processes, internal collaboration, quality and productivity, resource utilization, operational risks, and scalability.

American Express

American Express focused on capability improvement through leadership development, Six Sigma methodology, and cost reduction. Some of the strong improvements were achieved within risk management, information management, and online capabilities.

To accelerate performance, American Express has focused on driving organic growth and has established targets for increasing shareholders' value. The long-term financial targets are clearly spelled out here:

- Earnings per share growth of 12 percent to 15 percent
- Revenue growth of at least 8 percent
- Return on average equity (ROE) of 33 percent to 36 percent

To achieve sustained performance, group and team incentives were created, where the performance is assessed against the employee's potential rather then manipulated, negotiated targets. The CEO led the improvement initiative to communicate the message and its significance. Measures consisting of customer and employee metrics, along with the processes of goal setting, tracking, reporting, and evaluations, are implemented throughout the organization.

The Six Sigma journey was started in 1998 with a small group of Black Belts, and eventually it became part of the company's global reengineering initiative. Savings of more than $1 billion were attributed to the reengineering initiative in 2004, resulting primarily from the Six Sigma projects. To perpetuate performance improvement, Ken Chenault, CEO, had focused on leadership development, aiming to become one of the most successful and admired financial and business performance companies. The leadership development initiative included direct interaction with the CEO to understand the culture and leadership requirements and to raise issues in a no-holds-barred discussion.

Collaboration

Microsoft

Microsoft has a founding culture of collaboration in meeting customer needs and creating value. The first CP/M operating system that Microsoft sold to IBM was built on Seattle Computer Products 86-DOS, which later became MS-DOS. When the time came to overcome competitive pressures, Microsoft offered very friendly terms to its partners and offered competitive products. Similarly today, Microsoft offers the advantages of new market opportunities, resources to refine business strategies, and innovative solutions development. Microsoft collaborates to build business through partners by allowing them to use Microsoft products and platforms virtually free, developing their competencies, and exploiting partners' customer relationships. Interestingly, Microsoft has built a network of about 400,000 small to large partners who are expected to make more money with Microsoft products then by selling competitive products.

Microsoft generates revenue by developing, manufacturing, licensing, and supporting its various software product for customers, and by providing consulting and support services for integrators and developers. Microsoft develops new products delivering breakthrough innovation and high-value solutions. Creating new opportunities for partners and responding to partners' needs are fundamental strategies to support growth. Most of the manufacturing activities are contracted to third parties for producing Xbox, Zune, packaged products, and other hardware.

In a keynote address at the 2007 Consumer Electronics Show, Microsoft's co-founder Bill Gates said that building relationships with customers is critical to grow the business. Microsoft develops customer relationships through its partnership networks. Microsoft supports its partners in improving their financials (profit, revenue, and growth); in speeding up sales, delivery, and customer growth; and in developing systems for improving capacity utilization, billing, and execution throughout the service cycle.

Wal-Mart

Wal-Mart reported revenue of about $92 billion for the last quarter in July 2007, with an income of $3.11 billion or 3.3 percent, and with expected annualized sales of over $350 billion. Wal-Mart has mastered supply-chain management and is considered a pioneer in this field. By its very nature, supply-chain management involves collaboration with suppliers. Corporations doing business with Wal-Mart must be the best, the most efficient, and the most time-sensitive in order fulfillment to become a part of Wal-Mart's supply chain. Interestingly, Wal-Mart has also been named the best retailer with which to do business.

Analysis of Wal-Mart's performance between 1996 and 2006 shows that sales rose by 250 percent and cost of goods sold rose by about 242 percent, but the inventory increased by only 100 percent. Inventory management is Wal-Mart's mantra to sustain profitable growth. The inventory turns increased from 4.4 to 7.5 during this 11-year period. For Wal-Mart, inventory growth at a rate less than that of net sales is a key performance measure. When reviewing quarterly performance for investors, President and CEO Lee Scott said, "Our management is focused on inventory improvements, delivering quality products at low prices, and store execution at the highest standards."

To achieve inventory improvements, Wal-Mart continually looks for ways to eliminate disconnects and inefficiencies by having better sourcing, technology upgrades, and inventory optimization through virtually real-time reporting. Today, Wal-Mart sets standards for supply-chain automation. When collaborating with suppliers, Wal-Mart has clear expectations, such as the lowest price, that are nonnegotiable.

To help its suppliers, Wal-Mart has developed a Retail Link for accessing store-by-store inventory levels, point-of-sales data, and trends to stay tuned to optimally manage their product shipments. Suppliers must learn to use the Retail Link and its analytics. To increase direct communication with its suppliers, Wal-Mart deals directly with them without using third-party sales representatives. To keep the price low, Wal-Mart goes to unbranded producers, upgrades their capability, oversees their factories, and then depends on the Wal-Mart brand.

Still, Wal-Mart deals with branded products like Procter & Gamble, Mattel, and Levi's. Due to its sheer size, Wal-Mart becomes one of the key customers of its strategic suppliers. Such top suppliers are part of the long-term strategic discussions. Wal-Mart views its business description as a global retailer committed to improving the standard of living for its customers by providing quality merchandise at everyday low prices. Wal-Mart has utilized both the IT infrastructure as its key competitive advantage and collaborative planning to reduce the cost of carrying inventory for its suppliers and Wal-Mart, thus improving inventory turns, throughput, and income.

Innovation

Starbucks

Starbucks is one of the most successful and admired firms. In slightly over 30 years, it has grown from 1 shop to about 101,000 shops. The company is growing beyond coffee into a social meeting place with the convenience of music, drinks, snacks, and even a lunch menu. Starbucks has changed the taste of coffee into a wholesome experience of relaxing while sipping coffee. It is amazing how many people wake up in the morning on the weekend and head to the nearest Starbucks for their cup of coffee. One can judge from the queue for fresh coffee that it has become a "Starbucks lifestyle" for some, while it is the Starbucks experience for others. All of this has occurred by the transformation of an inexpensive cup of coffee into a high-end drink.

The Starbucks success began with the innovative thinking of challenging the current paradigm of buying a cup of coffee into finding a nearest Starbucks to meet people for social, business, or intellectual discussion. Thus, the innovation is not merely in the coffee but in its commercialization or usage. Another innovation is in the location of its stores. Sometimes they are found in clusters, and sometimes they are in every corner of downtowns or neighborhood locations. This location innovation makes Starbucks ubiquitous, allowing it to capture market share quickly. Other innovations include partnering with Barnes & Noble or other dominant bookstores to attract educated buyers, or with Pepsi-Cola for bottled drinks, or with Breyer's for coffee ice cream, or with Hyatt to have a footprint in hotels.

Starbucks's innovation in store design is being imitated by other coffee brands, that is, the European ambience, warm colors, and amenities such as furniture, Internet access, and even music. The driving force behind Starbucks innovations is its mission statement: "Develop enthusiastically satisfied customers all of the time." Enthusiastically satisfying customers implies continual innovation. Starbucks's commitment to innovation is evident in the trials of its new products or ideas being tested in some stores. Besides, the company is always looking for ways to have customers spend more money in its stores, whether through prepaid credit cards or by preordering the coffee.

Starbucks is one of the top innovators for its many innovations in all aspects of its business. Starbucks innovations occur in products, the supply chain, marketing, store designs and locations, food services, specialty stores, niche products, entertainment, or even the Starbucks card that can be reloaded. Starbucks is partnering with Pepsi for its vending and bottom line, resulting in CAGR of over 20 percent.

Federal Express (FedEx)

From a term paper in 1965 at Yale University leading to the founding of Federal Express in 1971, Fredrick Smith has raised customer expectations for delivery of mail and packages. FedEx provides supply-chain, transportation, and business and related information services through operating companies. To achieve its business objectives, FedEx has established its values addressing people, service, innovation, integrity, responsibility, and loyalty. FedEx has incorporated innovation from its early years. FedEx's commitment to innovation is described in its manifesto: "We invent and inspire the services and technologies that improve the way we work and live."

From 14 small aircraft and 186 packages to 25 cities on its founding day, to about 5.6 million packages daily to 220 countries, 280,000 employees, about 700 aircrafts, 75,000 motorized vehicles, and becoming one of the most admired companies, these achievements represent the power of FedEx innovations. Revenue for fiscal year 2007 reached over $35 billion, up from $1 billion in revenue in 1983.

FedEx innovated the application of information technology in logistics. Innovation at FedEx implies listening and anticipating customer needs and developing innovative solutions. This philosophy of innovation is fostered with a culture of openness, where people are empowered to present new ideas and serve customers and their community. The IT centers are specifically designated to improve existing methods and products. FedEx has innovated online tools and support for its customers and employees in managing and monitoring its processes in real time.

FedEx innovations include the many "firsts" in the transportation industry, including the following:

- Overnight package delivery
- Next-day delivery by 10:30 a.m.
- Saturday delivery

Being an innovative company and the industry leader, FedEx has received many awards, including the first Malcolm Baldrige Award in the Service Category. FedEx is leading its innovations in logistics to innovations in "access," which needs to be exploited for its impact on society, marketplaces, and a nation's strength.

Execution

Walt Disney

Visits to Walt Disney parks always turn out to be happy experiences, given the diversity of entertainment, number of customers, scheduling of events, number of employees, timeliness of events, and customer delight. Rarely is there an event that is disliked by customers. Every event and supporting operations must be well executed for achieving customer delight, while at the same time sustaining profitable growth.

The Disney Brothers studio, started by Walter E. and Roy O. Disney in 1923, has become a $35 billion entertainment conglomerate consisting of Media Networks, Parks and Resorts, Studio Entertainment, and Consumer Products. In any aspect of Disney products or services, the consumer can feel the cleanliness of its execution, because the customer experience is very smooth and enjoyable.

The Walt Disney World Resort is the single largest employer site, with about 58,000 employees, who are called cast members. In other words, every employee is a star! The enormity of its operations can been seen through the huge number of costume designs, with about 2 million total pieces; the 250 buses hauling people from the airport to the resort and various sites; the 3,000 weddings, 300 places to dine; and the millions of visitors.

At Walt Disney Parks, the main strength lies in its size and resources, experience in the entertainment business, and cost-driven operations strategy. To sustain profitable growth, Disney must achieve increases in attendance, increases in spending per guest, reductions in the cost of delivering its services per guest, and increases in the number of attractions to increase attendance.

Disney is known for its customer service methods to ensure customer satisfaction, processes for delivering entertainment services to customers, investment in employee training, attention to employee ideas for improvement and innovation, and practice of workplace standards. To improve its business performance and demonstrate its commitment to the environment, Disney has recently committed to business standards and ethics, corporate governance, community supporting activities, environmental stewardship, labor standards, and safety and security. Ultimately, the Walt Disney Company and its affiliated companies have committed to produce unparalleled entertainment experiences based on quality content and exceptional storytelling. As a business, Disney listens to consumers, works with suppliers, deploys technology, and takes care of employees.

Singapore Airlines

Since its beginning as a regional airline, Singapore Airlines has become a leading airline known for excellence and service. To improve its performance and strategy execution, Singapore Airlines reports its performance monthly. As a result, in its latest annual report it improved profit by about 70 percent over the previous year, and passenger load increased by over 70 percent as well. Singapore Airlines is now introducing the newest planes to its fleet, with innovative services such as the Cabin.

Most importantly known for its superior in-flight service, Singapore Airlines has focused on promptly getting baggage on carousels, as well as outstanding service by all employees, including pilots, ground staff, and cabin staff. To achieve excellence in execution, the airline spends 30 percent of its general resources on reviewing systems and procedures, thus ensuring continuity of its excellence in execution. This sense of superior service is transforming into pampering customers, especially the high-end customers. In doing so, Singapore Airlines is becoming one of the most admired companies.

Its four-month rigorous training program includes functional skills, soft skills such as grooming and laundering techniques, spoken skills, and simulation of a real airlines environment in serving meals.

Finally, customers love the Singapore Airlines experience, as is evident from the high ratio of compliments to complaints, which is rare in any industry.

Retention

Nordstrom

From a downtown shoe store, Nordstrom has grown into a nationwide chain focusing on catering to individual customer needs. Nordstrom's commitment to offer its customer the best possible service, selection, quality, and value has remained the same for over 100 years. Stories abound that employees are empowered to make decisions about refunds and exchanges.

Nordstrom's commitment to an extraordinary shopping experience includes the following:

* A prepaid return label included with every order
* Free exchanges by mail, by phone, or in the store

Today, Nordstrom's customer service has become a benchmark in the customer service industry, where people have been heard saying, "I will be the Nordstrom" of an industry. Just like Xerox in copying, Nordstrom is known for customer service. When an organization emulates Nordstrom's customer service, it implies creating a culture of providing a high level of customer service, making the customer's buying experience enjoyable, empowering employees to make decisions to keep customers, and providing the ultimate in customer service.

To create a culture of service to delight customers and earn loyalty, senior managers can create a customer-friendly environment, employee-driven customer service, and various choices to delight customers. Knowing that happy employees make customers happy, Nordstrom hires service-oriented people, develops their customer service skills, mentors them in the early days of employment, and rewards superior performance. With leadership support and management systems, it is up to the Nordstrom employees to care for and listen to customers, give them attention, and help them in their buying experience through personal relationships and teamwork with peers. Employees commit themselves to customer service following good service principles. Some examples of Nordstrom customer services include driving to a customer's home to deliver purchases, calling customers to alert them of new arrivals, or even writing thank-you notes to customers for shopping.

To enhance the customer experience, a feeling of luxury, simple store design, and personalized customer service are Nordstrom's way. The escalators are located in the center of stores, a baby grand piano is played nearby, spacious aisles are easy to navigate, and the popular Nordstrom's cafe is located on the third floor. Nordstrom salespeople are knowledgeable and trained; their job is not to push a certain brand or a certain product, but instead to enable customers to buy what they need. Irrespective of departmental territories, Nordstrom salespeople can help customers anywhere in the store, ensuring personal attention.

Ritz-Carlton

Ritz-Carlton Hotel Company operates luxury hotels and resorts for others. Ritz-Carlton has established three principles of service: warm welcome, anticipation and fulfillment of customer needs, and a fond farewell for customers to remember and thus return. Its motto is "We are ladies and gentlemen serving ladies and gentlemen." Thus, it establishes an expectation of mutual respect and dignity.

To serve and retain customers, Ritz-Carlton has established Gold Standards consisting of the following philosophy and values: Ritz-Carlton takes customer preferences into account while serving its customers. The strategy is driven by customers' needs and preferences, and detailed preferences are entered into the information system. Ritz also wants to react immediately to customer complaints and immediately correct the issue and satisfy the customer 100 percent of the time.

Employees have to be empowered to execute such a strategy. Ritz-Carlton provides comprehensive training and empowerment to its employees to execute a customer-driven strategy. The CLASS system links returning customers to their preferences. This memory of preferences and pleasant experiences is a major competitive advantage. The experience enhances customer retention.

To ensure that Ritz-Carlton guests receive best-in-class service, employees of Ritz-Carlton practice the following service values:

- I build strong relationships and create Ritz-Carlton guests for life.

- I am always responsive to the expressed and unexpressed wishes and needs of our guests.

- I am empowered to create unique, memorable, and personal experiences for our guests.

- I own and immediately resolve guest problems.

- I am proud of my professional appearance, language, and behavior.

- I am responsible for uncompromising levels of cleanliness and creating a safe and accident-free environment.

Ritz-Carlton is a two-time recipient of the Malcolm Baldrige National Quality Award. The Ritz-Carlton Leadership Center has trained leaders from other industries and helped them benchmark their performance. Product Quality Indicators (PQIs) include defects during the development phase. The Service Quality Indicators (SQIs) report the 10 most serious defects in the service provided. Aggregate numbers are reported to the workforce daily.

Ritz-Carlton has established a well-defined process for best-in-class customer service, earning customer loyalty and ensuring an enjoyable experience to bring the customer back.

Take Away

- The Service Scorecard is an aggregation of powerful performance measurements for a service organization.

- Sample service organizations using the key performance measurements presented are good benchmarks.

- Successful service businesses deploy a collection of service performance measurements.

- Collaboration and acceleration are emerging elements of the Service Scorecard that provide competitive advantage.

- Implementation of the Service Scorecard should begin with a commitment to sustained profitable growth.

Final Thoughts

This book answers three basic questions:

1. How different are services and what issues shall be considered while designing a performance measurement system for services?
2. What should be the architecture of service performance measurements system?
3. How should the Service Scorecard be implemented?

Corporate performance measurement needs have been impacted by the transformation of manufacturing-based economies to service-based economies. In this book, we viewed the length and extent of interaction with the customers, separating various types of services. Additionally, we viewed service not only from a provider's perspective, but also from a customer's perspective. Measurement in any service scorecard, therefore, should address both views. The performance measurement system of a service firm should be aligned with the service operations strategy and corporate objectives, should balance service innovation and process execution, and should have common understanding across the value chain partners and across various functions.

Our understanding of service performance measurement is evolving. For example, service inventory discussed in this book has been redefined for the services context. Other specific challenges associated with the understanding of service firms' performance are as follows:

- Inherent variation among customers, servers, time periods, and service processes
- Prominently including the engagement of employees

- Including the service innovation dimension
- Maintaining a partnership focus
- Existing in a solution-dominant world

The operations strategy of a particular firm depends on its business context, the life cycle of the offering, and other contextual variables. Considering the importance of innovation and challenges to implementation, a newly proposed Six Sigma methodology called DMAIE (Define, Measure, Analyze, Innovate, and Embed) was presented in this book. The DMAIE methodology can be applied to both transaction-based and experience-based services. The axiom-based service model provides a framework for our DFSS approach, as well as the criteria for evaluation.

Traditional models and frameworks fail to take into account the intricacies and specificity of services. Broadly speaking, three different classes of performance management systems exist. The first class of systems emphasizes being fully integrated with existing systems and processes. This class of systems requires a focus on all stakeholders, both internal and external. The second class places the focus on the customer and is continually striving to improve—not just to monitor. The third class of systems is focused on internal measures only, such as the cash flows and return on investment. Some of these requirements are fulfilled by all three classes.

Many performance measurement/monitoring and control frameworks exist for the manufacturing context. Examples of popular measurement systems are the Balanced Scorecard, Performance Prism, Six Sigma Business Scorecard, and Performance Pyramid. A few popular auditing frameworks are the Deming framework, Baldrige Award, European Quality Model, and maturity models for software firms. Only three systems that were designed specifically for the service context can be identified: the ServQual Model, the Service Profit Chain Model, and the Service Model presented by Fitzgerald et al. The Service Quality Model (ServQual) focuses on the customer satisfaction aspects of service quality and is not a comprehensive performance management model. The Service Profit Chain Model is a strategic tool and includes a service profit chain management audit. The Fitzgerald model is a performance management system, but no measures are provided in this model. None of these models is comprehensive.

The power of a scorecard lies in identifying opportunities to increase value realization and predicting the future performance with some confidence. The Service Performance Index (SPIn) is an aggregate performance measurement of the Service Scorecard that can be correlated to the financial outcomes or the business objectives. The seven elements of the Service Scorecard are Growth, Leadership, Acceleration, Collaboration, Innovation, Execution, and Retention. The seven elements were put together in a model (GLACIER) that represents certain intangible attributes of a service business. Each element of the Service Scorecard represents a significant aspect of business and has interdependency with the other elements. The business relevance of the scorecard makes it familiar to employees and improves its acceptability and visibility in the organization.

Each element of the Service Scorecard was discussed in detail in chapters of the book. Leadership and Acceleration in the GLACIER of the Service Scorecard form critical arch stones. The leadership element is critical to set the bar and helps align the organization to achieve business objectives. Leadership inspires employees to excel, and Acceleration drives improvement. A decision by leadership may lead to action by all employees, resulting in a significant impact on the performance. Thus, the leadership decisions are weighted at 30 percent of the total forming the SPIn.

The Service Scorecard places an unambiguous and clearly identifiable importance on the collaboration measure. The strategic importance of the collaborative service chain is understood by recognizing the importance of the competitive landscape in a particular service sector. Similar to the manufacturing world, competition is between service delivery chains and not between service firms. Ideally, we should measure the *overall health, reach,* and *relevance* of the collaboration. Collaboration health is impacted by various factors, such as the culture of a service firm, strategic considerations and alignment, and trust between partners. Establishing trust is one of the key considerations to a long-term partnership. Longer-term partnerships will focus on trust development, communication, and learning aspects. One obvious measurement is partner satisfaction.

Employee engagement directly affects employee turnover, employee satisfaction, and Innovation at a service firm. Employees at service firms deal directly with the customers and need to be engaged positively. Customers usually have longer contacts with employees at service firms. Therefore, employee engagement is even more important in the service context, because it influences customer retention and behaviors. Employee engagement drives human capital when employees are considered as assets. Execution is another important element of the Service Scorecard. Although services signify intangible offerings, the consumers demand reliability. Reliability builds trust contributing to customer loyalty. Reliability depends on reduction of variability. In the language of lean principles, service systems have huge waste. Waste can be in terms of wait times and servers sitting idle to redundant process steps. The Service Scorecard considers accuracy and responsiveness as two measures of execution.

Customer Retention and loyalty are observable constructs and usually are measured in terms of customer equity or lifetime value of a customer. Unobservable constructs, such as service quality, perception of the service, and intention to buy a service, are more important for a service firm. A service firm could grow by acquiring new customers, entering into new markets using existing services, creating and delivering new services, and selling more services to existing customers. Considering Growth through service innovation as a process, we could consider metrics at three different levels: input metrics, such as number of ideas per employees as discussed in the employee innovation section; process velocity metrics, such as tracking the employee responsiveness to ideas; and output metrics, such as revenue/profit growth from new services.

After identifying challenges and designing a Service Scorecard, we described an implementation strategy. Each company implements its scorecard in a slightly different way depending on the leadership style, corporate culture, business strategy, and performance objectives. Certain steps, however, are recommended to implement the Service Scorecard effectively. The implementation begins with the leadership commitment and ends with the ability to (a) predict corporate performance in the coming months and (b) adjust the business processes proactively to ensure realization of business objectives. Enthusiastically reporting the corporate performance, formally (or informally) measuring performance against goals, and rewarding superior performance in various elements (or measurement) of the Service Scorecard are good ways to demonstrate leadership commitment to the Service Scorecard. Most importantly, the leadership must expect significant improvement that is reported through Service Scorecard measurements and corresponding aggressive goals for improvement.

The majority of scorecard frameworks has not been tested rigorously. The Service Scorecard is not an exception. A rigorous statistical analysis of various scorecard frameworks provides higher confidence to the Service Scorecard users and justifies their commitment to the Service Scorecard. Chapter 13, "Service Scorecard Validation," provided validation of individual elements of the Service Scorecard, validation of similar methodologies, and a roadmap to rigorous validation of the Service Scorecard. However, this book should not be considered as a final work on rigorous validation of various frameworks.

There are companies that have implemented aspects of the Service Scorecard well and realized the benefits. Imagine if a company implemented best practices throughout its operations. One of the distinctive features of the Service Scorecard is that it considers the organization as a system. The performance of this system is managed for profitable growth. Although profit and growth are sometimes considered conflicting strategies when running a business, experience shows that successful companies do manage to sustain profitable growth. Such companies grow profitably over a long period. Implementing the Service Scorecard can enable more service companies to sustain profitable growth.

Bibliography

Adams, Chris, and Andy Neely. "The Performance Prism to Boost M&A Success." Measuring Business Excellence 3 (2000): 19–23.

Becker, Brian E., and Mark A. Huselid. *The HR Scorecard: Linking People, Strategy, and Performance.* Harvard Business School Press (2001).

Blattberg, Robert C., Gary Getz, and Jacquelyn S. Thomas. *Customer Equity: Building and Managing Relationships as Valuable Assets.* Harvard Business School Press (2001).

Brignall, Stan, and Joan Ballantine. "Performance Measurement in Service Businesses Revisited." *International Journal of Service Industry Management* 1 (1996): 6–31.

Curkovic, Sime, Steve Melnyk, Roger Calantone, and Robert Handfield. "Validating the Malcolm Baldrige National Quality Award Framework through structural equation modeling." International Journal of Production Research 38 (2000): 765–791.

Davis, Tim R. "Developing an Employee Balanced Scorecard: Linking Frontline Performance to Corporate Objectives." Management Decision 4 (1996): 14–18.

Easton, George S., and Sherry L. Jarrell. *The Effects of Total Quality Management on Corporate Performance: An Empirical Investigation. The American Workplace by Casey Ichniowski.* Cambridge University Press (2000).

Eckerson, Wayne W. *Performance Dashboards: Measuring, Monitoring, and Managing Your Business.* Hoboken, New Jersey: John Wiley & Sons Inc. (2006).

Edvardsson, Bo, Michael D. Johnson, Anders Gustafsson, and Tore Strandvik. "The Effects of Satisfaction and Loyalty on Profits and Growth: Products Versus Services." *Total Quality Management and Business Excellence* 9 (2000): 917–927.

Evans, James R. "An Exploratory Study of Performance Measurement Systems and Relationships with Performance Results." *Journal of Operations Management* 3 (2004): 219–232.

Fitzsimmons, James A., and Mona J. Fitzsimmons, eds. *New Service Development: Creating Memorable Experiences.* Thousand Oaks: Sage Publications Inc. (2000).

Fitz-enz, Jac. *The ROI of Human Capital: Measuring the Economic Value of Employee Performance.* New York City: AMACOM–American Management Association (2000).

Fleming, John H., Curt Coffman, and James K. Harter. "Manage Your Human Sigma." *Harvard Business Review - On Point* 7 (2005): 107–114.

Fleming, John H., Curt Coffman, and James K. Harter. "Manage Your Human Sigma." *Engineering Management Review,* IEEE, 1 (2006): 52–52.

Flynn, Barbara B., and Brooke Saladin. "Further Evidence on the Validity of the Theoretical Models Underlying the Baldrige Criteria." *Journal of Operations Management* 6 (2001): 617–652.

Fornell, Claes, Michael D. Johnson, Eugene W. Anderson, Jaesung Cha, and Barbara E.Bryant. "The American Customer Satisfaction Index: Nature, Purpose, and Findings." *Journal of Marketing* 60 (1996): 7–18.

Franco, Monica, and Mike Bourne. "Factors That Play a Role in Managing Through Measures." *Management Decision* 8 (2003): 698–710.

Gallouj, Fa'iz, and Olivier Weinstein. "Innovation in Services." *Research Policy* 26 (1997): 537–556.

Gates, Stephen. *Measuring More Than Efficiency: The New Role of Human Capital Metrics*. The Conference Board (2004).

Gibbons, John. *Employee Engagement: A Review of Current Research and Its Implications*. The Conference Board, Inc. (2006).

Goel, Parveen S. Praveen Gupta, Rajeev Jain and Rajesh K Tyagi. *Six Sigma for Transactions and Service*. New York: McGraw-Hill (2005).

Gupta, Praveen. *Six Sigma Business Scorecard: Creating a Comprehensive Corporate Performance Measurement System*. 2nd Edition. New York: McGraw-Hill (2007).

Gupta, Praveen. *Business Innovation in the 21st Century: A Comprehensive Approach to Institutionalize Business Innovation*. North Charleston: Amazon.com Company (2007).

Harris, Michael, and James H. Harrington. "Service Quality in the knowledge age – huge opportunities for the twenty-first century." *Measuring Business Excellence* 4 (2000): 31–36.

Heiskala, Mikko. *A Conceptual Model for Modeling Configurable Services from a Customer Perspective*. Helsinki University of Technology–Masters Thesis (2005).

Heskett, James L., Earl W. Sasser, and Leonard A. Schlesinger. *The Service Profit Chain: How Leading Companies Link Profit and Growth to Loyalty, Satisfaction, and Value*. New York City: The Free Press (1997).

Humphrey, Watts S. *Managing the Software Process* (The SEI Series in Software Engineering). New York City: Addison-Wesley (1990).

Jones, Christopher R. "A 'Scorecard' for Service Excellence." *Measuring Business Excellence* 8 (2004): 45–54.

Kaplan, Robert S. and David P. Norton. *The Balanced Scorecard: Translating Strategy into Action.* Harvard Business School Press (1996).

Keiningham, Timothy L., Bruce Cooil, Tor Wallin Andreassen, and Lerzan Aksoy. "A Longitudinal Examination of Net Promoter and Firm Revenue Growth." *Journal of Marketing* 71 (July 2007): 39–51.

Klassen, Kenneth J., Randolph M. Russell, and James J. Chrisman. "Efficiency and Productivity Measures for High Contact Services." *The Service Industries Journal* 18 (1998): 1–18.

Lambert, Richard A. *Customer Satisfaction and Future Financial Performance Discussion of are Nonfinancial Measures Leading Indicators of Financial Performance? An Analysis of Customer Satisfaction. Journal of Accounting Research* 36 (1998): 37–46.

Lees, Gillian. "Improving Strategic Oversight: the CIMA Strategic Scorecard." *Measuring Business Excellence* 8 (2004): 5–12.

Luteberget, Andreas. *Customer Involvement in New Service Development: How Does Customer Involvement Enhance New Service Success?* Agder University College Faculty of Engineering and Science Master Thesis Paper (2005).

Maister, David H. *Managing the Professional Service Firm*. New York City: The Free Press (1997).

Marr, Bernard, Alexander Fink, Jens-Peter Kuhle, and Andreas Siebe. "The Future Scorecard: Combining External and Internal Scenarios to Create Strategic Foresight." *Management Decision* 43 (2005): 360–381.

Marr, Bernard, and Gianni Schiuma. "Business Performance Management – Past, Present, and Future." *Management Decision* (2003): 680–687.

McIvor, Ronan. *The Outsourcing Process: Strategies for Evaluation and Management*. Cambridge, United Kingdom: Cambridge University Press (2005).

Melnyk, Steven A., Roger J. Calantone, and Joan Luft. "An Empirical Investigation of the Metrics Alignment Process." *International Journal of Productivity and Performance Management* 54 (2005): 312–324.

Miller, C C., and Laura B. Cardinal. "Strategic Planning and Firm Performance: A Synthesis of More Than Two Decades of Research." *Academy of Management Journal* 37 (1994): 1649–1665.

Niazi, Mahmood, David Wilson, and Didar Zowghi. "A Maturity Model for the Implementation of Software Process Improvement: an Empirical Study." *The Journal of Systems and Software* 74 (2005): 155–172.

Northhouse, Peter G. *Leadership: Theory and Practice*. Thousand Oaks: Sage Publications Inc., 1997.

Oliva, Rogelio, and John D. Sterman. "Cutting Corners and Working Overtime: Quality Erosion in the Service Industry." *Management Science* 47 (2001): 894–914.

Ogbonna, Emmanuel, and Lloyd C. Harris. "Leadership Style, Organizational Culture and Performance: Empirical Evidence from UK Companies." *International Journal of Human Resource Management* 11 (2000): 766–788.

Patel, Alpesh B., and Hemendra Aran. *Outsourcing Success: The Management Imperative.* New York City: Palgrave Macmillan (2005).

Patton, Fred. "Does Six Sigma Work in Service Industries?" *Quality Progress* 38 (2005): 55–60.

Phelps, Richard. *Key Trends in Human Capital: A Global Perspective - 2006.* PricewaterhouseCoopers, Saratoga (2006).

Phillips, Jack J and Lynn Schmidt. *The Leadership Scorecard.* Oxford, UK, Elsevier Butterworth-Heinemann (2004).

Robinson, Alan G., and Dean M. Schroeder. *Ideas Are Free.* San Fransico: Berrett–Koehler Inc. (2004).

Rust, Roland T., Tim Ambler, Gregory S. Carpenter, V. Kumar, and Rajendra K. Srivastava. "Measuring Marketing Productivity: Current Knowledge and Future Directions." *Journal of Marketing* 68 (2004): 76–89.

Samuels, David I., and Frank L. Admomitis. "Six Sigma Can Meet Your Revenue-Cycle Needs." *Healthcare Financial Management* 57 (2003) 70–75.

Segil, Larraine. *Measuring the Value of Partnering: How to Use Metrics to Plan, Develop, and Implement Successful Alliances.* New York City: AMACOM–American Management Association (2004).

Silvestro, R. and Cross, S. "Applying the service profit chain in a retail environment: Challenging the 'satisfaction mirror.'" *International Journal of Service Industry Management* 11 (2000), 244–268.

Spitzer, Dean R. *Transforming Performance Measurement: Rethinking the Way We Measure and Drive Organizational Success*. New York City: AMACOM–American Management Association (2007).

Sureshchandar, G.S., and Rainer Leisten. "Holistic Scorecard: Strategic Performance Measurement and Management in the Software Industry." *Measuring Business Excellence* 9 (2005): 12–29.

Tangen, Stefan. "An Overview of Frequently Used Performance Measures." *Work Study* 52 (2003): 347–354.

Tangen, Stefan. "Insights from Practice. Analysing the Requirements of Performance Measurement Systems." *Measuring Business Excellence* 9 (2005): 46–54.

Vargo, Stephen L., and Robert F. Lusch. "Evolving to a New Dominant Logic for Marketing." *Journal of Marketing* 68 (2004): 1–17.

Waldman, David A., Gabriel G. Ramirez, Robert F. House, and Phanish Puranam. "Does Leadership Matter? CEO Leadership Attributes and Profitability Under Conditions of Perceived Environmental Uncertainty." *Academy of Management Journal*, Vol. 44 (2001) 1:14–143.

Wilcox, Mark, and Mike Bourne. "Predicting Performance." *Management Decision* 41 (2003): 806–816.

Wilson, Darryl D., and David A. Collier. "An Empirical Investigation of the Malcolm Baldrige National Quality Award Causal Model." *Decision Sciences* 31 (2000): 361–383.

Wong, Alfred. "Integrating Supplier Satisfaction with Customer Satisfaction." *Total Quality Management* 11 (2000): 427–432.

Wongrassamee, S., J. E. L. Simmons, and P.D. Gardiner. "Performance Measurement Tools: The Balanced Scorecard and the EFQM Excellence Model." *Measuring Business Excellence–Emerald* 7 (2003): 14–29.

Woodcock, Neil, Merlin Stone, and Bryan Foss. *The Customer Management Scorecard: Managing CRM for Profit.* UK Kogan Page (2003).

Yang, Xiaoming, Peng Tian, and Zhen Zhang. "A Comparative Study on Several National Customer Satisfaction Indices (CSI)." Aetna School of Management (2005).

Zemke, Ron, and Chip R. Bell. *Knock Your Socks Off Service Recovery.* New York City: AMACO-American Management Association (2000).

INDEX

Symbols

4P (Preparation, Perform, Perfect, and Progress) model, process excellence, 220-222

4P model of process management, 198-201

A

acceleration, 117, 123-126
  best practices
    American Express, 256-257
    Infosys Technologies, 255-256
  defined, 123
  GLACIER, 90-91
  measurements, 126
    implementing, 126-128
  Service Scorecard, 15
  validation of individual Service Scorecard elements, 238-239
Accenture Human Capital Development Framework, 146
acquisitions and mergers, 62
ACSI (American Customer Satisfaction Index), 176
  validation, 244-245
activity blueprinting, 175
activity mapping, 175
adjusting measurements, Service Scorecard, 212
agricultural processes, 3
ambidextrous organization principle, 100

ambidextrous organizations, 100-101
American Airlines, implementing growth, 191
American Customer Satisfaction Index (ACSI), 176
  validation, 244-245
American Express, best practices, 256-257
Analyze
  DFSS (Design for Six Sigma for Services, 45
  Six Sigma, service, 44
Android, 132
approaches to implementing Service Scorecard, 196-197
Arrival variability, 30
assessments, Baldrige Award, 66
assimilation approach, 182
ATMs, 183
Austin, Rob, 26
axiom-based service design model, 46-49
axioms, 46
  for designing services, 49-52

B

Balanced Scorecard, 6-8, 21, 75
  financial measurements, 60
  perspectives, 60-61
  software solutions, 61
  validation, 246
balancing innovation and continuous improvement, 100-101

FINANCIAL TIMES

In an increasingly competitive world, it is quality
of thinking that gives an edge—an idea that opens new
doors, a technique that solves a problem, or an insight
that simply helps make sense of it all.

We work with leading authors in the various arenas
of business and finance to bring cutting-edge thinking
and best-learning practices to a global market.

It is our goal to create world-class print publications
and electronic products that give readers
knowledge and understanding that can then be
applied, whether studying or at work.

To find out more about our business
products, you can visit us at www.ftpress.com.